THE ECHO

STORIES FROM THE EDGE OF SURVIVAL

BARRY BLANCHARD

patagonia®

THE ECHO

STORIES FROM THE EDGE OF SURVIVAL

Patagonia publishes a select list of titles on wilderness, wildlife, and outdoor sports that inspire and restore a connection to the natural world and encourage action to combat climate chaos.

Stump (p. 61): Originally published in the *American Alpine Journal*, 1982

Kurtyka (p. 265): Originally published in *Alpinist 2*, 2003

Hardcover Edition
Published by Patagonia Works
Printed in Canada on 100 percent postconsumer recycled paper.

Hardcover ISBN: 978-1-952338-39-7
E-Book ISBN: 978-1-952338-40-3
Library of Congress Control Number: 2026944299

Editors: Matt Samet, Sharon AvRutick
Photo Editor: Kyle Sparks
Art Director/Designer: Christina Speed
Project Manager: Sonia Moore
Photo Production: Angelo Partemi, Tee Smith
Graphic Production: Tausha Greenblott
Creative Director: Michael Leon
Publisher: Karla Olson

Building mutual relationships with Indigenous peoples is part of our work to restore Earth, the home we all share. Patagonia's headquarters is located on the unceded homelands of the Chumash people in what is now known as Ventura, California. Because the people in this book are in locations around the planet, we acknowledge the many Indigenous communities who have stewarded the lands and waters of each of these places since time immemorial. We are also grateful for their continued leadership in the environmental and climate movement today.

Front cover: Barry Blanchard pops up on the Infinite Spur, Mt. Foraker, Alaska. Carl Tobin

Front endpaper: A tired man 588 feet below the summit of Mt. Foraker. Carl Tobin, June 3, 2000. Barry Blanchard

ENVIRONMENTAL BENEFITS STATEMENT

Patagonia Inc saved the following resources by printing the pages of this book on chlorine free paper made with 100% post-consumer waste.

TREES	WATER	ENERGY	SOLID WASTE	GREENHOUSE GASES
0	259,000	210	11,100	65,000
FULLY GROWN	GALLONS	MILLION BTUs	POUNDS	POUNDS

Environmental impact estimates were made using the Environmental Paper Network Paper Calculator 4.0. For more information visit www.papercalculator.org

1% FOR THE PLANET
MEMBER

FSC
www.fsc.org
MIX
Paper | Supporting responsible forestry
FSC™ C016245

For my fiancée, Nicole,
and our girls,
Rosemary and Eowyn

Left to right: Chamonix's Aiguille de Triolet, Les Courtes, Les Droites, and Aiguille Verte. Kevin Doyle and I made an ascent of the waterfall route on the north face of Les Droites in 1980. Eleven years later, in 1991, Mark Twight and I did the first ascent of the Richard Cranium Memorial route, also on Les Droites. Barry Blanchard

THE ECHO TUNES & WORDS

Ch 1 "Things Are Happening": Capleton

Ch 2 *Floodland*, especially "Lucretia My Reflection" and "1959": The Sisters of Mercy
"Our Darkness": Anne Clark

Ch 3 "51st State": New Model Army
"Behind the Wheel": Depeche Mode

The Shining Mountain: The First Ascent of the West Wall of Changabang by Peter Boardman
Sacred Summits: A Climber's Year by Peter Boardman
The Savage Arena: K2, Changabang and the North Face of the Eiger by Joe Tasker

Ch 4 "Willin'": Little Feat
"Like A Hurricane": The Mission

Ch 5 "Don't Leave Me This Way": The Communards
"Mining for Gold": Cowboy Junkies
"Anarchy in the UK": Sex Pistols

Ch 6 "Ribbons," "When You Don't See Me": The Sisters of Mercy
"Song to the Siren": Dead Can Dance
"Cool Water": Sons of the Pioneers

One Man's Mountains: Essays and Verses by Tom Patey
Run with the Hunted by Charles Bukowski
The Great Days by Walter Bonatti

Ch 7 *No Picnic on Mount Kenya* by Felice Benuzzi
Nine-Headed Dragon River: Zen Journals 1969–1982 by Peter Matthiessen
The Unbearable Lightness of Being by Milan Kundera

Ch 8 "This Is the Modern World": The Jam

Darkness Visible: A Memoir of Madness by William Styron
The Complete Posthumous Poetry of César Vallejo by César Vallejo
One Man's Mountains: Essays and Verses by Tom Patey
Iron John: A Book About Men by Robert Bly
The Mont Blanc Massif: The 100 Finest Routes by Gaston Rébuffat

Ch 9 🎧 "Folsom Prison Blues": Johnny Cash
🎧 "The Bottle Let Me Down": Merle Haggard
🎧 "Wicked Game": Chris Isaak
🎧 "Censor": Skinny Puppy

📖 *The Roominghouse Madrigals* by Charles Bukowski

Ch 10 🎧 "Low Self Opinion": Henry Rollins
🎧 "Straight to You": Nick Cave and the Bad Seeds

Ch 11 📖 *Gervasutti's Climbs* by Giusto Gervasutti

Ch 12 🎧 *Agate Lines:* Area
🎧 "King of the Road": Roger Miller

Ch 13 📖 *Everest: Kangshung Face* by Stephen Venables

Ch 14 🎧 "The Gift": Ian Tyson

📖 *The Letter of Marque* by Patrick O'Brian
📖 *This House of Sky* by Ivan Doig

Ch 15 🎧 *Unknown Pleasures:* Joy Division
🎧 *Nebraska:* Bruce Springsteen

📖 *Kiss or Kill: Confessions of a Serial Climber* by Mark Twight
📖 *Motel Chronicles* by Sam Shepard
📖 *Murder of the Impossible* by Reinhold Messner

Ch 16 🎧 "Beat on the Brat": The Ramones
🎧 "Real Wild Child": Iggy Pop
🎧 "The Wait," "Precious," "Tattooed Love Boys": The Pretenders
🎧 "Willin'": Little Feat

📖 *Alpinist* No. 2: "The Shining Wall" by Voytek Kurtyka

Ch 17 📖 *A River Runs Through It* by Norman Maclean

Ch 19 🎧 "Mercy Now": Mike Farris
📖 *A River Runs Through It* by Norman Maclean

Ch 20 📖 "The Dead" by James Joyce

TABLE OF CONTENTS

'eter Arbic and Troy Kirwan negotiate the
Kukuczka/Piotrowski route above the De Filippi
Glacier on K2. July 27, 1993. Barry Blanchard

INTRO

When I wrote my first book, *The Calling*, I took advice from Hemingway and wrote longhand with a pencil while standing. Over time I needed to be more productive with my writing, so I started composing with the keyboard on my computer. As I write this introduction to my second book I am back to Hemingway's advice with a pencil on paper as I stand. Next I'll edit on my computer. (Ernest would have used a typewriter.)

I am now older than Hemingway was when he took his own life at sixty-one. I was born above the banks of the Elbow River in Calgary, Alberta, Canada on March 29, 1959. As I write this I am sixty-six years old. If I divide my life, as is done in the Canadian Football League, into four quarters and given that the average Canadian male lives to eighty, statistically I am in my fourth quarter of life.

The Calling covered the first and second quarters of my life, when my passion and belief in alpinism was the groundwater that flowed through me. *The Echo* picks up where *The Calling* left off, with alpinism defining how I lived, but then there was a shift in my third quarter when my daughter Rosemary was born in 2004 and Eowyn in 2007. Fatherhood changed me. The last significant alpine route that I climbed was on the north face of Mt. Cromwell in the Canadian Rockies in 2010. Will I add to that? Time will tell. Eowyn is now eighteen and off at university with Rosemary, who is twenty-one. The average Canadian female lives to eighty-four, so they are both in their first quarters. Eowyn tells

I'm still guiding. Happy to be in the sun on top of Mt. Athabasca with my guests Erin and Phuong, July 16, 2023. Erin Lind me that I have to live to be over a hundred. Some Canadians do see a fifth and even a sixth quarter. Hmmmm....

I've tried to have the book that you are holding in your hands capture some of the love, loss, and life that has been part of my second, third, and fourth quarters. You, dear reader, will decide if I have succeeded.

“Things Are Happening”: Capleton

CHAPTER 1 — THE INFINITE SPUR

MT. FORAKER

MARCH 1984: Carl Tobin, David Cheesmond, and I established a new route on the east face of Mt. Fay in the Valley of the Ten Peaks in the Canadian Rockies. Twenty-six days later, Carl, George Lowe, and I made our first attempt on the northeast face of Mt. Chephren, in the Canadian Rockies.

I wouldn't climb with Carl Tobin again for another sixteen years.

SEPTEMBER: Carl and Matt VanEnkevort left their homes in Fairbanks, Alaska, and walked into the Hayes Range to attempt the unclimbed north face of Peak 9448. They encountered hard climbing and bad weather high on the face and fixed two ropes in anticipation of downclimbing to their snow cave to wait out the storm. Carl triggered a small wind slab. The avalanche swept him down the lower part of the mountain, over and through 1,600 feet of cliffs and gullies.

Death was there, arms open, but Carl survived, unconscious, with a punctured cheek, a broken rib, his left femur snapped in two places, and his right tibia "plateaued"—when the femur rams into and fractures the tibia. That knee also had all its ligaments torn off. Carl quit alpine climbing for pretty much a decade. But at one point in his recovery, he wrote, "You are never really free."

MAY 15, 2000: I found myself ankle-deep in the chaos of the Tobin household in Anchorage, Alaska. It was a three-story log structure built

ollowing a tightrope of steps high on the ıfinite Spur, as a sea of clouds stretches out ward Anchorage. Glen Deal on a concrete pad and added onto over time in the Alaskan way. Granted, there was no white polyethylene house wrap visible, and that gave the house an air of completion and permanence. The ground floor held a mayhem of mountain and road bikes, Nordic skis, downhill skis, touring skis, and bins of mountaineering gear including big-wall stuff and athletic and outdoor wear, plump and rising like multicolored muffins. The higher living floors were much better organized.

Now add two dogs and a bike chariot for Canyon, Carl and Nora's beautiful, flaxen-haired baby boy. It was a busy, busy household. A couple that was used to working, training, and climbing all their waking hours was now adjusting to being parents.

My room was on the ground floor. I boxed up bike gears and bulk bails of disposable diapers to make room to organize the twenty-five days' worth of food I'd bought at Costco in Anchorage.

Ropes, we needed ropes. Steve House, who would be flying into the Alaska Range with Mark Twight and Scott Backes in a couple weeks' time, told me to grab a 165-foot half rope from his cache in Talkeetna. Carl and I bought a brand new 200-foot half rope, the only length they had, to pair with it, and decided to cut it down so that our leads would be shorter and we could rest more, carry a single rack, and place protection more closely.

MAY 18: We drove to Talkeetna, where Carl asked Paul Roderick, the owner and head pilot of Talkeetna Air Taxi, to put us down on the west fork of the Kahiltna Glacier below the southeast aspect of Mt. Foraker. The landing plunked us closer to our objective, far removed from the peopled cattle track leading to the West Buttress of Denali—aka "The Butt." Paul was so proud of his new de Havilland Canada DHC-2 Beaver aircraft. I have a treasured, and much shared, image of him taking a piss under its tail.

My bank account was bloated on the bounty of *Vertical Limit*, the Hollywood movie I'd spent the previous year working on in New Zealand. Over the phone, I had said to Carl, "I want a lot of room in base camp. I'm thinking of buying a Himalayan Hotel." That was one of the bigger four-man tents being made by The North Face at the time.

"I LIKE that kind of talk!"

Problem was, I couldn't find one. That particular model of tent had been discontinued. We ended up pitching my new four-person dome and complementing it with Carl's pyramid tent to use as our kitchen, replete with a two-burner camping stove and a twenty-pound tank of propane.

MAY 19: Carl and I organized camp, then luxuriated in it. Carl is never one to luxuriate for long. Came the morrow, we skied off for Mt. Crosson, a 12,352-foot peak adjoined to Foraker along a 12-mile-long ridge that runs to Kahiltna Pass. Mt. Crosson would be our descent route from Foraker's Infinite Spur, egressed via the 4,000-foot-long Sultana Ridge falling to the northeast from Foraker's summit. Crosson would serve two purposes: acclimatization and reconnaissance.

Carl kicked my ass the first two days of the ascent. I had to tap out early—I was fighting and fretting about the cold. The altitude was choking me, grinding me to a funereal pace. Fully recovered from his injuries on Peak 9448, Carl was ox strong.

The altitude got to both of us the next day. Carl was human! We camped for two nights, eating, sleeping, reading, and catching up on the intervening decade and a half.

MAY 23: We descended from Crosson into a whiteout at the end of a long day. An ancient, primal fear closed down on me: Blinded by whiteness as nightfall and exhaustion amass, it is always easy to think, *What if I don't find the camp? What if this storm lasts for days? Where the fuck are our ski tracks!*

I dug out my map, compass, and altimeter and came up with a bearing and skied on in anxious dead reckoning through dusk and cold—not that it ever gets that dark at 63 degrees North in late May, but it does get a whole bunch colder. Then, I saw an apparition of a line like the faint slant of rain in a Japanese watercolor. I stopped and stared.

"What is it?" Carl shouted from fifty feet back along the rope.

"I think I saw something."

But the fine gray line had disappeared. I skied toward where it had been, and it sifted back into view, surfacing as the bright-purple and yellow sections of my spare avalanche probe, its neon-green stuff sack flapping like a banner. Camp!

"Wow, was that grace?" I asked Carl when he skied up to me.

"No, I don't believe so. That would imply the hand of God."

"Serendipity?"

"No, that would involve chance and beneficence. I think it was skill and intuition."

"Well, whatever the hell it was, I am mighty glad we're here. I'm going to move our stove into the vestibule of our tent."

"I like that kind of talk."

MAY 24: We gorged on goodies: blueberry pancakes with bacon, thick slices of salami on Sailor Boy pilot bread with mustard and jalapeño Havarti, tubes of Pringles, cups of Kaladi Brothers coffee, and shots of Laphroaig, neat. I bartered for a second rest day, but Carl had had enough languor.

"I want to get on the route and get home. I miss my son," he said.

MAY 25: We skied toward the Spur with day packs and our food, fuel, and climbing gear sliding along behind us in plastic kiddie sleds. Over the first pass, and across the eastern head of the Lacuna Glacier, we buried our cache below the second pass—the low point on the eastern bifurcation of the French Ridge (the southwest ridge of Mt. Foraker that was climbed in 1976 by six French men, one French lady, and one American fellow)—and skied back toward camp. That was when we saw the Lads skiing up our track.

"I wonder where they're going?" Carl said.

Soon, they were on us, making good time in our tracks. "Right, we're off to make the third ascent of the Infinite Spur," Gren Hinton said, beaming, his voice ringing with an Aussie accent. *Holy crap!* said the voice in my head. The route had only seen two ascents in twenty-three years, and now there would be two parties on it at once!

"No shit," Carl observed. "We're planning on climbing the route, too."

"Looks like we'll beat you to it," Glen Deal, an American, said with a smile.

We talked some, feeling each other out. Carl and I learned that they'd turned around on Mt. Hunter.

"How are you planning to get off?" Carl asked.

"The Sultana Ridge and down Mt. Crosson. I went up and down it last week, by myself, while he was sick," Gren said, pointing at Glen.

"I caught a cold, but I'm ready to climb now," Glen said.

"Carl and I spent four days acclimatizing on Crosson. We're planning on coming down that way too." There was a pregnant pause, then I added, jokingly, "Well, we've got a Bibler I-Tent, so if you guys could chop tent platforms to that size, we'd appreciate it."

"We don't have a tent. We're going with bivy bags," Gren said. There was another pregnant pause; Carl and I couldn't quite believe what we'd heard.

"You're going onto the Infinite Spur without a tent?" Carl asked.

"You bet, mate," Gren effused.

"Well, good luck with that." The Lads skied west while Carl and I skied east, back toward camp.

"Can you fucking believe there's another team on the Spur?" Carl spat when we got into camp.

"Ya, man, what are the chances? Sounds like they were gunning for the Lowe/Kennedy on Hunter. I guess if you get shut down on that route, the logical next step is to go for one that's twice as long and twice as hard."

"Hmmm."

MAY 26: We skied to our cache, dug it up, and added it to our packs, which now weighed over fifty pounds each. We left our approach skis there (both of us had a second pair, to facilitate retrieving the first pair, back in base camp). We followed the Lads' footsteps over the second pass. A 90-foot rappel got us over the bergschrund and onto the west fork of the Lacuna Glacier, where we followed more footsteps as close as we dared, to get to the 9,000-foot face. Here, a half dozen hanging and tumbling glaciers calve tons of blue glacial ice that trigger snow avalanches into the three-quarter-mile wide cauldron footing the south face. It is a killing zone. Carl and I gave it respect and pitched our tent out of its firing range.

MAY 27: We started toward the face, crossed the threshold of the avalanches, and picked up our pace. Carl and I wanted to be through the danger and onto the relative safety of the Spur as fast as possible.

"Holy shit!" Carl bellowed back along the rope. "The Lads camped here!"

A wall of snowballs fenced their sleeping platform from the face, while two tendrils of recent debris reached past their site. Carl and I scampered on and soon made out the Lads entering a large couloir left of the route proper. That gully served as a drainage for two hanging glaciers fronted by 200- to 400-foot-high seracs and two tumbling glaciers. Much of the ice and avalanches that the glaciers spat blasted through this gully, creating a massive fan of debris on the glacier below.

"Lads! Lads! The route is over here!" I bellowed. They yelled back but then continued. Carl and I soon lost sight of them as we jogged breathlessly through avalanche debris.

Soon we stood panting below the 'schrund, nervously flaking our ropes.

"Oh, man, can you believe where those guys are climbing?" Carl gasped.

"No. You couldn't get me to go in there with a gun to my head."

Carl hustled us up 700 feet of snow and onto the face proper, where we were finally out of the firing line of the seracs. Then we heard the Lads' bloodcurdling screams followed by the thunder and roar of an avalanche crashing down their gully and running out onto the glacier, like a slithering tentacle of the Kraken.

FUCK! bellowed in my head. The avalanche came to rest. I heard one last, loud scream...then silence. I yodeled and yelled but got nothing in response.

"Son of a bitch.... They're dead," I said, with no one to hear me. I climbed to Carl. We screamed and shouted some more but got no reply. A darkness descended. What could we do? What should we do?

"I don't know if anyone could have survived that hit. The debris took a full minute to come to rest on the glacier," I said.

"Well, if they need help, they're going to have to get themselves to the glacier. There's no way I'm going into that gully," Carl said. I agreed.

There was no help we could provide, so we kept on climbing. It was my turn to lead. I looked above to four parallel cracks splitting monolithic golden granite. Three were less than overhanging and held gunmetal ice

Glen Deal and Gren Hinton trying to hustle under heavy packs, breathing thin air. Gasping, gasping. Barry Blanchard and crusty blobs of snow; the fourth was over vertical, finger width, and darkened inside by black lichen.

"I'm going to have to haul my pack on this pitch," I said, surveying the options.

Carl squinted up from under the brim of his blue helmet with a blue handicapped sticker front and center on it. A sticker he'd earned the hard way. My helmet sported a Patagonia surfboard sticker on the front and a white rectangle on the back that read in bold black lettering: BAD COP NO DONUT.

"I think I can lead that with my pack on," Carl said.

"Man, if you can, we'll be way faster."

"Hand me the rack, youth," Carl said with a grin. He was forty-seven; I was forty-one.

Then it got a little hard to comprehend. Opting for the first of the four cracks, Carl cranked his way up the intermediately difficult climbing, 5.7 or 5.8, like he was enjoying a mixed pitch at a roadside crag. It was a breathtaking display of proficiency, élan, and POWER. That pitch set the tone for so much of the Spur: 5.4 to 5.9 mixed climbing clothed in crisp, fresh, frozen snow from the recent moist storm, iced-up cracks in

solid granite that yielded great drytooling—when the climber uses the pick of his ice-ax on the rock rather than his gloved, or bare, hands; we used our hands directly on the rock around 10 percent of the time—good protection, and secure anchors. We took to clipping our packs in with a locking carabiner and lanyard and shucking them off at every anchor; those rests, gained while we belayed, helped us recover.

We continued shouting for the Lads. The thought of their shattered bodies lying under all those tons of ice weighed on us. *Why the fuck had they gone there?*

Late in the day, amidst a pulsating mist, I led us onto the very edge of the Spur. Carl mounted a fantastically symmetrical pyramid of jigsawed granite blocks. We anchored and flattened the snow ridge on top and then set up our wee yellow Todd tent. (Todd Bibler was the designer and owner of Bibler Tents. We liked to call his gear "Todd stuff.")

"Blanchard/Tobin party on the Infinite Spur for Denali Park," I said into my VHF radio for the fifth time. No reply. We hadn't heard, or seen, the Lads since the avalanche; now that we'd stopped climbing, the possibility of their deaths towered ever taller like a dark shadow in my mind.

"I think they're dead," Carl said in a somber tone.

"Ya, me too. Fuck."

"I'll try to call Nora on my cell phone. I want to save the battery, though, so I can call her from higher on the route." No luck. Were we too low in the gut of the cauldron for either the radio or the cell phone to work?

MAY 28: I tried my radio again. This time I got a response from Kahiltna Base Camp. My heart beat a half dozen times as my trigger finger hovered over the push-to-talk button. As soon as I reported the accident, word would get out and our families would hear about two climbers lost on the Infinite Spur of Mt. Foraker. I pushed the button and explained the details.

By midmorning, a fixed-wing aircraft was making passes across the south face trying to spot the Lads with information supplied over my radio. The plane, however, had no success. Carl and I concluded that they were dead in the debris below the face. As that funereal moment passed between us, we lowered our heads.

As a counterpoint, the climbing was fabulous. Beautiful tawny granite. Carl and I had an absolute blast figuring out our pitches, ropelength after ropelength, our heavy packs snapping tight and weighty to each successive anchor. The kindness of direct sunlight in the morning was juxtaposed against yet another invasive mist in the afternoon, cold but also mystical and mythical, like climbing into an Arthurian legend.

Late in the day, we heard the baritone rumble of a Hercules circling somewhere above the clouds. Next, a Pave Hawk helicopter thumped into the cauldron and made a half dozen amazingly precise passes, contouring the topography of the face 100 feet out, like a wood router following a jig. The ship gained elevation with each pass. Carl and I gazed down dumbstruck at the prowess of the pilot.

"I wonder what kind of navigation devices those guys have on board."

"I don't think that they'd be allowed to tell us even if we asked."

Still no sighting of the Lads. The park declared them "missing and presumed dead."

The temperature dove and the mist withdrew. Carl was leading. I heard him shouting to someone out to his left—and then I heard shouts in reply! What in the hell? Another party on the Infinite Spur! Where had they come from? It couldn't be the Lads, because the Lads were dead. But it WAS the Lads!

And there they were, bedded down atop a serac in a tumbling glacier, with the deadly aquamarine arc of a higher serac rearing above like a big ocean wave poised to crash. They hadn't learned a fucking thing!

Carl and I gained the white edge of the Spur and flattened it out for our tent. We were camped at about 11,000 feet, with 3,000 feet of exposure falling dramatically from either edge of our tent. The Lads were level with us. I tried to contact Mt. McKinley National Park (now Denali National Park) on my radio. No luck. Carl tried his cell phone.

"Fuck! I can see fucking Anchorage. I don't know why I can't talk to Nora!" he cursed.

"Here, let me try calling my wife in Alberta," I said. Catherine answered on the second ring. The shock—and relief—in her voice was audible: All anyone knew was that two climbers might have been dead. For some fucked-up-money-grubbing-dogs-pissing-out-their-territories reason, Carl's cell provider didn't cover his call, while my provider did.

We'd made National Public Radio: "Two climbers lost on the Infinite Spur." I explained the situation and asked Catherine to call Nora. Nora called the park.

"The whole world thinks that you're dead!" I shouted across to the Lads. "Do you want us to call your parents?"

"No, mate," Gren bellowed. "They don't give a shit anyway!"

"Yes, please," yelled Glen. "Please call my mom."

I handed the phone to Carl and wrote Glen's mom's number in the snow as he shouted it to us. When I called, she was overjoyed to hear that her baby boy was still among the living.

MAY 29: We convinced the Lads to abandon their line of death and join us on the relative safety of the Spur. The park sent a Lama helicopter in to get a confirmed sighting of the Lads, which was accomplished via my instructions over the radio and the Lads waving to the ship as they crossed the snow slope from their glacial bivy to reach Carl and me on the Spur.

Carl and I packed up our camp carefully. Our situation felt so much like a picture I'd seen of Michael Kennedy and Mugs Stump perched atop a similar feature during their attempt on the Shining Wall—the west face of Gasherbrum IV—two corners of their Todd tent dangling over thin air. One shocking difference between the image in my mind and the reality around me was a thirty-foot-long line of frozen urine and feces that funneled away from our tent to disappear over the lip of the Spur!

We got the story from the Lads. Glen had finished a lead in their gully and was about to bring Gren up when he heard the rumble. Looking up, he saw the sky billowing white. He screamed and leaned into the wall and pulled his pack over his head. Then he got pummeled by chunks and inundated by dust-fine snow that got into any opening, including his mouth. The avalanche passed, and Gren bellowed the last shout I'd heard. Glen thought he had broken bones and was pleasantly surprised to realize that he'd suffered no more than bruises; likewise with Gren.

When I questioned their choice of line, Gren said, "Ah, mate, I don't mind taking a little risk to jump-start a route." Then he went on to explain how they'd observed the face the day before and only seen avalanches after 1 p.m.—the storm snow cleaning off, yes, but my suggestion that seracs don't observe the same timeline earned only a blank stare. Their further reasoning was that they'd planned to climb through the night and be out of the gully by 11 the next morning, but Glen's leads had taken too long. It was obvious that the Lads were not enjoying the partnership bond that Carl and I were. But now it was a beautiful day with the Lacuna Glacier stretched out behind us like the staircase

n outside the wee origami tent, with thirty
et of human waste trailing away below. May
, our second day on the spur. Carl Tobin

descending from Valhalla, and the Lads, despite their challenges, were ALIVE!

Midday we gained the ice arête, a 1,500-foot-long spine of ice canted at 50 degrees that somehow—and I still don't know if I understand how—held a three-foot depth of snow. The four of us leapfrogged up the arête using the only tool for the job: a shovel. With lethal falls to either side and no protection to be had, as the ice was unreachable underfoot, Carl and I shortened the rope between us in anticipation of one of us having to jump off the other side should the other fall.

The leader advanced by balancing to cut away snow from in front of his face, then chest, then knees, and only then stepping up onto the excavated platform to repeat. If you didn't shovel enough away, you ran the considerable risk of having the snow at chest level teeter you over backward. It was tedious and dangerous. At one point, I looked back to the Lads and was impressed to see that they'd excavated a saddle into the arête, stacked their ropes into it, and tethered themselves to each other standing on opposite sides, counterweighted, in relative safety.

We'd been wallowing up the arête for over a thousand feet, astride a razor's edge of insecurity with nothing anchoring us to the mountain. A small wall of granite now paralleled us 100 feet to the west. I left the arête to nervously kick steps across the snow to it. If the snow avalanched, Carl would have had to launch himself down the eastern side of the arête in hopes that the rope between us would cut into the spine of the arête and stop us. Big physics. It was such a relief to touch the diamond-hard granite and sink in three, beautiful, solid cams. Carl followed up to my anchor.

"Fuck, man," he said when he got to me, "I just had to play dad and break up an argument between the Lads."

"What do you mean?"

"They started swearing and threatening each other. I had to raise my voice and chastise, 'No! You guys can't be fighting up here—you have to get along up here!'"

The Lads came across in our footsteps. Clouds boiled up from the cauldron footing the south face and Spur, and we could see the thickening juggernaut of a front advancing from Cook Inlet. A storm was coming, and we were going to get smacked.

The granite wall abutted us against an intrusion of fractured, metamorphic-looking rock. Carl stitched together anchorage, and then we swung our axes for 2.5 hours to hack a modest six-by-three-foot ledge into armor-colored ice below the rock. The work was as exhausting as breaking stone with a hammer and chisel. Toward the end, my grip strength would fail, leaving my ax thrashing from my wrist loop like a fish pulled out of the water.

I'd brought a silk-weight guide's tarp, and we tied it to ice screws to form an awning over our partially pitched tent. The Lads dug into the snow slope fifty feet east of us, their position more exposed. The last thing we heard was Gren shouting at Glen, "Dig a fucking hole for your head, mate, so you can put your pack over it and have room to breathe."

It began to storm that night. All the spindrifting snow slid right over the guide's tarp, a miraculous improvement over all the other nights I'd spent getting out with a shovel to keep the intrusive snow from pushing me off the mountain. The Lads were soon totally buried and invisible under the snow.

It stormed for thirty-six hours.

"I like the way you handle yourself in the tent," Carl observed as I handed him another brew of sweet, milky tea. "I'm learning a ton from your systems."

"What do you mean?"

"Efficiencies, like the way you use the snow cup to pour water into the bottle over top of the hanging stove so that nothing gets spilled in the tent and wasted."

"Ya, well the last thing a guy wants is a wet sleeping bag. I'm trying to keep everything out to the borders of the tent so it insulates us from the ice and rock, but, as you can see, it all wants to live in the fucking middle."

"Let it rest at the point of least potential energy, that's what I say," Carl said, grinning. I thought of the first floor of his house and grinned back.

MAY 30: We ate and drank and slept. As concerning as it was, the storm wasn't necessarily a bad thing; Carl and I needed the rest! For the second week in a row, we were listening to the NPR radio show *Marian*

McPartland's Piano Jazz on the small shortwave radio I'd brought along. For the next half dozen years and five trips into the Alaska Range, I would come to measure time by the number of episodes of *Piano Jazz* and another weekly show, KNBA's *Prince Albert's Reggae Hour*, we listened to.

"He phones people in Jamaica every week," Carl declared of Prince Albert. "I don't understand a fucking word they say, but I love to listen to it, mahn. Jah!" We both strained to hear the lyrics of "Things Are Happening" being sung by Capleton.

MAY 31: We were able to get weather information from the shortwave and the repeating weather forecast on my VHF radio. The forecast promised an end to the storm. Carl and I crawled out to stand and piss for the first time in a day and a half. Once again, we were worried about the Lads. *Were they alive? Had they frozen to death?*

"LADS! Lads!" I bellowed. There was movement from within the whiteness. Gren's bloated face emerged, smiling. He told us that they'd been able to brew up only once during the storm. It was obvious that they'd suffered physically, while Carl and I had gorged ourselves and drunk gallons. Our tent and awning had granted us sanctuary, while our willpower had preserved a piece of reindeer Landjäger sausage for the two of us for the next three days; we couldn't eat enough of it, especially coupled with cheese sticks.

The fractured rock overhead looked hard—and proved to be the most challenging climbing on the route. I chose to leave my pack and haul it. The pitch delivered me into the miracle of direct sunlight. I watched it wash benevolently over the Lads at their tent site below, where they clung like lethargic caterpillars half-covered in the yellow cocoons of their nylon bivy sacks. My own days as a young alpinist came to mind—situations that I had learned from and become more tactical for having survived. An old joke, "I hope we don't die, so that we can try something harder," rang in my head.

Carl followed on jumars. It was the only time on the route that we used them: ninety feet. After several more challenging mixed pitches on the left side of the Spur, we gazed down a fine WI 2/3 gully that we should have climbed instead! It lay tucked into a crease between the wall we'd climbed and the cul-de-sac wall that Michael Kennedy had led in a storm, during the first ascent, farther east, twenty-three years earlier.

Carl and I finished our fifth day on the left flank of the Spur. Steely ice took hours of exhausting hacking to yield a platform. We gained six inches of horizontal by cutting one-foot cubes of snow and bricklaying them onto the shallow snow of the outer edge, saving ourselves an additional hour of hacking. The night was calm and cold, so we didn't string our awning.

An hour into our brewing, the Lads traversed the edge of the Spur above us. Waves of snow from their footfalls surged down to accumulate between the inner wall of our tent and the mountain. Our tent began to collapse like it was sinking into quicksand. Next it would be flattened and then pushed off our hard-won ledge by the snow.

"We worked so fucking hard," I pleaded. I felt so defeated.

Carl snapped. He'd had it with the Lads. He tore open the door and bellowed into the dusk, "You fucking fuckers! Don't drop anymore goddamned snow on us! No! Fucking! More!"

The snowfall stopped and there were some mumbles from above, but then it began again—until Carl reiterated his demands. We pulled our boots on and got out and shoveled the snow from our tent. I could have named things that I would have rather been doing.

JUNE 1: Carl and I climbed onto the amazing knife-edge ridge of snow that slices out from the upper bulk of Foraker to form the Infinite Spur. We profited from the Lads' footsteps. Within 150 feet, we came to the bivy ledge they'd left an hour earlier. It was flat and comfortable, but directly on top of a cornice—an unsupported wave of snow with nothing but 7,000 feet of air below!

"We came upon this flat spot in the dusk and decided to bivy," Glen confessed when we caught them up. Then he exclaimed, "In the morning, we saw that we were bivied on top of a cornice!"

"Why are you stopped here?" I asked. The Lads sat lassoed to a jumble of granite blocks in glaring sunlight.

"The snow is getting soft," Glen said. "We think the slope above us could avalanche. What do you think?"

The surface snow had been cooked to snowball in the last hour, but it was still holding together. I wanted to get up the slope quickly.

"I don't think that it's ripe yet," I said. I saw no recognition of my western-Canadian avalanche jargon. "It's not isothermal yet. I'll go feel it out."

Fifty feet into the slope, the sun swung to perpendicular. Within ten minutes, the surface snow had cooked to the consistency of porridge; wet, snotty sloughs began hissing down. *Fuck.* I was totally exposed and felt like I'd screwed up—I knew that I'd screwed up. I dodged some of the sloughs, dug in, and prayed nothing bigger was coming my way. It was a little mind-boggling to see how fast the snow had cooked to crap, but then the sun glided off and the slope fell into shade. Ten minutes later, the surface had frozen to plaster, and I couldn't have started an avalanche with a hand grenade.

"That was fucking dumb of me," I confessed to Carl when he arrived at my anchor.

"Man, I thought that big one was going to take you off. It looked like ocean froth when it surged around you. I was mighty glad to be anchored to rock."

The Lads played through, and then the four of us stepped from the breathtaking tightrope in the sky to stand anchored to golden granite against the broad upper swath of Mt. Foraker. I led off, turning the steep rock overhead to the east. The Lads planned to tackle the wall straight on.

Forty-five minutes later, Carl climbed up to my anchor.

"Fuck, man. I had to be the dad again," he spat.

"What happened?"

"They had another fight, and Gren took a swing at Glen!"

"He punched him?"

"Tried to. Glen ducked, and I had to start yelling and telling them to get the fuck along! That's when Glen said to Gren, 'When we get down from here, man, we're brawlin'!'"

I choked on a guffaw. "You're shitting me. He said, 'We're brawlin'?"

"'We're brawlin'!' But then Glen launched into a rage, charged up, and took a thirty-foot fall—and I'm sure it was because he was so riled up."

Glen and Gren emerge from the snow after thirty-six hours of being buried in bivy sacs. Barry Blanchard

"Are they okay?"

"Ya, the fall calmed them both down."

I let thirty seconds pass. "We're brawlin'?" I cocked my eyebrows.

"We're brawlin'!" Carl said with a grin, and we both burst out laughing.

One last tumbling glacier straddled the top of the Spur. East of it lay a wide snow couloir with intermittent rock on its right and the crumbling edge of the tumbling glacier to its left. If we could cross to it and ride its right-hand edge, we would be out of the range of serac fall. It looked like we'd be able to simul-climb—aka "fourth-class"—moving at the same time with pieces of rock equipment between us to hold a fall.

"Let's show the Lads how to deal with a serac," I said. Carl and I charged across the traverse and got to the rock and out of harm's way. It was heartwarming to see the Lads pop up above their steep cliff and, like a couple of wee and eager chipmunks, scamper to our steps. For the remainder of that misty, frigid day, the four of us took turns breaking trail.

Late in the day, we traversed west to get into the bergschrund topping the tumbling glacier, around 14,700 feet. The Lads got there first and invited us inside the crack, but when Carl and I saw the two-foot-thick blocks of windblown snow barely clinging to the roof, we politely declined and pitched our tent out from under the upper lip of the 'schrund on beautiful, heaven-sent, flat snow. We didn't even have to chop ice!

"Right then, I'll 'ave those, mate," Gren declared when he saw Carl set the half dozen pitons we were carrying, and no longer in need of, in the snow. Gren was a true dirtbag climber, I thought, and I couldn't believe that he was opting to shoulder more weight. The Spur had extracted a hearty toll on all of us. I felt ragged and raw, but excited about the prospect of reaching the summit the next day.

JUNE 2: Carl and I got away early, before we heard anything from the Lads. We moved together, simul-climbing up a broad gully. As we exited the gully, the slope angle backed off and we untied; by and by, ascending into clouds, we gained the apex of the south face and a fine, flat camp against a crevasse and sheltering wave of snow.

The morning brought beautiful blue sky and true Arctic temperatures. My fingers froze within minutes of exposing my liner gloves, and I rammed my insensate hands back into my double-layered expedition mitts and swung my arms through full and aggressive circles to get blood back into my capillaries. We climbed away, but I couldn't keep my hands from freezing. For the first and only time in my climbing career, I put air-activated hand warmers into my mitts. I was damn glad that I had them.

Some 16,812 feet above sea level, on the south summit of Mt. Foraker, Carl was ahead of me on our rope shortened for glacier travel. He stopped and bent over at the waist and braced his hands against his knees. I thought about how very, very hard you had to work Carl Tobin to get him to sink into that position.

One mile north-northwest and 588 feet higher, Carl and I walked onto the summit of Mt. Foraker. My hands were finally warm. I had a perfect view of the south face of Denali and could see the Cassin Ridge, which I'd climbed with Kevin Doyle eighteen years earlier, from top to bottom—that amazing and breathtaking line separating sunlight from shadow for two vertical miles.

"Bubba! We did it!" Carl bellowed, and then we bear-hugged each other.

"Let's leave some candies here for the Lads," he added, grinning. And there, at the base of a sole bamboo wand, we nestled two Werther's Originals in the glinting snow, then headed off to find our descent down the Sultana Ridge.

What ensued was 4,000 feet of facing out on hard, 30–35 degrees wind-packed snow and ice. I didn't quite understand how my quadriceps could smolder, so totally spent, and still do the job. Each step felt like my legs wanted to drop me to the ground. We took to rushing into forward-falling steps at any hint of a flat spot, or a break in angle, places where we might get a rest.

"I think we should stop here and wait for the night and the cold," Carl said at 2:30 p.m., Mt. Crosson still several miles of ridgeline away. "If we keep going and hit the Kahiltna during the heat of the day, we'll be up to our nuts in moist, unsupportive snow."

We pitched our tent, drank, and rested for five and a half hours, then we traversed to Mt. Crosson and down through the Alaskan dusk.

The very first people we ran into were Mark Westman, a man destined to do great things in the Alaska Range, and his partner. Carl and I wanted to go; Mark wanted to talk.

"Damn it! I want to climb the Infinite Spur someday, and you guys are the only guys I've ever met who can tell me anything about it," Mark declared, his partner a tad uncomfortable at Mark's detaining us. We answered Mark's questions for a time.

The second folks we ran into were Scott Backes, Steve House, and Mark Twight. That was just so absolutely bloody perfect. My brothers were on the way up to acclimatize for their blitzkrieg ascent of the Czech Direct on the south face of Denali. Big hugs, big smiles, and big, heartfelt congratulations and some fine catching up. It was so very, very good to see those three men with whom I'd spent so much time in the mountains.

Carl and I walked on top of the hard, frozen surface of the Kahiltna Glacier all the way back to the airstrip. There, Carl convinced one of the TAT (Talkeetna Air Taxi) pilots to fly us across to our base camp below Mt. Foraker, wait while we packed up, and then take us out to Talkeetna.

"What about our skis and sleds below the second pass?" I asked Carl.

"I talked to some young guys I know here, and they're going to go retrieve them for money."

"I like that kind of talk—how much?"

"A hundred bucks each."

"Deal!"

We climbed on board and flew out of the Alaska Range. After a shower and change into street clothes at the TAT office, Carl and I caught up with our good buddies Joe Terravecchia and George Lowe. They'd just come out from attempting a new route on the Moose's Tooth. When I asked George how it was, he replied in his nasal treble, "The rock was terrible! I got sick of carving bollards in it to make anchors!" and mimicked the downward raking of his ice adze: *shuuuck, shuuuck; shuuuck, shuuuck.*

"You could carve the rock with your ax?" I asked, bewildered.

"Total kitty litter. Like a beach tilted to vertical."

George's disgust got a laugh out of Carl, Joe, and me. Joe added, "It was total crap, man. Horrid—absolutely horrid."

It was fabulous to compare notes on the Spur with George, who had made the first ascent of the route, along with Michael Kennedy. Carl and I had indeed been spot-on on the route, save for the steep wall I'd led without my pack on our fifth morning. George and Michael had climbed farther east. When I told George about the gully between where Carl and I had climbed and where he and Michael had climbed, the three of us agreed it should be the route going forward. Carl and I committed to sharing that information in whatever trip reports we would write.

We got word the next morning that the Lads had hit the Kahiltna in the heat of the day. Postholing knee-deep into the glacier, they'd taken to crawling across the surface with their packs tethered behind them, dragging them like sleds. Glen's classic lament got passed on to us: "Eventually we could see, and talk to, all the people heading up the hardpacked trail to The Butt, but we just couldn't get to them!"

Back at their house in Anchorage, Carl, Nora, Canyon, and I listened to *Piano Jazz* and *Prince Albert* for one last time. The next day, I got back on the plane home to Canmore after twenty-two days. It had been a marvelous adventure in the company of a good man and a couple of Lads.

🎧 *Floodland*, especially "Lucretia My Reflection" and "1959": The Sisters of Mercy
🎧 "Our Darkness": Anne Clark

CHAPTER 2 — EVEREST EXPRESS I

SHOWING UP

JULY 1988: Mark Twight, Kevin Doyle, Ward Robinson, and I walked out of our base camp below the Rupal Face of Nanga Parbat in the Himalaya of northern Pakistan. We had lived under the Rupal, the largest mountain escarpment on Earth, for fifty-one days and had made two attempts to climb it in pure alpine style. We'd come close to dying in an avalanche on the first attempt. Each one of us left the Rupal twenty pounds lighter than when we'd arrived. We walked slowly back down the trail.

In just four weeks Kevin, Ward, Albi Sole, and I would be on our way to Beijing.

AUGUST 5: "Mate, I hate to do this to you..." Albi started. I'd been home for two days, and it was my first face-to-face with him.

"Well, then, don't do it to me."

"Sorry, man, but I have to. My mother died a week ago." Lines of despair bracketed his eyes, lines that I'd never seen on the man.

"I'm so sorry, Albi—I didn't know."

"I need to go home to Britain to spend time with my family. And I just can't leave my business. Sorry, brother, but I'm out." Albi had immigrated to Calgary in 1976 and then started a guiding business there eleven years later.

The pact we held was sacred to me; four hands stacked upon each other. I felt like our code had been broken and I'd been let down. Yet blood runs deeper. Family underpins everything.

undled up in my warmest layers and sweating
n my apartment in Edmonton, Alberta. Go big
r go home. Hank Van Weelden

"I understand, man. Do what you need to do."

And then we were three.

AUGUST 8: Ward, Kevin, and I walked into the Bow Valley Club and immediately felt like fish out of water. We were at the high-end gym, squash, and dining club for Calgary's professional movers and shakers to meet with members of the support team for our Everest Express expedition. Albi and Kevin were meant to lead this climb/guided trip, with the support team likely only going partway up the mountain, if that. The three of us felt more at home when Bushwhacker, the club's Aussie expat bartender, held up three high-test beers and said, "Here you go, mates! Come on and charm your gullets!" We'd met our man.

We were joined by Jim Hayhurst Sr., his son Jim Jr., Archie Louis, and Jim Law. For the next two and a half hours, we immersed them, and Bushwhacker, in the slides and story of our recent attempt on the Rupal Face (recounted in *The Calling*). Expletives flowed. Mark had sent a rough-cut video he'd created from footage he shot while ice climbing in the Rockies. His *The Adrenalin Cocktail* was pure punk, like being in a mosh pit of ice climbers while The Sisters of Mercy pound out "Lucretia My Reflection," and Anne Clark finishes with "Our Darkness."

"Crank it fucking up!" cried Ward, and Bushwhacker did. All of us bobbed our heads and slapped our feet and got really excited about going to Mt. Everest.

AUGUST 11: Kevin called. "Bubba, I'm not going to be able to go, man. The guy I left running my shop fucked things up royally. The guy is a good woodworker, don't get me wrong, but not a fucking clue on how to run a business. I'll lose The Joinery if I go," Kevin said, referring to the fine woodworking shop he'd started in Calgary three years earlier. "I'm pissed off about that, and mostly I'm finding it hard to stomach what I'm saying to you. Especially after Albi quit on you. I feel like shit."

"Wow. That leaves just Ward and me."

"I know, I know, man. I fucking hate this, but I need to have my business. I can't work for anybody else right now. I could when I was younger, but not now. No way. What about Twight? Do you think he could make it?

I don't think he had anything other than his fiancée tying him down over there."

I looked at the time difference and called Mark at midnight—it was 8 a.m. in Chamonix.

"Dr. Doom."

"Bubba."

"Do you think you could take the place of two of my Everest partners?"

"What? What the fuck happened?"

"There is lots going on over here—"

He cut me off, "Yes, I'll go with you. I'm 100 percent. I'm there."

"Oh god, thank you, Doom. This is the best phone call I've made since I got home."

"And you've been making some, haven't you?"

AUGUST 20: "My daughter was born this morning. It was the most incredible thing I've ever seen. I thought I'd be able to go to Everest, but I can't. I just can't leave my family right now."

"Huh.... I can understand that. I'm happy for you, man. What's your little girl's name?"

"Jenna, her name is Jenna." Ward paused for four seconds, then added, "I'm sorry to let you down, man."

"No reason to apologize, Ward. Some things are far more important than Everest." And then we were two. Just Mark and me. We would need to talk about trying to get someone else on short notice, but that could wait. I had to remove the phone from my head. I needed to go climbing. Solo.

Soloing was of paramount importance to my alpine brothers and me, an imperative we'd gained through reading the writings of the great alpinists Walter Bonatti and Reinhold Messner. To be an alpinist was to climb grand glaciated peaks by their steepest flanks, alone. We held "The Solo" (the first solo of a route) in reverential awe, an awe that was culturally supported in the climbing community, triply so if the solo was a first ascent accomplished onsight. I believed in testing myself solely against the mountain, making all the decisions and being accountable to only me. Below that, deep within the roots of my heart, I felt the ties that

bound me to the people I loved. It is dumbfounding to me now—knowing that my head could outspeak my heart. Yet could it really? Maybe for several hours in a forest of stone and ice mirrors.

Soloing could have lethal consequences, but I believed I was one of the "very best climbers on their very best days." When the climbing went well, I flowed, rhythmically in the present, moving instinctively, feeling the presence of my totem animal—a gray timber wolf—as he loped through the forest, hunting.

I decided to do some soloing the next day.

AUGUST 21, 4 A.M.: I dreamt that I dropped the phone into the sink and listened to it go *bzzzzzt, bzzzzzt, bubble, bubble.* A contented smile stretched across my face as I hopped out of bed and dressed for climbing. I grabbed a day pack (more of a man-purse really, similar to what guides carry in Chamonix), two liters of electrolyte-rich athletic drinks, a couple sandwiches, two malt-flavored PowerBars (thank the Lord they came up with more flavors; the malt tasted like particle board), a windshell, a fleece jacket, rock shoes, and a chalk bag.

In the parking lot below the south face of Mt. Yamnuska, I plugged The Sisters of Mercy—*Floodland*—into my yellow-and-black Walkman, snapped it shut, and stormed off up the approach trail, which gains 1,500 feet in 1.2 miles.

Fifteen minutes later I was halfway up the approach, with my heart thumping and sweat running down my temples. Andrew Eldritch's deep baritone rumbled through "1959." I looked up at 1,000 feet of vertical gray- and yellow-streaked limestone above me, put my head down, and kept pumping in sync with the Sisters.

AUGUST 21, UNNAMED ROUTE, 700 FEET, 5.7: The ashen limestone was over five hundred million years old and warm to my touch. I was alone on the west end of Mt. Yamnuska, starting up the Unnamed Route. I pronounced the mountain's name, which is a Stoney Nakoda word, as best as I could: Îyâ Mnathka, meaning "flat-faced mountain." Below, just across the Old Banff Coach Road that ran beneath the mountain, I could see the Stoney Nakoda reservation. I remembered a powwow there during which the chicken dancers strutted and the young

raveling with Mark is always interesting. Here
e's training above our interpreter, Samson,
nce we finally got to China. Barry Blanchard

fancy dancers preened like acrobatic peacocks to the four-count beat of the drummers' circle—which reverberated with my heartbeat—as the singers' voices wailed a plaintive upward spiral. I'd felt the dancers and the drummers and the singers meld. Their union imbued my blood with power; it was in my pulse.

I was climbing well, making the right moves with my first touch, flowing. At the crux, I thought of one of my heroes, Brian Greenwood. He'd made the first ascent of this route in 1961 with Norwegian partner Jim Steen. Brian was THE climber in the Rockies in the 1960s and '70s. Thinking of him brought my own family history to mind. My people are Métis—the mixed-blood—half Canadian First Nations, half European ancestry (Cree, Scottish, and French, in my case). We seem destined to have a foot in each world. Half of me was in the powwow, the other half scaling the mountain like Europeans had for the last 150 years, starting in the Alps. At times, I never really fit into either and felt like an impostor in both. Yet as I climbed, I knew that I was creating a place for myself.

I lifted my right foot into a wide bridge and set the outside edge of my rock shoe onto a pencil-wide incut edge. On Halloween 1968, four climbers had spray-painted a four-foot-wide pumpkin in orange, black, and green onto a clean vertical wall just shy of the top of the route. I gazed into the jack-o'-lantern—one part graffiti, another part climber pictograph. *Perhaps climbers are tribal!* I held the thought as I left the ledge. Then I noticed a spearpoint-sized piece of limestone holding two fingers of green spray paint. It looked like a miniature peak. It had broken from an edge of the pumpkin. I picked it up and carefully placed it in my breast pocket. This talisman of Yamnuska has sat on my bookshelf ever since.

I topped out. The back slope was warm, and I scampered back to the base of the wall in my rock shoes.

AUGUST 21, EASY STREET, 770 FEET, 5.6: Easy Street shares its start with Unnamed Route but then continues across a large ledge to round onto an off-vertical wall of clean gray limestone. John Martin and Stewart Slymon made the first ascent in 1968, one month before the pumpkin was painted on Unnamed. They named their route after the 1917 Charlie Chaplin film. I'd guided the route dozens of times

The North Face of Mt. Everest, wind from the west throwing snow to the east. Barry Blanchard and often had to convince my clients that the name "Easy" was inspired by the film, not the difficulty of the route. All came to agree with me as they searched for holds on the clean gray wall.

When I topped out into the heat of the sun, I didn't miss a stride shuffling back down to the base. My feet felt the second trip down in rock shoes. I changed into my runners and jogged to the start of the next solo, Grillmair Chimneys.

AUGUST 21, GRILLMAIR CHIMNEYS, 970 FEET, 5.6:

Hans Gmoser and Leo Grillmair had recently immigrated from Austria in 1952, when they and the young British climber Isabel Spreat hiked up to the virgin south face of Yamnuska. It was November 23. Hans and Leo had packed a nylon utility rope slightly larger around than a clothesline. Not expecting anything other than to poke about to see if the face would be possible later, they chose the most striking and prominent line. Steep, dark chimneys and cracks stacked up like stairs between sections of shallower ground, but the top looked impossible, rent by a 150-foot, bottomless pitch-black chimney that soared into an architecture of massive, Gothic roofs. Late in the day, Leo spied light inside the bowels of that chimney; he climbed into the darkness and up to the light. A three-foot-wide hole birthed him onto the back slope, and he giddily pulled up his friends. The south face of Yam was not impossible! Leo had worn holes into his soft-soled shoes, "but I didn't give a shit about that!" he later told me.

My body loved the shade and cool. My sandwiches were gone; both liters of water, too. At the base of the final chimney, I tore chunks of leathery PowerBar with my teeth and then chewed and chewed and chewed. “Thank God there is athletic good stuff in this,” I said to the rock. Then I bridged up into the chimney, feeling the hyper-chilled air seeping from deep down in the bottomless black and wondering, as I always had on the dozens of times that I'd guided, or climbed, or soloed the route, just what was down there.

Ninety feet up, I bridged into my widest splits and marveled at the fact that I was directly over the belay stance. I spit, and I hit it—the chimney overhung. Twenty feet higher, I squirmed into the darkness, and the route became a cave. My eyes took 120 seconds to adjust and see features in the crepuscular vault. Leo's light beckoned like sunlight reaching into a cathedral. I climbed toward it and then squeezed out into the sun.

I'd climbed 2,500 feet, all of it in control. I wanted more. Runners on, I sprinted the back slope, careering downhill like a fell runner.

AUGUST 21, RED SHIRT, 885 FEET, 5.8+: Named for the red shirt that Brian Greenwood wore to tatters pioneering a new age of climbing in the Canadian Rockies. Greenwood put up the route in June 1962, with Heinz Kahl and Dick Lofthouse, declaring that “the second phase of exploration on Yamnuska” had begun. “In the second phase, it is the less obvious, and to some extent, artificial routes that will be climbed,” he said in the *Canadian Alpine Journal* in 1963. I'd soloed the route once before, in the spring of 1981. It was my first year working full-time as a mountaineering and rock-climbing instructor with the Yamnuska Mountain School, and I had, since 1979, been climbing 200 days a year. My finger strength and endurance were the best they'd ever been.

Now, six years later, I no longer had those reserves, yet I had amassed 1,000 more days in the mountains between climbing and guiding. My mind was stronger. I stepped up to the rock, laid my hands onto it, closed my eyes, and brought my attention to my breath: *in and out, in and out*. A dozen breaths and my right foot left the ground. I'd begun.

One-hundred-foot-high spruce trees passed, then compressed to green dots as I ascended. Some of the time I was scared; most of the time I was not. At the crux—a short, steep corner on the fifth pitch—I had to breathe my fear down, my forearms burning as I searched to find the right holds and pull on them at the most advantageous angles. Lower on the route when I'd been stymied, like in the chimney on pitch two, I'd been able to retreat to a place where I could shake out and get the lactic acid out of my forearms, but at this steeper crux I couldn't do that. I had to pull through. The rehearsed faith and boldness in me were a dangerous combination.

The sun had left the top when I stepped from the finishing moves. I felt tired and calm. I sat beside the wind-tortured Engelmann spruce that I'd anchored to when Ron Humble and I'd climbed Red Shirt for the first time, back in 1978. The gnarly old spruce had gained about a foot over the last decade, its roots reaching deep into the rock of Yamnuska.

I rose to my feet. I was ready to face the phone again.

AUGUST 28: Mark walked through the arrival gates at Calgary International Airport. He looked like a chiseled version of Tom Cruise, but with one front tooth tarnished. Mark was twenty-six years old; I was twenty-nine.

"Bubba!"

"Dr. Doom." We shared a backslapping bear hug.

"Are you ready to go and climb this thing?" he asked.

"I was born that way."

"Bald and chubby?"

"Born ready. Bald and chubby, too, as I recall. The doctor said I'd wrapped the umbilical cord around myself in a dülfersitz, rapped to the floor, and shouted, 'Off rappel!'"

We drove to my in-laws' house in Calgary to try to make sense of all the climbing gear we had to cram into duffle bags. I remember Mark's strong hands reefing the edges of the zippers together as I forced my knee in to compress the contents.

🎧 "51st State": New Model Army
🎧 "Behind the Wheel": Depeche Mode

📖 *The Shining Mountain: The First Ascent of the West Wall of Changabang* by Peter Boardman
📖 *Sacred Summits: A Climber's Year* by Peter Boardman
📖 *The Savage Arena: K2, Changabang and the North Face of the Eiger* by Joe Tasker

CHAPTER 3 — EVEREST EXPRESS II

CROSSING TIBET

The valley floors are verdant with barley crops, sparse trees stand out like grain elevators on the Canadian prairie, and hills of rust and ochre badlands rise for thousands of feet. Every hour as we cross Tibet, we see bright clusters of prayer flags, images of the Buddha carved into cliff faces and painted gold, or mounds of Mani stones carved with the mantra Om mani padme hum. *Vast spaces lie between small villages of whitewashed, flat-roofed houses; two- and three-story monasteries form the nexus of each community. The stupa of each single, square, central burnt-sienna building looks to me like it has large, rectangular pieces of tiger's eye laid into medieval gold.*

Tibet feels like a country I'd want to ride a horse through.

SEPTEMBER 3, 1988: From Beijing, Mark and I boarded a CAAC flight for Chengdu, accompanied by Samson, our interpreter, and Mr. Zhang, our liaison officer, both of whom were from the Chinese Mountaineering Association (CMA). Traveling in Communist China was always interesting. The country was opening up but, as Westerners, we were monitored and not popular. Like on my previous trip in 1986, the stewardesses tossed us our in-flight lunch boxes backhand while looking away from the indignity of serving Westerners. Mark and I got bright, plastic-bobbled key chains for our lunch-box prizes.

ark in Xêgar, small-town Tibet, the last stop efore Everest. Monasteries, mud, stones, and arley. Barry Blanchard

SEPTEMBER 5: "We pay four times what a Chinese person does to fly from Chengdu to Lhasa," I said to Mark as we rode away from the Chengdu airport.

"These guys all LOVE greenbacks. I think we look like fatted calves to them. Shy from the abattoir, beware the slaughter."

Mr. Zhang stopped our two cars, and Samson asked me for renminbi, the official currency of China, money I wasn't supposed to have.

I said, "I don't have any renminbi. You all don't let us have renminbi—all I've got is yuan." (At the time, yuan was the tourist currency of China, redeemable only in government souvenir shops. It was changeable for renminbi on the black market, which is how the Chinese got ahold of luxury items normally unavailable to them.) Mark put his headphones back in. I could hear New Model Army's "51st State" from my side of the car.

Samson whispered to Mr. Zhang in Mandarin, and Mr. Zhang whispered back.

"Yuan is okay. Mr. Zhang would like yuan."

"*Please* is a nice word."

"Ah yes, please."

"What is it for?"

More whispering.

"A stove—it is for the stove for the base camp of Qomolangma," the local name for Mt. Everest. We needed two of the big Chinese-made kerosene single burners. I'd asked Mr. Zhang to buy them for us, assuming that, as our liaison officer, he knew what he was doing.

I handed over a bunch of yuan and asked for it to be accounted for, knowing that Mr. Zhang would have to keep it and use his own renminbi, or exchange the yuan with somebody. Mr. Zhang walked into a big concrete box of a store. An hour later, he waddled out with a chest-sized cardboard box gaudily printed with bold red lettering slashed across a blue template. It looked like something from late-night TV, and it was only one stove.

"Samson, we need two stoves for base camp," I objected. *Whisper, whisper, whisper* with Mr. Zhang.

"This is a very good stove, and we will only need this one."

"How do you know?" More whispering.

Hanging out with Mark under prayer flags in the late-day Lhasa sun. Barry Blanchard

"Mr. Zhang talked to the cook."
"Really?"
"Yes."
"How?"
"On the telephone."
"When?"
"When we were in Beijing."
"Okay, great. Let's get on to Lhasa then."

SEPTEMBER 6: Before we left, we started the day in a meeting with Samson, Mr. Zhang, and two representatives of yet another government bureaucracy for the opening of "accounts." I saw pretty much everything we'd done in Chengdu for the last twenty-four hours itemized by hand in a legal-sized accounting ledger, including our upcoming transport to the airport and outward flight to Lhasa. Nothing was cheap. I would finalize accounts on our return from the mountain.

In Lhasa, we met with Samson, Mr. Zhang, and our account manager from the government agency China Tibet International Sports Travel (CTIST), which was organizing the shipment of our gear and supplies. "The cargo will arrive in Lhasa on September 17," Samson said. "We must be here until then."

"WHAT?! That's twelve days from now. We can't wait around for that long. We have to get to higher altitudes to acclimatize, or we will have no chance of climbing Qomolangma," I replied.

"If we don't get to base camp this week, we might as well just turn around and go home now," Mark said, glaring.

"That is impossible," Samson replied.

"How many words for *impossible* do you have?" I challenged. I saw the bafflement on Samson's face as he blurted, "A number." And then he flushed crimson and began a rapid-fire exchange in Mandarin with Mr. Zhang, who also boiled to red. The CTIST guy looked on, poker-faced.

The negotiation degenerated. Mark and I pushed for leaving for base camp with supplies we could buy in Lhasa, while Samson and Mr. Zhang declared "impossibilities" and insisted on more trucks than we needed.

"We damn well don't need three six-ton trucks. We only have one and a half tons of cargo! If I pay for two empty trucks, I might as well throw that money away!" I performed my strongest bluff yet by standing defiantly and hurling a handful of American twenty-dollar bills onto the beige carpet, then sitting down. The three sets of Chinese eyes in the room locked onto the greenbacks like they were bricks of gold, which they probably were in the Chinese economy. As I kept hammering my point, Mr. Zhang took a huge pull on his cigarette, reddened, and then lost it, shouting in Mandarin at Samson, who in turn shouted at us.

"You are arrogant Westerners who have no respect for China! You are bad. We will not leave Lhasa until the cargo arrives. It is impossible!"

"Fuck this," Mark spat.

"Yes, screw this shit!" I barked and bolted upright, then bent to scoop up the twenties. "C'mon, Doom, we're out of here." We marched out the door as a hush fell over the room.

Back in our room, I composed a telex to the CMA in Beijing outlining the challenges we were facing and the support that we needed. Our telephone rang at 11 p.m. Samson effused apologies for the "misunderstandings." Mr. Zhang had been in touch with the CMA, said Samson, adding, "Yes, it is possible to proceed to base camp in one jeep and one small truck as soon as we are provisioned."

SEPTEMBER 9: With our cook and two drivers aboard a Land Cruiser and half-ton truck, we hit the dusty road from Lhasa, headed for Xigazê, then Xêgar, and finally, two days later, our base camp on the stony outwash of the East Rongbuk Glacier. We sped through Tibet, spewing clouds of dust in our wake, save for when we were stopped by washouts, landslides, and the occasional police checkpoint.

Best of all were our stops for lunch. Waiting at one establishment, Mark Francis Twight sat on a chrome-plated folding chair coated in bright-red Naugahyde, the tacky artificial leather that adheres to bare flesh. Our table was rough cut and covered with thick plastic over a floral print. Hand-sawed shelves displayed exactly seven tinned essentials, including oranges, pork, and some kind of fish. A water-stained fabric of flowers lined the ceiling, and from it hung a chain of purple, green, and gold banners made of tinsel and crisscrossed with unlit Xmas-tree lights.

It felt like the Wild West, Tibetan style. The men wore traditional black wraparound coats with sleeves reaching a foot beyond their hands. Young men sported long, single braids, with multiple gold and silver rings, lacquered bone, beads of red coral, and turquoise and red tassels woven in. Many young women had 108 braids to reflect the number of sacred qualities that constitute an enlightened mind in Tibetan Buddhism. Their culture and piety glowed, in juxtaposition to the cookie-cut Chinese and their dull olive-green army garb. Mark and I felt that we fit in. We were definitely into black clothing—as well as somber poetry and music, and the dark places in our being.

"Black is the sun's favorite color," Mark commented. "The Tibetans wear it out of necessity, as most people who live at altitude do. It keeps them warmer."

"And don't they look cool?"

"Hell yes—kinda like a high-altitude motorcycle gang."

Mark had wrapped a colorful woven scarf around his forehead. He'd bought handmade sunglasses in the market in Lhasa—more James

Dean than Mr. Zhang. We'd bartered spiritedly for "real silver" Tibetan rings. I wore them on six fingers. I was trying to be like Mark; he knew that he was influencing me, and I knew that made him happy. Mark looked like a member of Depeche Mode, the band he was listening to at the time. Above the breast pocket of his purple pile pullover were the words "Till Death." His fiancée had embroidered them there. Also in black.

"Is she going to be okay with you being gone for another two months?" We had already been away for two and a half months that spring, attempting Nanga Parbat.

"I told her to do whatever she needed to do."

"You're okay with her sleeping with someone else?"

"Yes, because I know that it would just be sex, and if that's what she needs, it's okay with me because I know it wouldn't be love."

"What about you?"

"I'll be okay for two months. I have the mountain to climb, and that is what I need."

We picked up our boxed lunches and stood beside the Land Cruiser. Three young Tibetan kids, grimy but with big smiles and lots of giggles, came over. There were dogs, always dogs, but the kids shooed them away by pretending to wind up with rocks. Mark and I peeled our hard-boiled eggs and gave our bread and cakes to the kids.

For dinner that night, we sat in the motel restaurant, our five Chinese personnel at a separate table, as they almost always were, Mr. Zhang and the drivers inhaling cigarettes like they were oxygen.

"What do you think this is?" I flipped over a battered piece of something tabular, like a piece of shoe leather, on my plate and leaned over. "Samson, what is this?"

"Food."

"Yes, but is it an animal or a plant or a mineral?" Samson consulted with the others.

"It comes from the sea. It is good for your health."

From Xêgar, we lumbered up the switchbacks of amazingly even graded roads until we gained the Pang La pass, 17,000 feet, from which I'd first seen Everest two years earlier. The spine of the Himalaya held so much snow and ice that the chalky white contrasted abruptly with the barren brown of the Tibetan Plateau. It almost looked too simple: Could the Earth really be so black and white, and on such a mountainous scale? Everest was the proudest pyramid on the horizon. Mark and I wanted to climb it in pure alpine style with only a rope, a rack, and the packs on our backs. We would eschew established camps, fixed ropes, and supplemental oxygen.

In the pre-monsoon, in 1986, Everest had been a black banner against the sky, with a kilometer-long plume of snow that disappeared into thin, thirsty air. Midafternoon in 1988, we rounded the final ridge, and the north flank of Everest sat squat and wide and as white as a drive-in movie screen. We motored slowly by the remains of the Rongbuk Monastery, which had been mostly destroyed during the Cultural Revolution.

"They must have really wanted to blow the shit out of the Tibetans if they came all the way up here to bomb this place," I said.

"No monastery too far, no chorten too high."

SEPTEMBER 11: We rumbled on. A half hour later, the terminal moraines of the Rongbuk Glacier rose like dappled waves rolling onto a barren black beach. Flanks of shattered rock cupped the narrow valley floor. We had arrived at our home for the next couple of months.

Another expedition—the Wyoming Centennial Everest Expedition, aka "Cowboys on Everest"—was already camped on the very last small meadow of compact lichen and moss, nestled in the lee of a terminal moraine where we'd pitched our base camp two years earlier. The meadow had been preserved by virtue of a small spring the Cowboys had tented over with plastic to protect the only pure water source around. Everest Express would have to settle on something more austere.

The Land Rover's tires crunched around the moraine on rounded alluvial stones. We pitched our camp on its up-valley side. A cluster of bright-blue tents from a French expedition sat 200 meters farther on, across the flat and dry braided channels of the Rongbuk's glacial outwash. In the rarefied air at 17,000 feet, pitching two Chinese army-surplus tents was hard work; only our young, scruffy-haired cook, who'd joined us in Lhasa, enjoyed full and normal breaths.

"It's a fucking heater—it's not a stove!" I shouted to Mark. Mr. Zhang had unboxed the "stove" he'd bought in Chengdu. The blue metal cube sat on rounded river rocks in the center of our twenty-foot-square cook tent. It wouldn't be supplying any cooking, or any heat for that matter.

"It's some kind of oil-drip heater," I said as Mark stared on, slack-jawed. "Samson, how are we going to cook with a heater? How is it even going to work with no oil?"

Samson and Mr. Zhang ramped into rapid-fire Mandarin with much snap-of-the-wrist finger-pointing and sideways jaw-jerking. Shit flowed downhill, and they were soon glaring at Chyangba Sherpa, our young Tibetan cook, with their hands planted on their hips just like my mother use to do when she was pissed at me. Chyangba was tough and pragmatic. I'm pretty sure he told them to "get stuffed" and then went around to the other base camps and returned with a proper kerosene stove, the exact model that the CMA had contracted to supply for us. Mr. Zhang claimed credit, via Samson, "We have consulted with other Chinese personnel, and we now have a stove."

Chyangba soon had the pressure cooker hissing. The sun set, and frost reached through the perimeter of the cook tent. Mark and I trudged to our tents to layer up on clothing and pull on Canadian felt pac boots. The Himalayan night tasted cold and steely on my tongue; the mountain was freezing and in good shape. As I looked to its huge black shadow, my movements were slow, like I was wading through sludge.

Only half the normal pressure of oxygen was coming into my lungs; my body was in the process of multiplying red blood cells to transport more O_2 to my cells. That process takes time, and it hurts, especially the higher you go. Each and every cell lets you know that it's not getting enough oxygen. Thankfully, it gets better with each night spent at altitude, except when it doesn't—and then you may be in trouble. Above 7,500 meters (about 24,600 feet), all you do is survive and deteriorate; the deterioration multiplies exponentially above 8,000 meters (about 26,250 feet) and becomes death in a handful of days.

Mr. Zhang and Samson were shocked by the 5 degrees of Fahrenheit, suffering from it and even more with less oxygen in their

The ever-exuberant Archie Louis unpacks boxes of delicious Canadian food from a five-ton Chinese truck. We would be eating good.
Barry Blanchard

blood. They crowded to the stove, hunching to conserve heat. Soon they had on all the insulated clothing we'd brought for them. That first night was rough on all of us, save for the cook. In the morning, Mr. Zhang and Samson moved their tents inside the cook tent to try to stay warmer. I don't think they'd felt cold like that before.

Mark and I escaped our camp—where Samson and Mr. Zhang continued bitching about the cold—and made our way to the Cowboys' upscale base camp. We hit it off particularly well with Matt Ellenthal,

aka "Yak"; Jim Robinson, aka "Mr. Jim"; Carl Coy, a hardcore climbing lifer; and the young, bright-eyed Brad Werntz. Yak had a bra hanging like a coat of arms above his tent's portal; he and Mr. Jim shared our irreverent sense of humor. We could all talk trash and ratchet up the absurdity and the raunchiness. We were good at being boys.

SEPTEMBER 16: Mark and I felt acclimated enough to head up the East Rongbuk Glacier and reconnoiter a site for Advanced Base Camp (ABC) at 21,000 feet.

Outwash led to moraine, and moraine led to stone-covered glacier. We followed a cairned trail dotted with yak crap. A medial moraine lay like a landing strip up the center of the East Rongbuk, and we wobbled up its teetering plates of slate, stabilizing ourselves with trekking poles. Pure white penitentes—pyramids of ice that form on high-altitude glaciers, from the Spanish for "penitent-shaped snows"—lined our boulevard of slate like frozen phantoms, some thirty feet high and others at head level. Mark wheezed, lowering his camera, his lungs bellowing huge draws of cold, dry air.

"They look like gargantuan shark's teeth. I feel like I'm walking into the gullet of the earth."

"Nice image, but we're going up, not down."

I pivoted to face Everest, reflexively thrusting a ski pole out wide to catch my balance. I clenched my eyes and dragged dry lips wide over gritty teeth, my forehead furrowing like I had a bad headache. I heaved in a full lung-load of air.

"Up there," I pointed, and then I folded, dropping my hands to my knees, breathing fully. We were tottering around 19,000 feet. Enough for the day.

We pitched our wee, yellow origami tent on slates we had laid flat like stonemasons, and then we lethargically melted ice and hydrated and shuffled around. While we remained mildly active and erect, our thickening blood circulated advantageously. The challenges would come when our circulation slowed as we lay flat to sleep.

SEPTEMBER 17: Snow had fallen late afternoon and into the night, yet the morning dawned clear and cold. I woke to a headache that wanted to keep me down; my body wanted to be anywhere else. The only time I got headaches in the normal course of my life was when I was hungover. Of course, much of my life was spent at moderate and high altitude; the aching head of acclimatization had become familiar. In the last year, I'd guided a trip to the Cordillera Blanca of Peru, taken two trips to the high volcanoes of Mexico, and climbed close to 8,000 meters on the Rupal Face of Nanga Parbat. I'd suffered my share of headaches. By far the worst were while being hungover at altitude. One of the blessings of Pakistan is that there isn't any booze.

I pushed to sit up. The pain slapped me like a hit to the head. I breathed and brought my cold hands to my temples and delicately exited the tent to get our stove going.

The morning warmed and we trudged on. Slowly we rounded the shoulder of Changtse, the 25,500-foot peak just north of Everest and whose southern ridgeline, an extension of Everest's north ridge, defines the North Col of Everest. Two square miles of flat white glacier planed north and northeast. I could see the broad saddle of the Rhapu La footing the northeast ridge of Mt. Everest. Over that pass lay the mythical Kangshung Face, where my buddies George Lowe, David Cheesmond, and Carl Tobin had opened the hardest climbing on the great peak in 1983.

A broad white shield of snow formed the first third of the northeast flank and ran two miles from the edge of the Rhapu La to the North Ridge. The flank bulged a bit above the shield—not muscularly but maybe just to vertical. Higher, a broad couloir led plumb into the foreboding black rock of the Pinnacles, which look like pikes on a castle wall. The summit jutted as a hint over the North Ridge. From where we stood, it looked to be the same height as the third pinnacle, about 27,000 feet. But that was an illusion. The near-mile-long traverse from the third pinnacle to the summit lay out of view behind the North Ridge; the summit was in fact 2,000 feet higher and way off to the west.

"That's where Boardman and Tasker disappeared in '82," Mark said softly, looking toward the Pinnacles. The British climbers Peter Boardman and Joe Tasker were attempting the first ascent of the northeast ridge with Chris Bonington and Dick Renshaw. Boardman's body was found ten years later by a Japanese-Kazakh expedition (he lies at

8,200 meters on the Kangshung side of the ridge). Tasker's body has not been found.

The partnership of Peter Boardman and Joe Tasker was legendary for us. Boardman's book *The Shining Mountain* had moved me with its honesty when I'd read it six years earlier; *Sacred Summits*, published posthumously, convinced me that I could make a living as a mountain guide and travel the world. Mark had said, "If Boardman is honest, then Tasker is brutally honest." We both ranked Joe's book *Savage Arena* among the best of the dozens and dozens of mountaineering books we'd read. It had helped point us to alpinism, to becoming "hard" men. It was eerie to think that our heroes might be frozen in ice up there. In my fantasy of finding them, I saw myself kneeling to touch them, bless them, and even pray for them. Would I be praying for the dead or, more truthfully, for my living dream of Everest?

At 21,000 feet, on a lateral moraine being gouged from the flanks of Changtse, the Cowboys had two rectangular car-camping tents set face-to-face and adjoined with a blue tarp. We plopped our dome tent down close to the Cowboys to talk more bull with them, or at least as much as our shortness of breath would allow. We breathed the air up there for two nights, and then descended to Base Camp, feeling better with every step.

"I don't believe it," Mark said. "Is that Mr.-fucking-Zhang?" A figure bundled in down was busy arranging rocks into a levee to steer a creek, swollen from the afternoon sun, away from our tents.

"Well bugger me, Doom. It is!" As we crunched up, Mr. Zhang stood up and actually smiled. His rockworks were impressive, a number of square meters of stones stacked dry into a canted wall, which was diverting the silt-saturated water perfectly. I would never have guessed he had it in him; he wasn't even smoking.

"This is cool." Mark dropped his pack, walked to Mr. Zhang's quarry, and picked up a ten-pin-sized rock and carried it back to Mr. Zhang, who beamed and took the rock and placed it precisely. I left them and walked onto camp thinking about how Mark valued action to the exclusion of almost anything else. He'd once sent this equation to me: "Talk – action = zero."

Samson perked up on seeing me. Amazing what sheer and utter boredom can do for a guy. Chyangba made us tea with milk and sugar, and Samson was soon telling me about his hero.

"I think Mr. Lee Iacocca is the greatest man from your country."

"He's not from my country, Samson. I'm Canadian—Iacocca is American."

"Uh, yes. But he is still a great man. I have read his biography, and I want to be as successful as Mr. Iacocca."

"He made a really cool car in 1965." Samson's face pinched in confusion, so I added, "The Mustang." I got a lightbulb moment from Samson. "Other than that, all that guy did was make a lot of money." His face blanked with incomprehension.

"But Mr. Iacocca was the president of the Ford Motor Company, and he is now president of the Chrysler Motor Company. He is a great leader." Samson sat up straight and proud, as if having his picture taken.

"It would be cooler to be the president of Lamborghini, but I would dearly love to have a '65 Mustang, that's for sure," I said. Samson was processing the void between our values, though it may not have been as yawning as it appeared. I valued alpinism and style, he valued money. Somehow, we were closer to common ground with cars. I wondered if Samson had ever driven a car.

rad Werntz, me, Hank Van Weelden, Mark wight, Jim Robinson (Mr. Jim), and Matt llenthal (Yak) all sporting new punk rock aircuts. John Morel

"Willin'": Little Feat
"Like A Hurricane": The Mission

BASE CAMP

But there was no need to stop. Freedom was my catalyst as I deliberately and methodically made each placement. As I pulled over the top and onto the summit slope, I envisioned a crack like this running for days. Where could I find it? I didn't want the feeling to stop.

—Terry (Mugs) Stump, "Hunter's North Buttress Direct," Mountain *No. 85* and American Alpine Journal, *1982*

SEPTEMBER 19, 1988: We saw people milling about the French camp, which had been pretty lifeless. Mark walked over; he was back a half hour later.

"It's Benoît Chamoux. They're calling it quits on the North Face, but there's still one guy up there. Benoît's here with his L'Esprit d'Équipe project. He's fully sponsored by Bull computers." (Later we learned that in 1995 Benoît's team tried to rescue Michel Parmentier, but a storm stopped them. Parmentier's body was found later that season, at 25,300 feet on the North Face by a Spanish team attempting the west ridge. By then, Benoît had climbed thirteen of the fourteen 8,000-meter peaks. He disappeared close to the summit of Kanchenjunga, number fourteen on his list, that autumn.)

"Wow, that explains the cool blue tents. I know that guy—I met him when he was crashing at my buddy Tim's house in Calgary about five years ago. He was climbing in the Rockies, and he showed me how to

Mark Twight and Jim Robinson discuss routes and tactics up the North Face of Mt. Everest. Barry Blanchard do L-sit pull-ups." Benoît had raced up both K2 and Nanga Parbat in twenty-three hours apiece.

Their camp was well supplied. I immediately envied their tables and chairs; the massive, fresh plate of macaroni snowed over with parmesan and chunks of fresh-cut Italian salami made my mouth water. Benoît and four of his team sat around the table. They'd all been baked by the sun. Dramatic outlines of goggles were stenciled on their faces, delineating blistered and cracking mahogany skin from fish-belly white. Then I noticed that one of Benoît's team was missing the end of every finger yet was unselfconsciously gathering chunks of salami in his stumps. I knew he could tell that I was shocked, but he just kept on living his life. The words to Little Feat's "Willin'" rang in my head, and I liked the guy—loved his endurance, his willingness.

"Yes, it is quite hard to have succeeded on six 8,000ers and now to have failed here," Benoît stated, his English accented. He looked wistfully up at the Big E, and then went back to stuffing his down suit as he chatted with us. "We are out of time, and the face continues to avalanche. There is much snow, too much."

"Here's hoping that it changes for our attempt," I said.

"Yes, perhaps it will." And he paused and then let out the dismissive French *Pssst*.

On the way back to our unfurnished Chinese army tent, Mark said, "Benoît told me about a French guy who died here. The guy wasn't part of Benoît's team. He'd been sleeping in a hypobaric chamber in Paris every night for a month to acclimatize, and then he blitzed from Paris to here in five days and dropped dead twelve hours after getting here. They couldn't get enough juniper up here for a proper pyre." Mark stared at the stones at his feet, stones that could be inscribed with prayers to become Mani stones. "His chest cavity is sitting in the river."

"Poor son of a bitch. I don't think I want to see that."

But in time, we did. Brown water flowed through white ribs. Part of a skeleton stretched over white skin.

SEPTEMBER 20: Midday, four Land Cruisers and a three-ton truck pulled into Base Camp. Chris Considine, Tom Christie, Carl Hannigan, the Jim Hayhursts (Sr. and Jr.), Jim Law, Archie Louis, John Morel,

Ric Singleton, Dixon Thompson, and Hank Van Weelden all stepped out. I counted eleven Everest Express members where there should have been thirteen.

"Where are Goguen and Gault?" I asked Dixon.

"They went home," he said.

"Why?"

"There's been some issues."

"Like what?" My pulse, already pounding hard because of the altitude, pounded harder.

"Leeches and rain. A lot of the guys had some hard times, and then a lot of us got the shits, including Jeff and Gary. They said, 'screw it' and flew home." I could feel my blood pressure rising. Much thought and preparation had gone into the trek, and it had not gone to plan. I shelved the thought and went back to concentrating on the now.

Our half-full three-ton truck lumbered around the moraine, and we all began happily unloading and organizing the food and equipment that we'd shipped from Canada.

"We are going to eat well tonight, Doom."

"Yes, we are! Where the hell are the Pringles?"

I'd scavenged a bunch of wax-coated cardboard boxes from our 1986 Everest Light Expedition. The boxes were white, with the Everest Light logo—a five-toed dragon—emblazoned in red. We brought it all into our second army tent, using wood planks we'd bought in Lhasa to fashion the boxes into a table and benches.

When the support team went to set up their dome tents, Hank, who'd been with Mark and me for the first month of our Nanga Parbat trip, hung back.

"How's the 'do'?" I asked.

The most pleasant and endearing man you could hope to meet, Hank Van Weelden was also a hardcore punk rocker. Before leaving for Nepal, he'd had the Everest Express logo shaved into one side of his cinderblock-sized noggin and the Grivel logo on the other. An inch-wide mohawk divided Express from Grivel. He yanked off his pirate's bandanna. The logos and mohawk were three weeks grown out, but still proud and buttery blond.

"You should have seen the little kids on the Annapurna circuit! I'd get into camp and pull off the bandanna, and they'd all laugh and laugh and point. They all wanted to touch my head!"

"How were the leeches, the rain, and the butt-sickness?" I asked. "How is the support team?"

Hank hesitated, and then said, "The mountains were amazing. But not all of the guys saw that."

"I think everyone here is fine. If they get up to Advanced Base Camp and stand right below Everest, it'll be the trip of a lifetime."

Allwest Supermarkets of Calgary had sponsored our trip. Back in August, I'd gone into their store and filled a couple dozen shopping carts with whatever I wanted. Top of the list was Magic Pantry boil-in-a-bag, basically foil-wrapped military rations marketed to the public. Now, with our two MSR XGK stoves firing like jet engines under a large stock pot, I piled Magic Pantries in a dozen at a time: Salisbury steak in gravy, chicken supreme, beef stew, cannelloni, lasagna, and chili con carne! Our cook provided the rice, and we all sat down to our table and gorged ourselves on North American food washed down with cans of Star Beer and Twizzlers for dessert. It tasted so bloody good and raised everyone's mood.

SEPTEMBER 21: "The yaks will not be here for another five days," said Mr. Zhang, with Sampson translating.

"They were supposed to be here today, to start our trek to Advanced Base Camp tomorrow," I complained.

"Impossible."

"But our contract says they'll be here today."

"So sorry, that is impossible. The yaks will be here on September 26."

I shared this latest challenge with Mark, prodding him, "Can the Chinese Money Association [what we'd began calling the Chinese Mountaineering Association] do anything more to make sure that we don't climb the mountain?"

"Let's be careful what we wish for."

Over breakfast with the support team, we came up with yet another contingency plan. The support team and I would carry tents, food, and fuel to 18,000 feet, and then return to base camp; on September 24,

Everest Express base camp on the outwash of the Rongbuk Glacier. Geodesic domes for sleeping, Chinese military tents for cooking an eating. Barry Blanchard we would pick up that cache and occupy Camp I a bit further on; the next day, make a blitz to Advanced Base Camp; then return to Camp I and descend to base camp again. The support team would leave for home on September 27. Hank and Mark would stay in Base Camp to organize the yaks if, and when, they arrived.

SEPTEMBER 22: I zipped open the door to my tent and there was a copy of one of Mark's poems. Over the next two decades, I'd see a number of his poems written out on yellow, legal-sized notepads. Often similarly structured and—at least initially—as confrontational as an artificial mohawk bolted into a shaved skull, they became less melodramatic over time, as did we. My favorite alpinist in agony had added in longhand "Whether we make it or not, this is the most real experience we're going to have together. I'm loving it! Mark, 22, Sept, 88."

I read the poem four times and then headed back to our mess tent.

"Thanks, man," I said to him.

"You're welcome, Bubba." And we held eye contact for seven heartbeats.

SEPTEMBER 23: Our support team came to life. Dixon, Archie, Tom, Jim Jr., Jim Law, John, and I made the carry to 18,000 feet. Chris had pulled some intercostal muscles during a coughing fit (a common injury while acclimatizing in thin, dry air) and was sidelined at base camp. Ric wasn't acclimatizing well; Carl stayed behind to care for him. Jim Sr. had walked a couple hundred meters above Base Camp and decided that Everest wasn't the right mountain for him. He told his son to be safe and, panting, turned back.

"Barry, we've got a problem." Carl's Scottish brogue broke the absolute silence of the Himalayan night. I struggled from my pit and wiped a pool of saliva from my left cheek, and then unzipped my tent.

"What's up, man?"

"It's Ric. He's sitting upright, and his breathing is rapid and shallow. I think he's developing pulmonary edema. I'm going to give him some Lasix and put him on oxygen. I think he needs to get to a lower altitude."

SEPTEMBER 24: "What do you mean there's no jeep?" Yet again, I was squared off with Samson and Mr. Zhang. It was getting old.

"We have no jeep."

"Our contract says that we'd have a jeep and driver in Base Camp for evacuation. Mr. Singleton needs an evacuation, or he is going to die!"

"Our jeeps went back to Lhasa."

"What?" and then I snapped. "Fucking China!"

Samson and Mr. Zhang jerked back like I'd swung at them, which is exactly what I wanted to do. Their faces darkened. Samson did a double take and grabbed me by my shirt front, and I grabbed him by his and wound up to hit him just as he wound up to hit me. It was one of the two times that I've come to the edge of male-on-male physical violence in my adult life. Both Samson and I snapped to our senses and released each other. It was like the fighters in each of us had to see what would happen if we got pushed up against a wall. Now we knew.

I stormed out of the tent and Mark and I made the rounds of the base camps. By utter, dumb luck, a China Tibet International Sports Travel Land Cruiser pulled into the Cowboys' camp to deliver their mail. We negotiated transport back to Lhasa for Ric for the next day.

Ric sat in our mess tent. Clear tubing connected the medical oxygen mask covering his nose and face to a bright-orange O_2 tank—one of the four tanks we had for emergencies—set to two liters/minute. He wore our navy-blue and yellow expedition suit with Sunice, our clothing sponsor, boldly stenciled in white on the right thigh and in black on both sleeves. He managed a smile. I had to leave to retrieve our cache at 18,000 feet and to continue onto Camp I. As hard as it was to leave, with the responsibility for Ric's well-being ultimately resting with me, walking away from an ailing client was doubly hard because it flew in the face of all my mountain guide training.

"How are you doing in there?" I asked as I kneeled to look into Ric's eyes.

"A lot better with this oxygen. I'll be okay. Don't worry—Carl and I will take care of this." I'd just have to trust him, Carl and Mark, and Samson—who was to travel out to Lhasa with Ric.

I shouldered my pack, grabbed my ski poles, and trudged off for Camp I.

SEPTEMBER 25: The altitude continued to stalk us, turning most of the guys around until it was just Archie, Tom, and me walking up the glacier late in the day. Of the seven who'd started from Camp I, only Tom—the tough, no-nonsense stockbroker from Calgary—and I rounded the corner to 21,000 feet.

"Bloody aye, man! Good work! There it is!" I blurted.

"It's one bloody big hill!" Tom put his hands on bent knees and panted white clouds. We were in the shadows, and the night frost was on us. He looked up to Everest and asked, "Where are you and Mark going to climb?"

I pointed out the new route that Mark and I hoped to climb, a broad couloir leading into the Pinnacles, and then Tom posed for some pictures and we started down into the dusk. We picked Archie up from the black moraine that we'd left him on. He was cold but smiling—always smiling.

"How was it?" he asked Tom.

"Incredible, just fucking incredible."

Into the night, all of our headlamps dimmed, and then died. I led by the dark shadows of landmarks catalogued in my mind, most of my footfalls calculated by faint differentiations in blackness in my peripheral vision. Archie and Tom stumbled behind like blind men, focusing on my voice. They trusted my dead reckoning.

SEPTEMBER 25, 3 A.M.: I made out the circular silhouette of one of our tents, reached to touch it, and stumbled. It was a yard beyond where my depth perception told me it was. We heard the voices of our teammates. Dixon and John stumbled out into the black, cold night to help us into our tents.

"Well, that was amazing," Tom stated. "I don't know how the hell you found the way to our tents in the dark."

"I used my peripheral vision mostly."

"Man, you were born a hundred years too late. You would have been one hell of a frontiersman. Amazing."

"I tell myself the same thing all the time, man. Let's get some sleep."

SEPTEMBER 26: We descended to Base Camp, where Mark and Hank had our yaks organized. We had asked for three but got, and paid for, six.

"Easy work for the yaks," I observed.

"Well paid, too," Mark added, and then clicked on his Walkman.

"What are you listening to?"

"The Mission, 'Like A Hurricane.'"

"A Canadian cover, a Neil Young cover. Cool."

"Raine and I listen to it when we're..." And I cut him off.

"Don't say it, man—I don't need to hear it right now." He smiled a closed-lipped grin and said, "Yeah, it is getting to be too long. Wouldn't Himalayan climbing be great if you could have your woman at Base Camp?"

"Yes, I'd love to have your woman at Base Camp," I said, beaming.

"Touché!" Mark belly-laughed and then strode away.

Most of the support team was to leave for Lhasa the next day. Dixon and Carl planned to stay eighteen days longer, and John and Hank would be there until the bitter end.

Hank Van Weelden modeling the Grivel logo he'd had shaved into one side of his cinderblock sized butter-blond head. Doug Hofstede

There have been many conversations I wish I could go back in time to ameliorate. The one I had with Dixon that day is one. He and Carl wanted to try the mountain. I can't remember why I thought that would compromise, or compete with, or threaten, our own chances. But suffice it to say I lost it and pointed my finger like it was a pistol.

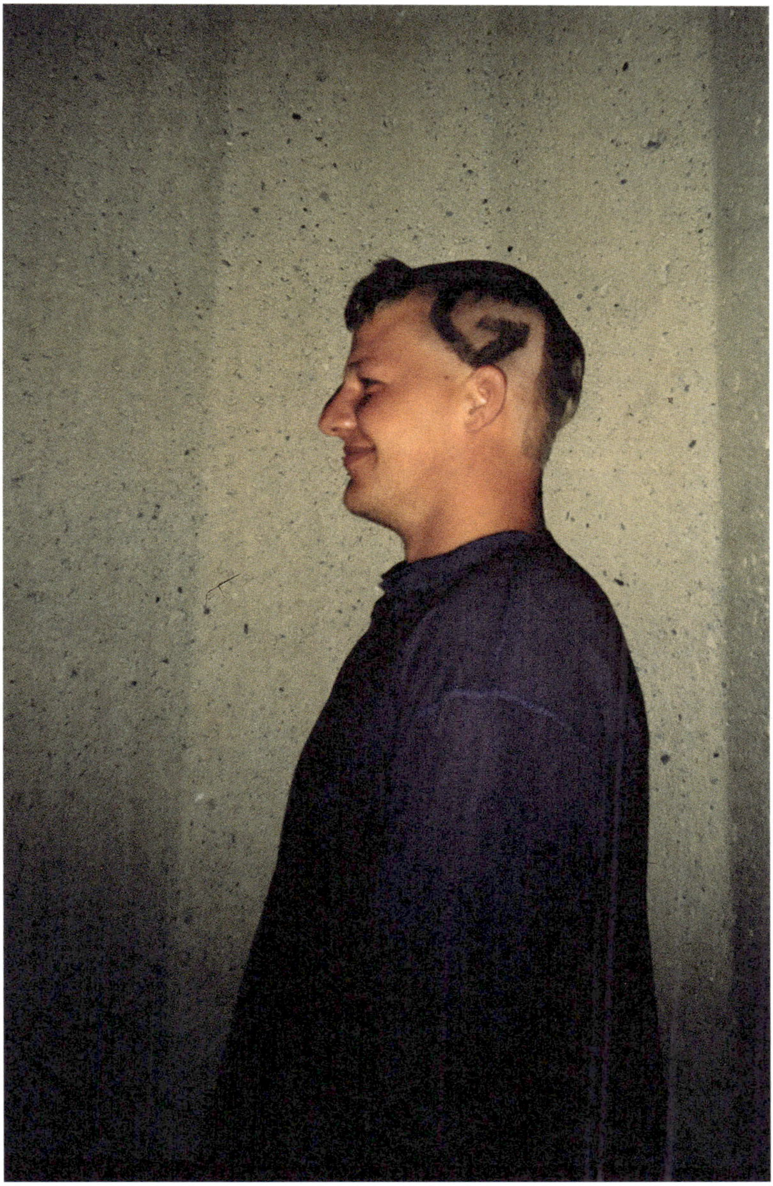

"I came here to climb this mountain! I'm not going to let you, or anybody else, stop me!" I bellowed.

"Fine!" Dixon swatted his hand down through the air. "It doesn't matter what anyone else's goals are. Fine!" He turned and marched off. He and Carl left with the rest of the support team the next day. Dixon would be at the airport when I arrived home a little over a month later, and we would drink a beer together and get beyond our spat. But our reconciliation still doesn't keep me from wishing it had never been necessary.

SEPTEMBER 28: I woke with the warming of the sun. The luminous line of its heat slowly sank down the wall of my tent; I felt like I was slowly surfacing from underwater. Then, I was awash in bright light and radiant heat, and my sleeping bag immediately felt stifling.

Only Mr. Zhang, our cook, and I were at base camp. The simplicity of that felt good; now it was just for Mark and me to climb the mountain. I felt strong, like I'd finally acclimated to Base Camp. Midday, I packed rock shoes and began switchbacking up the scree and talus slopes that bordered us to the east. A solid-looking cliff of sand-colored rock reared vertically about halfway to the ridgeline.

I settled my hands on the steep stone, breathed, and felt the sun's reradiated heat. The climbing felt as good as it had on my day alone on Yamnuska a little over a month before; I flowed up corners and cracks of intermediate difficulty to the top of the solid cliff. I felt like I could take flight from the final holds. The visionary American alpinist Terry (Mugs) Stump wrote in the *American Alpine Journal* (Mountain No. 85), "I screamed in order to release the fullness." I held my head back and howled like a wolf. A half dozen yellow-beaked choughs lit out from the slopes above and swooped by me in pairs, their underwings flashing silver.

SEPTEMBER 29: I left Base Camp by myself.

SEPTEMBER 30: I met up with Mark, Hank, and John at Advanced Base Camp.

"Right, then, what will you have?" John asked, his British accent audible despite two and a half decades in Canada. He stood in command of a small stone corral that he'd constructed with Mark and Hank. Our two Markill Stormy stoves were humming away melting ice; black in hue, the stone-age slate benches and table created a pleasant hang when it was warm. That was some of the time. The rest of the time, it was snowing, blowing, or cold.

"Warm Tang, please, squire. I'll have warm Tang."

"Coming right up, my liege." Forty-five years old with salt-and-pepper hair, John had a pace and a manner that came from an earlier time. To three young punks, it might as well have been Victorian England. He'd taken the "support" part of support team to heart. This wood artist who made his living with his hands had mastered our most important tools: the stoves.

"Don't Leave Me This Way": The Communards
"Mining for Gold": Cowboy Junkies
"Anarchy in the UK": Sex Pistols

CHAPTER 5 — EVEREST EXPRESS IV

THE UNCLIMBED NORTHEAST FLANK

At the end of the monsoon, two years earlier, Erhard Loretan and Jean Troillet started up the North Face of Everest at night with no tent, sleeping bags, or rope. Their revolutionary style was coined "night naked." Ascending the Japanese Couloir (first climbed by Tsuneoh Shigehiro and Takashi Ozaki in 1980) to the Hornbein Couloir (a gully that Tom Hornbein and Willi Unsoeld traversed into from the West Ridge during their amazing 1963 traverse of Mt. Everest), Loretan and Troillet stopped in the heat of the day to brew and doze, sitting on an Ensolite pad. They summited that day and were up and down the face in forty-three hours! Their blitz of the 9,000-foot face shocked, and shook up, the high-altitude climbing world. Their time has never been bettered.

SEPTEMBER 18, 1988: Mark and I talked a lot about Troillet and Loretan; we wanted our own night nakedness. But first, we needed to acclimatize. Mark's spikey punk hairdo sprouted from our tent, and he looked at me bleary-eyed and recited a fresh poem:

Altitude is rude!
Altitude is rude!
Troillet can't tell me he doesn't hurt!

OCTOBER 2, 5 P.M.: Mark carried a single sleeping bag that we intended to share; my pack held our stove, a shovel blade, and food.

ark Twight climbing new ground just as the n disappears, the shadows are long, and the ld is about to clamp down. Barry Blanchard

We had left John and Hank in the stone corral and crunched off toward the northeast flank. We planned to climb through the night, then dig a snow cave to rest and hydrate in during the warmth of the day. We hoped to be up and down the peak in three days.

The East Rongbuk Glacier glowed in voluptuous folds of pure white. The magic of its untouched surface excited me. Mark and I stitched a thin line of tracks into the firm snow. In stark contrast, the Cowboys, attempting Changtse, had stomped down a two-foot-wide groove leading to the fixed lines of the North Col. I remembered doing the same on the West Ridge two years earlier. It felt good to be going light.

"How is your ski-pole-cum-ice-ax treating you?" I asked Mark. Grivel had been forging ice-axes and crampons since 1818, out of Courmayeur, on the Italian side of Mont Blanc. The company's president, Gioachino Gobbi, had handed Mark a light ice-ax prototype with a length of ski pole that could extend from its shaft. It was a cool piece, and I wished that I had one. More to the point, I longed to be a sponsored alpinist like Mark.

"It's good so far. It looks like I'll be using it as a ski pole."

The shallow snow apron that footed Everest grew larger with every step we took; we could see no steep ground until far up the face. A crevasse scythed across the head of the valley as far as we could see: the East Rongbuk Glacier flowed away from Everest, Changtse, and the rest of the valley. Here, in its birthing zone, the bergschrund was bridged with monsoonal snows.

A slab avalanche had added a thick layer of debris over the 'schrund, and the wind had since drifted snow between the angular snow blocks, as fine as desert sand. We balanced up the blocks, grateful for the structure they added to the snow bridging the dark, linear crack. In my mind, the 'schrund was as deep, dark, and unknowable as Hades. The angle increased, and the 'schrund passed beneath us.

We were finally actually climbing on Mt. Everest.

"YO! YO! Doom! We are on the Big E now!" I shouted to Mark, and he looked up from twenty feet below and shouted back, "Hell yes, we are!" In that moment, I felt like I'd become the alpinist I'd always dreamed of being.

Climbing into the shadow of a big mountain is never abrupt. The defined line of sun and shade exists only at a distance. Up close, your shadow grows hazy then disappears over the course of twenty steps. What is absolutely abrupt is the dive in temperature, like you've stepped into a meat locker and closed the door. *Click!* I huffed a frigid cloud, kicked into the snow harder, and pushed my ski pole and ice-ax deeper to fire more heat.

Some 1,500 feet higher, we were punching up fields of inclined, arctic-cold snow. Cascading steps had been carved into the surface by torrents of spindrift. I could hear the wind raking through the Pinnacles 3,000 feet above me, as wave upon wave of snow glided down the northeast flank to flow around our legs like swash. Mark had been falling behind, stopping to swing blood back into his feet with fifty large, pendulous kicks of each foot. At 23,000 feet, he caught up to me and said "I can't keep my feet warm. I have to go down."

"Are you kidding me?" My spirit stumbled.

"I haven't felt my toes for a half hour. I'm going to have to add overboots to my system. We can try again tomorrow. I'm not losing my toes for this mountain."

I saw frank resolve in his eyes, and then a twitch of embarrassment that touched me. "Okay, brother—let's get out of here."

OCTOBER 3: That night we tried again. The spindrift had doubled in frequency and volume, and it felt like we were striding into surf. A bitter westerly strafed the slope. I put on goggles to protect my right eye from the rasp of airborne ice crystals, pivoted the insulated hood of my one-piece suit to shield the right side of my face, and instantly bemoaned the loss of much of my starboard vision.

At midnight, Mark said, "We should stop and hydrate for a couple of hours. This wind is going to be too hard to deal with all night. It's going to weaken us. I think we should climb into the heat of the morning."

"Okay, man," I huffed, "I'll start digging a cave. How about you anchor our packs and get the stove going?"

"Roger that, Mr. Blanchard." And he gave me a quick salute.

Cold snow came away in chunks. I dug hard and soon had a hollow that Mark could hobbit into and brace the stove between his knees. He fed snow into the stove and handed me a warm cup of Gatorade. I panted and slurped and panted some more. I passed the empty cup back to Mark and went back to hacking hard at the snow. My breathing grew rapid and shallow, a pattern I didn't recognize. That scared me. I kept digging until we had enough room to lie flat on our pads with our packs blocking the door and the wind. I was hyperventilating.

"Fuck, man, I can't seem to warm up. How are you doing, Doom?"

"I'm okay. Get into the sleeping bag and I'll keep the stove going. Try lying down and resting."

I squirmed in and zipped the big bag up; it took an hour for my shivering to stop and my breathing to resume a normal, deep, high-altitude rhythm. The stove hissed on, and we drank and dozed.

OCTOBER 3, 3 A.M.: We started climbing again. Within twenty steps, I was panting again. I rested often, letting my head hang. Mark pulled away from me in leaps and bounds. When he stopped and waited, his headlamp bobbed back down to me.

"I can't get enough air. It feels like my lungs are about a liter each."

"Ya, something is not right, Bubba. You are stronger than this."

"I think I'm getting pulmonary edema."

"I guess we're going down."

Down went better for me; I stumbled into our rock corral at dawn. Soon Mark, John, Hank, and I were in the Cowboys' car-camping tent, and Dr. Bob Bohus had his stethoscope pressed to my chest, confirming congestion in all quadrants of my lungs and pressure in my pulmonary artery.

The four of us headed down to Base Camp. I was anxious to get there. *Could this be the way my dream died?*

OCTOBER 5: A trickle of trekkers had arrived at our base camp, adventurous world travelers with the Lonely Planet's Tibetan phrasebook pressed tightly to their breasts and a need to get as close to Mt. Everest as possible. Not all that different from Mark and me, really. Samson had also brought mail when he returned from Lhasa. We ripped, literally, into it.

"Do you think that's a guy's foot?" Mark asked.

He held a fresh picture of Raine traversing the granite blocks on a railway bridge in Chamonix. She was reaching with her right hand and, aware of the camera, smiled beguilingly over her right shoulder, her gaze

I'm working hard and breathing harder to excavate a snow cave in the bitter shade of Everest. Mark Twight

set out of the frame, to the right. She was following someone. In the bottom right corner of the photo, standing on the small edge of a granite block, was a solitary left foot wrapped in a purple rock shoe, four inches of ankle and Achilles tendon exposed below the bottom hem of tight Lycra. I studied the picture.

We concentrated on the mysterious foot.

"I think it's a woman's foot," I said. "See how deep the hem is biting in? Don't women have an extra layer of subcutaneous fat?" Mark looked more closely.

"Ya, maybe you're right. A guy's ankle would be leaner."

"Do you think it's a guy?"

"I don't know."

After a couple of days in Base Camp, I was feeling better. That night, Samson approached me looking stern and asked that I come to meet with him, Mr. Zhang, and three other liaison officers. I pulled the flap to our cook tent and stepped into cigarette smoke as thick as fog and a mood as heavy as body armor. One of the liaison officers was over six feet tall, and broad. Samson beamed as the big guy talked at me in halting English, his black eyes unwavering,

"You said 'fucking China.' You don't say 'fucking China.'"

"I said Fukien, China—it's a place in China." There was shock and lots of Mandarin and the big guy repeated his warning, "You don't say 'fucking China.'"

"Okay, I won't say 'fucking China.' Nice to chat with you fellas." I got up and left. Out of earshot I hissed, "Fucking China."

OCTOBER 8: Two more Chinese army tents had popped up in Base Camp. Mark and I were soon having green tea with the Japanese alpinist Tsuneo Hasegawa and his wife. Tsuneo had soloed the north faces of the Eiger and Matterhorn and the Walker Spur on the north face of the Grandes Jorasses, all in winter, during the late 1970s. Mark and I respected him as an accomplished alpinist.

That day, we learned that he had specific permission for the broad couloir we had been trying to climb into! We had taken a liberal definition of our permission for the northeast ridge; now the jig was up. We'd need a different plan. We assured Tsuneo that we wouldn't try to climb into his couloir anymore. I lifted the tent flap, and Mark and I walked out.

"Fuck," Mark said.

"*Fuck* is right. We're going to have to change our objective. I think we can connect those slender gullies a couple hundred meters to the east. Might even give us more interesting climbing, and it will still be a first ascent."

"Did you see that Hasegawa had a pleasure tent set up inside the cook tent?" Mark asked.

"Ya, wouldn't it be nice to have your gal here in Base Camp?"

"I'd love to have *your* gal here in Base Camp!" Mark blurted, then he burst into cackles.

"Touché! You got me back, dude."

OCTOBER 11: We crunched into Advanced Base Camp early. Mark and I puttered around camp and watched Hank and John cross the flat white plain of the East Rongbuk Glacier and ascend a lovely, wee snow peak (22,398 feet) a little more than a half mile north of the Rhapu La.

Hank and John returned to our rock corral happy. "Ha, ha!" beamed Hank. "John and I got the first summit of the trip!"

"Yes, but now it's *your* turn," John added, nodding his head to Mark and me.

OCTOBER 12, 10 P.M.: Again, not quite naked. Scantily clothed, maybe. Mark and I carried a tent, two sleeping pads, and a stove. We did not take ropes, harnesses, or sleeping bags. The night was calm, and there was no spindrift. We climbed well, ten hours by headlamp.

OCTOBER 13, 8 A.M.: I attached the shovel blade to my ice-ax, and we hacked out a platform for our tent, then lay on our pads inside the tent and fed snow into our hanging stove. Hour on hour, liter by liter, we drank the yield until we were pissing gin-clear again. That took three liters each, with an additional four filling our water bags.

"The sun should be hitting you guys in about fifteen minutes," Hank said over our small personnel radio. We brewed and we shivered.

Forty-five minutes, later Hank repeated, "The sun should be hitting you guys in about fifteen minutes."

"Are you s-s-sure?" Mark chattered into the radio.

"Ya, I think so. It just has to clear the rock band over your tent."

A half hour later, he repeated his prediction—but it had become a cruel joke.

"The sun is never going to f-f-fucking get here!" I hissed over chattering teeth. And it never did. Our small yellow tent sat in eternal shade, 24,800 feet above sea level.

"Wow! You guys picked the only place on the whole face that's stayed in shadow all day!" Hank exclaimed.

"God hates us," I replied.

OCTOBER 13, 2 P.M.: We broke our tent down and packed it away along with the pads, and the stove, and then started climbing again.

The sun! the sun! We entered a couloir of good, firm snow and climbed into the sun. God loved us; the warmth of the sun was marvelous, miraculous. An hour later, the wind came and hauled away all of the sun's heat save for what was reflected from the snow and absorbed by our faces. My skin was baking browner yet.

OCTOBER 13, 5 P.M.: At 26,300 feet, the west wind screamed over the north ridge and slapped at our right flanks. Wind-borne ice crystals rasped my right eyeball. We donned goggles and pulled up our hoods. Spindrift was washing down from the Pinnacles again.

Mark was outdistancing me. I watched him climb into a thirty-foot-high chimney splitting a steeper rock band. My chin slumped to my chest and heaved on the thin air, but my airway felt like it was folded. So, I threw my face to the sky and dragged in lungfuls of air.

Mark waited atop the chimney as I entered it. I watched my gloved hands grab holds in the black rock, yet it felt like my hands were not attached to me, like I was sitting in the front row of a movie theater and watching hands projected onto the silver screen. Intellectually, I recognized the danger of that disconnect, but even that information seemed to be coming from behind a closed door. Most of my mind was content to sit back and enjoy the show. I climbed to my feet beside Mark.

"Something is going wrong in my head. I've been out of my body for the last half hour, just watching myself climb," I said. I saw Mark's eyes register. For the first time, I tested my head by shaking it side to side. A white strike of pain bridged my temples. It blinded me and took my breath away.

"It feels like spikes are being driven into my temples, and I've lost my peripheral vision. It might be cerebral edema."

"Okay, we're going down."

ark, about to climb over the bergschrund, njoying the warmth of the sun. Gotta love the ın when you're cold. Barry Blanchard

I hesitated. *Was I overreacting? Could I spend the night here and continue in the morning?* I shook my head again; another blinding bolt.

"I'm scared."

"We're outta here."

"I've gotta get out of here, but you don't. You should go for it."

"No. No way," he said, shaking his head side to side. "You're my partner and you've got cerebral edema—there's no fucking way I'm leaving you alone."

"I'll be okay. I can get down this."

"No. I descend with you. That's it, man—we're going down."

I've always liked the ánalogy of spinning a suspension cable to describe the passing back and forth of the strands of trust that connect one soul intimately to another. At that moment, high on a virgin flank of Mt. Everest, the cable that bound me to Mark doubled its strands.

I followed him across the northeast face, losing elevation toward the North Ridge. We strode across Hasegawa's couloir like we were bounding over an alpine meadow. In less than an hour, we'd crossed 2,500 feet to walk onto the ridge at 25,500 feet. As we left the lee of the ridge, the wind drove into us like a strong ocean current. We staggered to our knees, then dug our heels and axes into the wind-hammered snow, sat, and put our backs to the pounding.

Down at Advanced Base Camp, Hank and John hustled over to the Cowboys' tent. Dr. Bob Bohus was soon on the radio to Mark.

"Dr. Bob says to take these," Mark shouted. We sat shoulder to shoulder, still shuttering against the wind. He held ten little yellow pills of dexamethasone, a steroid, in his palm: ten milligrams. It would help reduce swelling in the brain. I slapped the pills into my mouth and washed them down with water that was beginning to freeze. Ten minutes later, the wind abated some; Mark and I teetered off down the ridge, leaning into the wind.

I felt so tired and hazy, like I was wading through a swamp of ether. Each footfall was an effort, and I had to sit down often and rest—when I did, I wanted to lie down and sleep. Mark waited patiently. Every so often he'd coax, "C'mon Bubba, we have to get down this thing." And I'd get up and continue forcing my way down.

The Cowboys had four yellow dome tents at the North Col, 23,000 feet. Unrelenting westerly winds had stuffed their attempts to get higher. I staggered into their camp just about as buggered as I've ever been. The Cowboys got to work on Mark and me. They gave us hot liquids, food, plus an extra jacket for me, as I couldn't keep warm. I tried to refuse their offer of oxygen, but Carl Coy said, "Just take the fucking oxygen, man. You need it. You can give us one of your bottles at ABC."

Four liters per minute. Mark and I started down the Cowboys' fixed lines at dusk, and I got it on! I felt like I could run, and I did. A thousand feet lower, I'd pulled away from Mark. I was hot, sweating. I stopped and peeled off the extra jacket, marveling at how the oxygen had given me my lungs back.

"Holy crap, Bubba, you bolted like a spooked horse!" Mark panted. We were at the end of the fixed lines, and his headlamp was on. Below, I saw four headlamps bobbing up the glacier toward us. Our rescue team—Hank, John, and the Cowboys' Jeb Schenck and Quint Barney—met us with sweet, milky hot tea. They took our packs and walked us to Dr. Bob.

"Well, you've got cerebral edema," Bob concluded. "I'm going to keep you on oxygen, and I think you need to spend the night in the Gamow bag."

The Gamow bag is a portable hyperbaric chamber. Ingeniously, its heavy, red nylon fabrics, ribbed with yellow, one-inch military-spec webbing, could be inflated with a foot pump, increasing the air pressure within the chamber and effectively lowering the patient inside—me—by 10,000 feet of elevation. Inflated, it looked like a cross between a commercial river raft and a torpedo. It was the length of a coffin. Thankfully it had several clear, plastic windows; without them, anyone going inside would lose it and exit screaming and punching. The Gamow bag was freaky to lie down in, but one of the side effects of the dexamethasone was a euphoric feeling. I settled into a happy place. A mind far finer than mine had even devised a bladder to collect my exhaled CO_2, which bled out via its own pressure.

The foot pump had to be stepped on rhythmically all night. Hank, John, and the Cowboys set a schedule. I remember looking up at Dr. Bob as he stepped onto the pump every minute, a book in his hand and such a calm expression on his face. He was a urologist by profession; earlier, in Base Camp, he'd had Mark and me in stitches describing how he made good money reversing vasectomies. Warm and safe inside the bag, I fell into a deep, sixteen-hour sleep.

OCTOBER 15: The four of us descended to Base Camp. After two months of wind, the Wyoming Centennial Expedition was calling it quits on the North Ridge. The beer came out, and so did Hank's hand-powered hair clippers.

Getting drunk and giving each other haircuts.... What could possibly go wrong? Mark, Mr. Jim, and Brad Werntz all went for wide mohawks, I got a racing stripe shaved over one ear, and Yak (Matt Ellenthal) took the cake by having horizontal lines shaved every half inch up the right side of his beard and head. For the next several days, we cajoled him to shave vertical lines into the other side of his head so that when his parents picked him up at JFK he could say, "I passed out on the barbeque and my friends flipped me."

The Cowboys left the next day. In parting, Bob Skinner said, "If you ever come to Pinedale and don't visit us...we'll kill ya." And then he grinned hugely and lumbered over to each of us, mauling our hands like a silver-tipped grizzly.

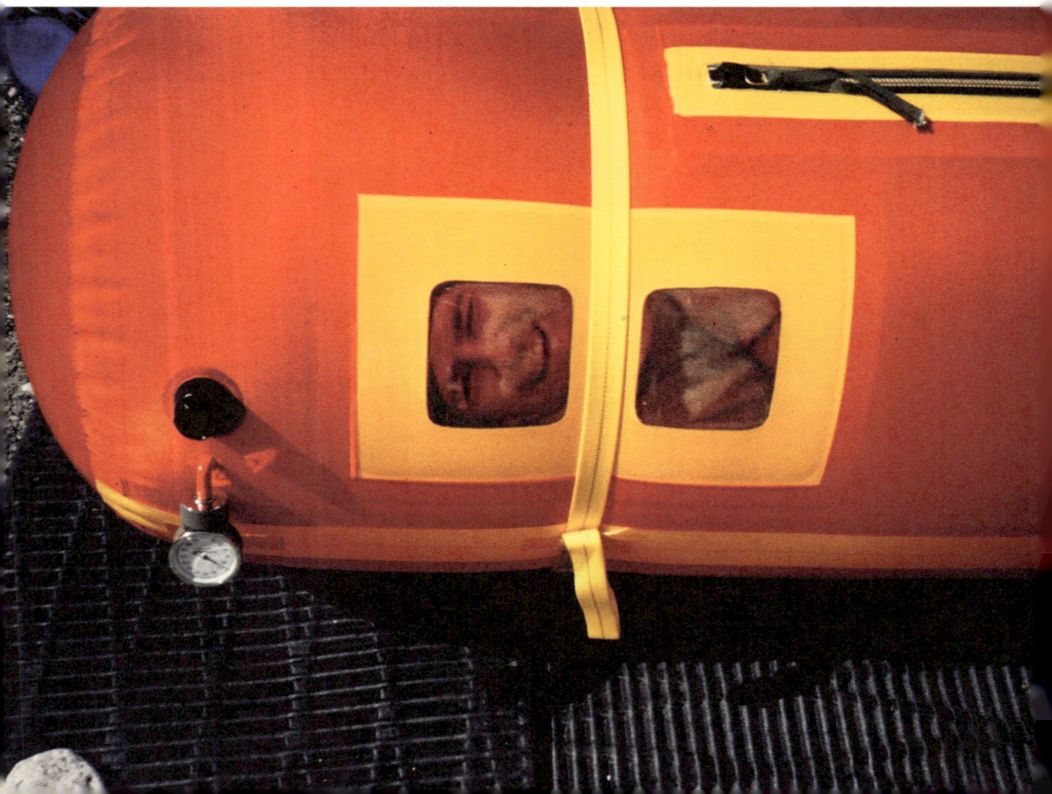

I was getting better, but for the next four days, Mark vomited and hobbled to our latrine with his arms wrapped over his gut to support gouging cramps of diarrhea. When we'd rolled into Base Camp a month and a half earlier, he was 145 pounds of lithe, marble-hard muscle; now he was 130 pounds, a web of blue veins extending from the diaphanous white skin at his waistline.

"I don't know if I can make another attempt," he said, sitting doubled-over in our mess tent. "But I will try."

"We need to go tomorrow. We're running out of time, our yaks are showing up in five days, and it's just getting colder."

"I know. Let's plan on Camp 2 tomorrow, and I'll see how I'm doing. You may have to try it alone."

"I don't want that."

"Me neither. I'm hoping I get better—I have to."

"You will. Let's leave at noon. That'll give us enough time to make it to Camp 2."

OCTOBER 20: I walked out of base camp alone. Mark had planned to leave within the hour and meet me at Advanced Base Camp, but he didn't show up that night. I spent the next day and night alone at ABC. Every hour brought me closer to concluding that Mark was done. Sadness piled up like sand in an hourglass.

OCTOBER 22, NOON: Good old John Morel, our rock, walked into Advanced Base Camp and told me that Mark had gotten sick on the way up and that he'd retreated to Base Camp.

"I don't think he'll be making it," John said. It felt like my anchor line had been cut and I'd started to slowly drift. I breathed and noted that that finally felt normal, like it did back home in the Rockies. I started preparing for a solo attempt. I planned to leave at 10 that night.

OCTOBER 22, 7 P.M.: Footsteps crunched up to my tent door. I thought that John had come to try to talk me out of going alone. I sat up as the tent's zipper ripped open and Mark's blue eyes met mine. His eyes threw sparks.

lark and I both had turns in the high-pressure amow bag, a portable hyperbaric chamber. He's austrophobic, so his joy here is feigned. But nere was no doubt about his actual happiness hen he got out of it. Barry Blanchard

"NEVER QUIT!" he howled. "At your service, Mr. Blanchard, and ready to climb!"

"Are you kidding me? I'm not soloing?"

"Not with me around you're not."

Relief and optimism flooded my core; more strands in the cable that connected us.

"I started out from Base Camp an hour after you. About a half mile out, I stopped to take a drink and woke up on the ground with sore knees and no water bottle."

"You passed out?"

"Oh ya, and when I came to, I sprinted the hell back to Base Camp. One of the trekkers was a doc, and he told me that I was salt and potassium deficient from being butt-sick and vomiting. I started pounding electrolyte pills. I left Base Camp at two today and made it up here in five hours. I feel good, but I'm going to need to rest some."

OCTOBER 23, 2 P.M.: We walked toward the Headwall. Three hours later, we pitched our two-man tent at the North Col. We had one shared sleeping bag with a half-length zipper. We slept warmly by pulling the bottom of the bag over our feet and draping the open top over us like a blanket. The only way to fit was if we spooned. That left the facing-away guy's back exposed, so the spooner would hold a big, insulated jacket against the spoonee.

OCTOBER 24: We walked up the North Ridge with ski poles in hand. The westerlies were moderate; I wished that the Cowboys had been there to see that. By early afternoon, we reached our high point from eleven days earlier, at 25,500 feet. Our traverse into the Great Couloir began there. One horizontal mile away, and 1,000 feet higher, we saw a promising place to pitch our tent under rock that defined the eastern edge of the couloir. We thought we'd be there by 3 p.m.

The traverse ground us down and then began to torture us. My heart and lungs were finally doing well, but my body felt beaten. "Another twenty steps," I told myself. "Keep going, keep going." But I'd give in and stop, and lean on my ice-ax and will the bivy spot to be closer. When I looked up, it wasn't.

OCTOBER 24, 7 P.M.: We trudged up to the rock that would shield our tent for the night.

"Altitude is rude, altitude is rude. Troillet can't tell me he doesn't hurt."

I smiled, dug the shovel blade out, and slowly started hacking out a platform, 26,500 feet above sea level. My body throbbed.

Mark and I got in the tent and started the hours of melting snow. On the inside walls, feathers of frost grew a quarter inch an hour—our exhaled breath expanding in clouds to cool, condense, and freeze.

OCTOBER 25, 12:30 A.M.: We shut off the stove and I snuggled down as the spooner and Mark as the spoonee. I had my massive altitude mitts on, and with my left I held a jacket onto Mark's shoulder blades. With no place to put my right, I let it flop over Mark and immediately realized that it had landed right in front of his crotch. I felt a nervous tremor of energy pulse through him, and then he coughed to camouflage his hand sweeping mine onto his hip, and I thought, "Ha, he's homophobic." Then, I felt a second tremor of nervous energy pass through him, and I knew that he was thinking, "Huh, Blanch must be thinking that I'm homophobic." He coughed again and moved my hand back. I fell asleep.

OCTOBER 25, 2 A.M.: The alarm whined. Frost rained down from the tent walls as we pivoted into sitting positions to light the stove. We guessed that it was -15°F inside the tent.

OCTOBER 25, 5 A.M.: We stepped into the Himalayan night and started climbing toward the top of Mt. Everest. Twenty steps, then stop, then lean too heavily on both ice-axes: My balance was off. I felt ridiculously feeble; the slope was only 40 degrees! I'd ski it in the Rockies or the Alps—hell, I'd ski it here, if I had my skis! Mark stopped every twenty steps to swing blood back into his feet. He couldn't keep them warm and told me that he was descending to the tent to wait until it got warmer.

Watching him start down, I knew that half of my chances went with him. I stood at 27,000 feet and turned back into the slope, planting one crampon in front of the other, forcing twenty steps then tilting my head back to haul thin air into my lungs. Muscles in my back and neck not usually involved in breathing pulled to help expand my lungs to their maximum. The brightness around me felt restricted; I wore goggles, a neoprene face mask, and an earflap toque, and had two insulated hoods cowling my head.

And then I started losing consciousness every time I changed direction, like I'd blinked asleep at the wheel. At 27,500 feet, I realized that if I went unconscious for more than a blink, I'd fall over and accelerate down the slope. I doubted that I'd be able to stop myself.

Okay, Barry, this is too much. You've got to go down, I told myself. Twice I descended a hundred steps only to shout inside my head, *You're not trying hard enough. You don't have to quit. It's not that bad. You're so close!*

On my second time turning back uphill, I pushed a hundred steps higher and passed out for a heartbeat when I changed directions. I stopped. At this pace, the summit would take me another eight hours; I would not have the energy to descend.

This is TOO much. I have to go down. I planted an ice-ax in the bright white snow and cautiously stepped my feet around 180 degrees. I slowly began back down my tracks, the top of the world at my back.

"I'm going to wait here to descend when it's warmer, Bubba. I'll bring the tent and bag down," Mark said back at our high camp.

"Okay, man—give me the stove. I'll take that down. Let's go home."

"Yes, man, I want to go home."

As I walked down the North Ridge, it was obvious to me that I'd made the right call. I was beat. I felt it with each and every footfall.

OCTOBER 26: We met Hank and our yaks as they came up to haul our stuff off the mountain. We sat on broken black slate and told him about our attempt.

"Sounds like you guys gave it your best. I don't think you could have done anything more, and I'm mighty glad that you're both down here," he said, smiling.

In my tent back at base camp that night, the air felt rich and thick, and I knew that it had taken me six weeks to gain full acclimatization—twice as long as Mark—something I would not forget.

And then, out of the blue, there was a plaintive whine outside my tent: "Mr. Blanchard, Mr. Blanchard. You MUST help me." It was Samson. He sounded distraught, on the edge of tears. I let him into the vestibule, and he pleaded with me for money to go to university and for his family.

"Samson, I wish I could help you, but we don't have any money." More wailing. It felt like I was watching an acting class gone bad, yet there was true desperation behind Samson's drama. He lamented for minutes and minutes.

"Okay, Samson, okay." I dug out $200 in US twenties, handed them to him, and hoped I'd have enough to get out of China. He launched into the gratitude part of his act; thankfully it was a short scene, and I was able to go to sleep. The next day he was back to himself, with nary a hint of his nocturnal thespianism. We sold our last two oxygen bottles to Hasegawa; his wife paid us in yen, about double the amount I'd handed over to Samson.

Jangbu was a lone Tibetan who'd taken to helping us out around Base Camp. We'd paid him some cash, unbeknownst to Samson and Mr. Zhang. I walked over to Jangbu's tent, and he invited me in for tea. I sat cross-legged on a pile of black blankets and marveled at the fact that his tent was hand spun: woven yak-hair blankets supported with sticks and anchored by river rocks. The ceiling had a yard-long, canoe-shaped hole, below which Jangbu had a battered, charcoal-blackened pot balanced on three upended rocks above a yak-dung fire. As always, the dung fire smelled sweet, like incense. I remember how I'd been surprised by that on my first visit to Tibet, two years earlier.

Jangbu crumpled a handful of black tea leaves into the pot with his creased, soil-lined hands. We sat and drank tea and communicated awkwardly via sign language. He fit so well into the high barren landscape of Tibet; it was obvious that he was part of that land, while I was just a tourist.

OCTOBER 27: Sarah trekked into our base camp—with sass and a cut-glass English accent. Mark and I invited her for tea and had a great time talking music and movies and hearing the hilarities of her travels across China to Tibet. It was fabulous to flirt with a woman.

OCTOBER 29: Mark, John, Hank, and I were determined to leave our base camp immaculate. Our Chinese personnel did not share that ethic. Soon we were arguing with them about not leaving any garbage.

Samson walked away from a smoldering pile of half-burned refuse, saying, "This is China and China is clean. We will leave now." Mark did a Mark thing: grabbed Samson by the shirtfront, hauled him back to the pile, and thrust him to it like he was rubbing a puppy's nose in crap. "Clean it up!" Mark commanded.

Samson wiggled, pitched a hissy fit, and spewed hysterical Cantonese at Mark's back as Mark walked away. Samson stormed off and returned with Mr. Zhang, a camera in hand; Samson then grabbed Mark by the shirtfront and stood wide-eyed and accusatory, staring into the camera as Mr. Zhang clicked off a photo. It was funny in a way, as Samson's attempt to reenact Mark accosting him resulted in a photo of Samson accosting Mark. Mark, of course, swept Samson's hand from his person and stood ready to fight. Samson was blathering more hysteria, red in the face with forehead veins bulging and pulsing.

For the second time that trip, I snapped. I strode in between them and shouted for them both to "BACK THE FUCK OFF! And I mean right FUCKING now!" Mark acquiesced because I was on his side; Samson and Mr. Zhang backed down because I scared them. After the cool-down came the talk-down, with Samson threatening to have us imprisoned and me saying, "You do what you think is right, Samson."

A dozen trekkers had amassed. We'd hoped to give some of them rides in the half-empty back of our cargo truck, but after the meltdown with Samson, the Chinese refused to allow anyone but us in the vehicles. From the back of the truck, Hank giddily played Santa Claus, throwing Magic Pantry boil-in-a-bags out into the crowd of bummed-out trekkers, laughing all the while. Sarah made an agitated pass through the crowd, and then just stepped into the Land Cruiser and sat down beside Mark. I don't think that Samson or Mr. Zhang noticed, and if they did they didn't say anything.

Jangbu stood to the side. We'd loaded him up with food; as a parting thought, I walked over and gave him my water bottle, something I knew he'd use until the sun baked it brittle, and then he'd use it as a cup. He smiled hugely for several beats, and then his face fell in befuddlement. He asked me something in Tibetan that I didn't understand until he pantomimed pissing into the bottle. I reassured him that it hadn't been a pee bottle by shaking my head "no" while wagging my right trigger finger, "Uh, uh, uh," and my left trigger finger in front of my crotch, "No, no, no." He beamed again and stashed the bottle into his rolls of blankets. Hank climbed down from our cargo truck and got in the front seat of the Land Cruiser. I climbed in the back beside Sarah, sidling into her aura of warmth, and we pulled away from Everest.

Soon the burnt-sienna hills of Tibet were passing outside the windows. Hank had commandeered the cassette player and played The Mission's cover of "Like A Hurricane." Midday, Sarah said, "Here, Hank, I have a tape you can play." "Don't Leave Me This Way" chimed out of the speakers.

"Is this the fucking Communards?" Hank gasped. Sarah closed her eyes and smiled and started bopping her head side to side. Mark groaned and pushed the play button on his Walkman.

"You honestly like The Communards?" Hank continued, and Sarah grinned wider and bopped more fully, enjoying the jolt she'd given us.

OCTOBER 30: We rolled into Xigazê, got into our hotel, and started drinking beer. Hank seldom drank; I soon knew why. He got high fast, his Dutch heritage bubbling to the surface. He shouted across the corridor to a tour-busload of gray-haired Germans, "Give us our bicycles back!" and "Did you kill my grandmother?!" Mark and I pushed him up the stairs to our room, where we got our base camp boombox going and more trolleys of Star Beer arrived. We NEEDED to party. John joined us for a couple and then excused himself.

The empty, green, one-liter bottles piled up. Sarah began swaying to Cowboy Junkies, and Mark, Hank, and I started dancing too. The music got faster and louder. I accounted for more than my fair share of Star bottles. When Mark cued up the Sex Pistols—the first bars of "Anarchy in the UK"—I roared like a berserker and sprinted around the room vaulting from the beds, pulling the curtains down, and then the light fixtures. I grabbed the TV by its handle, did one revolution, and was about to put it through the third-story window, when Mark grabbed it, and me.

"Woah, Bubba, easy boy. Let's put the nice TV back on the nice TV table." My chest was heaving, clamped tight inside Mark's chiseled arms.

"Wow!" said Hank, smiling. "You took the 'get pissed and destroy' part seriously."

"Barry," Sarah asked coyly, "did you actually want to be a rock star?"

"Oh, yes, we've always wanted to be rock stars. Right, Doom?"

"No. I'm punk to the bone. I wanna be a punk star."

And then there was a knock at the door, and I cracked it to Samson and one of the hotel guys dressed in a suit. I stepped out.

"Mr. Blanchard, you have a woman in the hotel with you. This is not allowed—she will have to leave."

"She is not just a woman, Samson. She is my wife."

"How can she be your wife?"

"Mr. Twight married us yesterday in Xêgar."

"How could Mr. Twight do that?"

"Mr. Twight is a reverend minister. He has the authority to marry people. His church has ordained him."

"Mr. Twight belongs to a church?"

"Mr. Twight has his own church."

"What is it called?"

"The Church of Mark Francis Twight."

Samson and the hotel guy exchanged some Cantonese and then left. Soon came another knock at the door, and the hotel guy was back with Samson and a bellhop.

"Mr. Blanchard, I am pleased to tell you that the hotel has prepared the honeymoon suite for you and your bride!"

Sarah smiled beautifully and boldly strode forward to lock arms with me. I looked over my shoulder; Hank was already on the floor, one hand on his gut, the other over his mouth. Mark's cheeks inflated to blow a high note like a young Chet Baker—he was choking on laughter. Sarah and I followed Samson, the hotel guy, and bellhop to the honeymoon suite, where I swept a smiling Sarah into my arms and carried her over the threshold. The hotel guy closed the door behind us, and then we burst out laughing. And our laughing continued as we looked about the rose-colored room. Cheap sparkling wine on ice, soft light, plastic flowers

Mark in Advanced Base Camp, the North Col of Everest rising white like a drive-in screen behind him. Barry Blanchard aplenty, pictures of puppies and colts on the walls. The Communist Party was so obviously taking steps to up the birth rate in Tibet.

"All this is lacking is a banner that says 'breed' over the bed," I said with a laugh.

"Yes, they might add one of those, mightn't they, my dear?"

I chuckled, then stepped over the emotional threshold as we lay on the bed and talked and talked until we eventually passed out in our clothes.

My hangover was ferocious, but the vision the next morning of Mark and Hank, feet sunk into a gaudy bedcover, working together to

reaffix the curtain rods and light fixtures, made me smile. Hank gently held a faux-gold light fixture while Mark coaxed screws back into the concrete with a red Swiss Army Knife. My buddies were making amends for my being a drunken asshole. We drove to Lhasa that day. Sarah's presence felt magnetic. *Did I want to be a rock-star climber? Or did I want a family?* Selfishly and unaccountably, I just wanted her.

I left Mark out of the meeting to finalize accounts with China Tibet International Sports Travel (CTIST). Mark always needed something to push against, and Chinese bureaucracy proved to be as dogged and indefatigable as he was. The meeting went a lot smoother without him. I enjoyed sitting across from the CTIST guy as he pulled away on his cigarette while jotting down our give-and-take in a ledger.

NOVEMBER 2: Mark, Hank, and John boarded a flight to Kathmandu to connect for home. Sarah and I attended a final banquet with the CTIST. She looked stunning in a vintage Tibetan opera dress she'd found. We made love that night. The next day, I boarded a plane for Chengdu with Samson and Mr. Zhang. By the time we got to the Jin Jiang Hotel, I felt like a match had been struck in my throat. I was fully in the throes of a fever when Samson and the Sichuan Mountaineering Association (SMA) guy knocked on my door.

"Can we settle these accounts in the morning please, Samson? I'm sick right now."

An "Aha!" spark slashed through the SMA guy's eyes, and Samson translated, "No. It has to be now. There will be no time in the morning."

"Really?"

"No, it has to be now."

"Well, okay, let me sign the damn papers then." I signed. The SMA guy beamed and scampered off. When he was gone, Samson said, "Mr. Blanchard, you shouldn't sign these papers without reading them." It occurred to me that I'd just been had.

It took three days in Beijing for the Chinese Mountaineering Association (CMA) to settle my accounts and take all my remaining money, save for 25,000 yen and a few Canadian dollars. China somehow knew exactly how much money I had. Then they banqueted me with mystery meat and plum brandy. Mr. Zhang had a grand time standing to joyously toast Canada, "Canada is a very big and great country! *Ganbei!*" And then it would be my turn, "China is very wide! *Ganbei!*"

NOVEMBER 5: Jan Wong was *The Toronto Globe and Mail*'s correspondent in Beijing. Jan was intense. She took offense when our Chinese servers didn't clear our lunch plates.

"I grew up working in my dad's restaurant. This pisses me off, and I know they aren't doing their job because you're white."

"I wouldn't go as far as to call me white. I prefer red."

"Whatever." And she harangued our waiter into taking away the used plates.

I spent our lunch telling Jan about our attempt on Everest and my frustrations with the CMA. The headline "China nearly as tough as Everest, climber says" would make the front page of *The Globe and Mail*. Jan told me that she'd phoned Mr. Zhang and learned that he'd never actually been in the mountains before; his previous experience had been organizing waterskiing competitions.

The next day, Mr. Zhang approached me alone in the hallway of our hotel and asked, in sign language and broken English, about the money I'd given Samson. I handed over the 25,000 yen I'd hung onto, telling him it was equal to $200 US. Then I went to the airport and got on my flight for Vancouver, with $135 Canadian in my wallet.

Jan's piece ran on November 7, 1988, while I was in the air. "With his ponytail and cowboy boots, his silver rings and bracelet, he is just the iconoclastic, irreverent type guaranteed to irritate Chinese mountaineering officials." When I saw the story later, I smiled, realizing I'd dodged being arrested and forced to write one of the self-criticisms other irreverent climbers had, I'd heard, been made to pen.

Much worse, I had a confession to make to my wife. My first wife, but not my last confession.

🎧 "Ribbons," "When You Don't See Me": The Sisters of Mercy
🎧 "Song to the Siren": Dead Can Dance
🎧 "Cool Water": Sons of the Pioneers

📖 *One Man's Mountains: Essays and Verses* by Tom Patey
📖 *Run with the Hunted* by Charles Bukowski
📖 *The Great Days* by Walter Bonatti

CHAPTER 6 — ASPIRING ALPINIST I

CONVERSATIONS *WITH* BONATTI

MARCH 1989: *I tried to solo a route on the north face of Mt. Temple but ended up retreating from snow that I thought might avalanche. That night, I read Walter Bonatti's* The Great Days, *for his dauntless courage, his simple search for a personal purity, and truth.*

MARCH 1990: *I backed away from the Grand Central Couloir on the north face of Mt. Kitchener. An eggshell crust had collapsed under my ice tools; my chest thumped into the lower lip. Sparkling snow particles swirled in the vortex of my headlamp's beam then dissolved into black. Climbing alone, I asked myself,* What would Bonatti do? *One of many conversations I would have with my "inner Bonatti." Bonatti would go down and get his skis and come back up and bury them as an anchor then belay himself across this hole.* Well, I guess Barry Blanchard just wasn't Walter Bonatti.

When I wrote of my self-doubt to Mark, he replied, "No. I wouldn't keep going. But that's because I believe that the next crevasse that I ski into will kill me.... And dude, soloing the GCC is one bad-ass project. I'm really impressed that you even had the emotional smash to get to the 'schrund. Then again, you know how much those mountains up there [in Canada] scare the shit out of me...."

JANUARY 28, 1991: I said goodbye to Jim Elzinga and our five clients in Puente del Inca, Argentina. All but one had summited Aconcagua.

sting and melting water in the perpetual wind Aconcagua. Looking past my crampon points the approach of the night. Barry Blanchard

I walked back into the hostería, intent on resting a couple of days before walking into the Plaza Francia base camp at nearly 14,000 feet to solo the south face of Aconcagua. I sat and sipped strong black tea and pondered my haloed reflection in my teacup while listening to the *Vision Thing* album by The Sisters of Mercy. When I'd written to Mark, declaring that the album had saved my life, he replied, "It saved my life, too. INCOMING!" (That's from the chorus of the song "Ribbons," meaning the opening of a door and/or a warning of enemy fire.)

Wind came in the night and pounded the hostel in waves; dirt particles rattled the windows like heavy rain. I felt my commitment ebb and flow. *I know I can do this.* And, *I should just pack up and get home.* My last slurp of tea had gone cold. The Sisters were singing "When You Don't See Me." Good point. *Did I exist outside my wife's vision and consciousness? When she breathed out, did I breathe in?* I had married into that ideal, then pushed it over with Sarah, nudging the bride and groom off the top of the cake into the thick, sticky icing. *Could I—could we—re-create the ideal?* I wasn't dealing well with the sticky mess in my heart.

The windowpanes quit rattling; I would approach the south face the next day. First, I'd have to pack, then organize a muleteer to pack my stuff sixteen miles and 4,500 feet up to Plaza Francia. In the last year, I'd accomplished several first ascents that boosted my credibility as a world-class alpinist and connected me with several sponsors. When I packed a small voice recorder—my press agent's suggestion—into the lid of my day pack, to document my climb as I went, I could feel the tension rise between wanting to promote myself and make money from climbing and wanting to experience the climb and find moments of grace. I hoped that the south face of Aconcagua could sort that out for me and purge me of infidelity. It was a lot to ask.

JANUARY 29: The morning sky was the color of the Mediterranean, and I hustled up the trail feeling excited, alive, and purposeful. By afternoon, I was tromping up the valley of the Horcones Inferior Glacier. I hadn't seen my muleteer, off to the Plaza Francia, since the morning, nor anyone else since I'd branched away from the main trail at the Confluencia, where the Upper and Lower Horcones rivers meet. Two people were descending toward me, growing taller with each step. Eventually I shook hands with Tom and Dudley, two Canadian guys from Vancouver. Wind had turned them around halfway up the south face.

"Between the Korean siege and Bubendorfer's filming, the route is fixed," Dudley said. There had been a Korean siege ascent of the route earlier in the season. The Austrian climber Thomas Bubendorfer had also made a solo ascent, and then soloed the route again while the climber and filmmaker Steve Marts documented it.

"I think I'll leave my self-belay and rope behind." They raised their eyebrows at a decision I could see made them uncomfortable.

"We have some topos, if you'd like," Tom offered.

"Yes, please."

The young guys walked away, growing smaller again as the trail stretched between us. My research had always fallen somewhere between being fully prepared and being completely uninformed upon trying a mountain the first time. Had I been more studious, I might have been more successful, but I also knew that following a plan might have robbed me of the hundreds of decisions that had helped form my intuitive sense of route-finding.

It took time to round the forehills. I crunched along over the burned and rusted remnants of an eroding volcano. Aconcagua's volcanic base had cooled out of existence about ten million years ago. Since then, the bulk of the mountain had been lifted by thrust faults. At 22,840 feet, it was the highest peak outside of Asia, also the highest in the Southern and Western Hemispheres. I knew that a lot of the rock would be friable like the Canadian Rockies, but for different reasons. I hoped that, as in the Rockies (except flipped 180 degrees: north faces in the Northern Hemisphere; south faces in the Southern), ice, snow, and permafrost on the steep, shaded face would bond the rock together.

Coffee-colored pebbles ground under my feet. I was feeling good. I thought that I'd start climbing the next day. One mile farther on, a sudden cramp twisted my guts. I knew all too well the panicked pulsations pushing against my anus. I ripped at my pants, racing the release, got my ass out, and splattered the ground with diarrhea.

Butt-sick! My guts gurgled like air sputtering from a garden hose. I sprayed again and enchained six distinct obscenities so loud that they echoed. It just felt so bloody unfair after having been so careful for the last eighteen days.

"God hates me," I said as I cleaned myself up.

Eventually, I came to see the south face head-on. I was in awe. I'd stood below bigger faces—the Rupal Face of Nanga Parbat, the north flank of Rakaposhi—but those have slopes that ease the transition from horizontal to vertical. Aconcagua is breathtakingly abrupt, like 8,000 feet of sea cliff rising straight from the ocean. A lenticular cloud was pulled tight over the summit; I could see, and hear, the wave of the wind as it roared over the top. I scanned left and right from the central line of the French Route. Tiers of seracs scythed over much of the face; the French Route was one of the safer lines, although safe is relative, as the line took the seracs of the Middle Glacier direct.

Like a scene out of a Western, my muleteer rode down toward me, his image shimmering with the late-day heat rising from the dark gravel. He sat his horse next to me, his pack mule on lead in his left hand, the thick bulge of the *cojinillo*—the sheepskin that tops a gaucho's saddle—wrapping his thighs. He had no English and very few teeth, but through my rudimentary Spanish I understood that my duffle bag was in the Plaza Francia, about an hour farther on. He tipped his wide-brimmed hat and trotted away. I was alone again.

My rotund blue duffle sat on the burnt-umber gravel flats of Plaza Francia, looking as foreign and alone as a probe on Mars. I walked over and sat on it, trying to gauge the state of my guts. There was a percolation, and then a dash to a boulder. More splattering and more swearing. I was going to have to shovel a pit for all of the shit, so I walked back to my duffle and set up camp: my tiny yellow tent, a rock stool and table outside the front door with my stove balanced in the middle.

The sun set. Slivers of ice crept across my open-mouthed water bag. I crawled inside the tent and squirmed into the 2.5-pound, zipperless sleeping bag that Feathered Friends, of Seattle, had made for me. They had eliminated the cold line of the zipper and made the bag lighter. It was a hassle to worm into, but great once you were in. I'd brought *One Man's Mountains: Essays and Verses* by the Scottish climber Tom Patey. I twisted on my headlamp and was soon beguiled by Patey's masterful storytelling, wry Scottish wit, and to-the-bone insights on the climbing game. His "Creag Meagaidh Crab-Crawl" had me crying with laughter and quivering with the cold, my gloved hands too numb to flip the pages. I had to pry the book from my own hands.

JANUARY 30: I had a semi-solid bowel movement in the morning and thought, *Applesauce is better than apple cider. I must be getting better.* The shadowed south face greeted me when I stood, the sky cloudless and pale blue. I thought that I'd be able to start climbing the next morning.

The approach to the face proved to be straightforward when I scouted it, so I piled up marker cairns on the way back and settled into an afternoon of reading and drinking tea. Patey's "A Short Walk with Whillans" had me laughing out loud. It is one of the greats in the canon of climbing literature, as is the satirical piece "The Art of Climbing Down Gracefully." I was in stitches again and finished the book that day wishing that Patey had written more. (Dr. Tom Patey died in 1970 rappelling from The Maiden, a sea stack off Whiten Head on the north coast of Scotland.)

JANUARY 31: Four squat fingers of cloud reached from the summit ridgeline; I watched them mature to a full fist. A couple of hours later, I spoke journalist-like into my recorder: "4:45 p.m., January 31, 1991, a Thursday. Well, I've been here for over twenty-four hours. The weather seems to be observing the same pattern it did yesterday, relatively calm with clouds building up about three in the afternoon. In today's case, cumulus clouds that I hope are fair-weather cumulus clouds. My diarrhea, I hope, has taken a turn for the better."

The billowing tower of cloud turned cannonball-black over the next hour. The wind—Aconcagua's perpetual wind—raked across the valley, careering grit before it and cracking like a whip. I got inside my tent and read as the walls billowed and popped and rattled. I'd joked to our clients that you didn't have to brush your teeth on Aconcagua—rather just step outside and smile into the wind, which would sandblast them clean.

FEBRUARY 1, 8:45 P.M.: The cumulonimbus cell had collapsed and the sky was clear, the wind calm. To the left of the French Route, the Yugoslav line had been dusted with snow, but the French had been missed by the storm, and that was good enough for me. I really wanted to be alone climbing up the wall, hungered for it. I set the alarm.

A pleasant calm settled down through my chest. The south face didn't look overwhelming. It looked quiet, interesting, inviting. I stood over the small glacial tarn I'd been drawing water from and meditated on its surface, as clear and clean as glass.

I was ready to climb.

FEBRUARY 2, 1:04 A.M.: Light glowed through the half-moon opening at the top of the tent door! I jerked to full consciousness as if slapped across the face. "Shit!" Had I overslept? Was I too late? I grabbed my watch, it was 1:04 a.m.... Aaahh. It was the soft silver light of the full moon, perfect, mythical; in fifty-six minutes, it would be a blessing. I fell back asleep—a gift from having spent enough nights sleeping next to, or on, big mountains. I'm able to relax around them.

I'd affixed a small steer's head stamped out of tin to the top lid of my pack, with darts pushed through the cloth then folded over like staples. A Texas longhorn with a 1.5-inch span that I'd bought in a punk-paraphernalia shop in Vancouver. Quarter-sized skulls and six-guns adorned the blue jeans I wore around town. Mark had noticed them immediately and said, "Those are fucking cool—where did you get them?"

Moonlight gleamed off the bull's wee horns, and I thought about Mark possibly walking toward a winter solo in the Alps at that exact moment. Inside my day pack: my zipperless sleeping bag, a three-quarter-length ultra-light Thermarest, a bivy sack, my stove with an extra gas cartridge, two pounds of food, a small down jacket, a spare pick. Strapped to the outside: my crampons, two Stubai Tirol ice-axes with hammerheads attached. The tape recorder and my camera were sardined into the pack lid along with sunglasses, sunscreen, and toilet paper (more than usual). It all weighed twenty pounds.

I hefted the pack and pivoted it onto my back. It felt light. I bounded for the face, skimming over the broken rock that carpeted the glacier like bomb-shattered cinderblocks. I followed my moon shadow, skirting low out of the firing range of the face; the stacked glaciers and calving seracs scared me. To walk over serac debris, with its aquamarine

A self-portrait early in the day. Moving hard, working hard, breathing hard. Going for it. Barry Blanchard chunks of intact ice glinting and encased inside a pulverized matrix of ice shrapnel and snow, is to know how little chance you'd have of surviving a hit. A compilation of Charles Bukowski's writing captured the anxiety of it for me—*Run with the Hunted*.

FEBRUARY 2, 5:15 A.M.: Once I was perpendicular to the French Route, I hightailed it through killing fields of shattered ice to the sanctuary of the basal rock wall. The moon would be setting in fifteen minutes. I had a choice: stay here safe from the seracs and wait forty-five minutes for daylight or go out and gamble that the bergschrund would be straightforward and that I'd be able to find the start of the route by headlamp.

I gambled. The bergschrund was choked with fallen debris, and I cramponed over it hastily. The moon set just as I touched the first of the rock, panting, knowing that once I was a hundred feet up, I'd be out of range of the falling ice. *But where was the route? Fuck, would I be stuck standing out in the open for a half hour waiting for daylight?* I twisted my headlamp on and had to laugh. A yard in front of me, Thomas's blue ropes hung like garlands on a Christmas tree.

I followed the ropes, ever conscious of not touching them, telling myself that it would be cheating. Shattered plates of wind-polished rock offered sharp edges for my gloved hands and plastic boots, but almost all the rock was loose. I had to distribute my weight between my limbs and not pull out on anything, always pushing down. The climbing felt like the worst of the Canadian Rockies—vertical, broken pottery.

Dawn came to the upper wall first. Soon, the seracs of the Middle Glacier were glowing in a golden arc, beautiful, but deadly. In my head, I heard the haunting "Song to the Siren" by Dead Can Dance. Off-balance, my vision blurry in the gloaming, I felt like Aconcagua was moving ever so subtly beneath me rather than me moving over it. *No Barry,* I said to myself. *No decisions now—this is your bad time; you never make good decisions at dawn. There is something weak inside you at dawn. Keep moving.* I twisted my headlamp off, scraped it from my helmet, and let it dangle from my neck. I'd deal with it later when my position was less exposed, when I hoped to have better balance and confidence.

The mountain presented crumbling gullies between fins and towers of crap-colored rock that reminded me of hoodoos in the Bow Valley. Those hoodoos formed because a cap rock insulated the weak glacial till underneath from direct rain erosion. The rest of the till had been washed away, leaving the hoodoos to stand as fairy chimneys, their vertical flanks as friable as dried mud.

I stuck to secure rock on the edges of the gullies, pushing myself to keep moving. Where the ropes ended, a series of small Korean croquet flags guided me in a traverse around the ridge. I had to chuckle; my situation seemed in total juxtaposition to smacking a croquet ball across a manicured lawn! Then a terrifying contraction rocked my rectum: "Oh fuck!" Instantly, I was ripping at zippers, collapsing into a squat and scraping layers of fabric across hard, bulging glutes, my right hand clinging like a talon to one of the few solid pieces of rock. No more chuckling—rather, I was cursing Argentina over the rapid-fire mix of hydraulic explosions bursting from my butt. Oh! The glamour of being an elite alpinist!

The first real move of the route: 5.6, with a death fall down a dirty brown gully to the glacier yawning at my back, more of Thomas's blue rope.... I clipped it with a locking carabiner daisy-chained into my harness. Wouldn't it be irrational not to? My onsight, free-solo ethic eroded in human time like Aconcagua did geologically. *"Poco a poco,"* as they say, "Little by little."

FEBRUARY 2, 9 A.M.: I stepped onto a tent platform, 15,000 feet. Above me, the Central Spur—the prominent feature of the lower wall—looked like a staircase of ruin. Twin blue ropes wound a double helix up the arête. I thought about cutting them and letting them fall, snakelike, to the glacier. The mountain would be cleaner, offering a purer ascent. But then, it was an Argentine mountain and not for me to decide. Beneath that nobility lay self-interest; if I couldn't make it up the face, I would need the lines to get down. *Poco a poco.*

The higher I climbed, the more horrid the rock became, as granular and loose as kitty litter. Initially, I ignored the blue ropes, then I started using them as a handrail over short, vertical steps of disintegrating stone. At the top of the spur, I scrambled into a field of scree. I clipped my locking carabiner onto the blue ropes, pushing it up with my right hand while holding the lines with my left. The climbing was disgusting, the scree unstable, and I told myself that no one in his right mind would forgo a handrail.

FEBRUARY 2, NOON: At 16,400 feet, the first crux of the route was above me—a vertical groove glazed with patches of ice, the rock some type of mud conglomerate with embedded chunks of dark, harder stone. I couldn't shut off the exposure; several thousand feet of air pulled at the back of my shirt. If I made a mistake here, I would fall to my death. *What if I misjudged a hold and it broke? What if there was a move that I couldn't figure out and I wasn't able to downclimb? What if I grabbed the rope and it broke?*

The Koreans had fixed a white, half-inch-diameter hawser-laid rope up the groove, but I couldn't see what it was anchored to. I wove a sling around it, passing the lower loop through the upper to form a Klemheist knot. Then I clipped my locking carabiner into it, pushed the Klemheist as high as I could, and slowly squatted my body weight onto it, all the while maintaining a separate attachment to a good, fixed piton in my right hand. The rope held. Hopefully it would hold if I fell on it. I needed to do everything I could to keep from falling.

The climbing was true 5.8. Rock rained down as I felt around, trying to find, or unearth, something solid. Steve Marts had filmed Bubendorfer free soloing this pitch in rock shoes. "He just started soloing up it," Steve had told me, "and it is loose and icy, and he's climbing without a rope.... Scared the hell out of me." I placed my double plastic boots onto holds and climbed, advancing the Klemheist as I went.

Then it got hard. My calves began to tremble with the pain of holding a wide split-legged, tiptoed position while I felt and felt and felt for a trustworthy handhold. Fear rose within me, my throat dried up and started to close. I had to move, but I was too scared of breaking the rope if I fell. I hooked a finger into the Klemheist and pulled down as gingerly as possible. I set my boots onto better holds, and my hands wrapped onto good edges. My throat relaxed as my fear subsided. I was in a secure position, and I hung my head and breathed and breathed. I climbed on.

Toward the top of the groove, I could see that the rope was intact to the anchor—a cluster of pitons in an alcove. I lifted the rope to set it more in line with me. Loose rock cascaded down, crackling off my helmet and thumping into my pack; dust filled my eyes, and I clenched them shut. "Aw fuck!" I spat, as the reports ricocheted off down the mountain. I looked down and the exposure grew, like the toes of my boots were balanced on the edge of a skyscraper, with the heels out over air. "Screw it!" I rasped and wrapped my left hand around the rope and heaved myself up into the alcove to grab the anchor.

Standing there, I felt no pride. I wasn't doing a very good job. *I should have brought my self-belay and rope,* I told myself. *At least then I could have climbed that pitch properly.* But self-belaying would have taken more time, more time under the seracs, more time lolling about underneath the scythe. I considered retreating and leaving with some dignity, yet I still wanted to climb the wall. My desire won out. I wriggled into the primal security of a chimney and started scraping my way up.

At 17,000 feet, the fixed ropes ran out. I balanced on the ridge with 4,000 feet of mountain falling away to my left and 4,000 feet to my right. If I were to drop bowling balls from each hand, they would come to rest at the base of the wall, thousands of feet apart. The first icefield lay 100 feet above me, beyond a slab of brittle rock. My plastic boots smeared on the low-angle, flaky rock, about as useful as hockey skates. All my handholds broke like crackers when I lifted out on them, and I was committed to going up because it was too insecure to climb down. I hated that piece of Aconcagua; I could feel more hair turning gray. It was too much of a crapshoot. When I got to the ice and stood into a secure hollow, I screamed obscenities until I was hoarse.

Paradoxically, the icefield was secure. A field of knee-high penitentes reached from the mountain like lines of bleachers in the Astrodome. It would be impossible to fall there. Some 1,800 feet higher, I stood onto the lower of several tent platforms that had been chopped into the final stretch of the ice arête, the logic having been that the serac would part and fall to either side of the ridge. *Hmmm.* I questioned that. I'd climbed a vertical mile on one liter of water and a chocolate bar. It was time to brew, eat, and record: "3 p.m., February 1st. I'm just below the second rock band. Got a big gray cloud moving in here. I think it would probably be prudent for me to look at bivouacking, at least until tonight and hopefully the clouds will clear off, possibly till tomorrow morning. Just drank a warm liter of tea with sugar and milk; feel real rejuvenated and ready to continue this thing."

That made it sound like I had calculated control of the situation, a wishful image that stood in such contradiction to reality. The lower half of the French Route had been horrendously rotten and insecure. There was no calculated control to be had there. I was spewing BS.

FEBRUARY 2, 4 P.M.: I touched the second rock band and gazed to the murderous serac leaning over top of it. As if on cue, an office-building-sized sheet of ice calved off 500 feet to my right. The sun-bleached ice shattered to azure then exploded like an artillery shell hitting the chalk cliffs of Dover. The thunder of the collapsing ice cramped my guts, and I wrapped my arms over my stomach, rolling forward to squeeze.

The sky darkened to charcoal. It started to snow heavily, huge flakes driving obliquely and quickly piling up. I had to get into my pit and wait it out, hoping it would be over by 7 or 8 p.m. and I'd be able to continue.

Twenty feet to my right, the rock wall bulged. I hacked into fins of ice tight to its base, hoping the rock would provide protection from falling ice should the serac fail. Having seen the aftermath of many such failures, I knew that a lot of erratic trajectories were caused by collisions of ice chunks with the mountain and the chaotic billiard-balling that ensued. Not all the motion was downhill; some pieces exploded out and back, and some even ricocheted skywards.

The wind clawed at my hood, and I snapped it tight around my helmet. *Should I just bail?* I asked myself. *But if I do, and the snow stops, I will lose.* Anxiously, I squirmed into my bivy sack, reached down to my feet, and blindly removed my gaiters and boots. That took fifteen minutes; wriggling into my sleeping bag and peeling off neoprene socks and liner socks took another ten. Like stones, the falling snow piled up and pressed its weight onto the bivy sack, pushing it down on me. I'd shake and punch at it and feel the snow settle and press into my flanks and I'd squirm and wiggle to create some space between me and the heat-stealing snow.

FEBRUARY 2, 6 P.M.: Eventually, I looked out onto a raging blizzard. I retreated into my pit to continue punching the snow off and trying to keep my air hole sheltered.

When the first thunderclap exploded, I jolted into a fetal position. My body was tensed as hard as a fist, and the terror of being pummeled to death by ice shrieked inside my head. I held my breath, but the impacts didn't come, and I realized that it was literal thunder and not the serac collapsing. "Uuuhh!" I grunted, and then I breathed in long and deep.

My feet got cold, and I reached down and blindly slipped my inner boots back on. I wished that there was some way to run the stove inside my pit, but it was just too cramped. I lay there for ten hours, occasionally wrestling off snow, sometimes sleeping, and waking to the black, cold pressure of the snow pressing down on me. I'd punch and wiggle and worry.

FEBRUARY 3, 4 A.M.: I looked out onto the soft, feminine light of the moon. Snow lay like lunar dust all around me, calm, magical. I twisted to a sitting position, and the moon snow cracked and fell away like an eggshell. The stove "popped!" to life and then settled into a hiss of burning blue butane that looked oddly electric and luminous in the moonlight. I brewed four liters and guzzled it all. One man in the moonlight sitting on an ice ledge below a rock band, 5,000 feet up, 3,000 more to go, the blue light of his stove like a pinhole to a brighter universe.

Dawn revealed a white valley that had been black the day before. I convinced myself that going up was the safest option; my hubris had yet to be eroded.

Above me lay solid rock the color of dark oak—I couldn't believe it! Had it not been covered with several inches of new snow, the climbing would have been enjoyable. Instead, I tediously brushed off snow and advanced nervously, rarely knowing if my gloves would slip on a residue of snow or if my crampons would skate against the rock. The Koreans had fixed 9 mm rope there, and I safeguarded myself with a Klemheist. About 200 feet up, the 9 mm changed to 7 mm strung tight as a guitar string and crossing horns of jutting, snow-glazed rock—not the best

undling up and brewing as the sky blackens
nd the maelstrom amasses. Soon I'd be
rawling into my bivy sac and sleeping bag.
arry Blanchard

climbing line. I pulled on the Klemheist on every move, fretting over what the rope was anchored to.

Some 200 feet higher, the 7 mm was tied around a solid horn. The ropes ended there, below a mountain covered in fresh snow. I slid my Stubais ice-axes from their holsters and smacked them into the ice above. Seventy feet up, the ice ended against more steep, good stone. I holstered my tools and began brushing snow from holds, but I felt clumsy, off-balance, my gloved hands shifting on the icy holds. The last particles of my hubris fell away with snow that carried minute grains of oak-colored rock. It was too risky. I did not want to fall. I started down.

I expected the descent to be a horror show, and it was. The Korean lines creaked when I rappelled on them. Thomas's blue rope tightened to the diameter of a ballpoint pen when I weighted it. Twice my feet whipped out from under me on the new snow, and twice I was caught by that darling blue line.

At the bergschrund, I realized that I hadn't eaten in twenty-four hours. One chocolate bar satiated me.

FEBRUARY 3, 4 P.M.: I transitioned from the slope of the wall to the relative flat of the glacier. The snow had settled to a couple inches, and it coated the broken rock; some of it was slippery, but much of it had bonded to the surface and provided good footing. Several miles farther down, the snow had melted from the valley floor and the ocherous hues had returned, funnel and ridge, funnel and ridge, hourglass and blade, hourglass and blade. "Twenty-four hours can be a long time in the life of a mountain," I stated. Fingers of cumulus cloud reached from the top of Aconcagua, and they were building. I congratulated myself on being where I was. Retreat had been the right decision. I strode on feeling light and alive, lighter than normal, like the mountain was gifting me reprieve from gravity.

Farther on, I heard the wind-chime trickling of water running under the broken rock, washing the skin of the glacier clean. At a small rivulet, I got down on my hands and knees and slurped greedily. Time folded back, and I suddenly remembered listening to Sons of the Pioneers sing "Cool Water" with my paternal grandmother's second husband, Harold, on a vinyl LP in Medicine Hat, Alberta, in the late 1960s. A cold pulse shot through my temples—an ice-cream headache—and I clenched my eyes shut. When I reopened them, I was back in the present and arrested by the perfection of four finger-width pillars of ice directly before me, sitting on a small disk of ice afloat on the slowly running water. Ringed with sensuous bulges, like bands of gold, yet as clear and beautiful as horizontally ribbed glass, the columns supported a dirty arc of glacial ice above, oaken grains of Aconcagua caught and held like jewels within. It was a structure that bridged the gap between the black scythe above and cool, clear water below: life and death, two phases of the same element.

I stared for some time. Eventually I wondered if Carlos Menem, the president of Argentina, was aware of this small area of perfection in his country, or if my prime minister was aware of similar areas in Canada.

I rose to my feet and walked down the glacier. The sound of water grew until it was flowing in streams the size of my forearm. Turbulent from snowmelt, the water was murky with sediment. The sediment hid things. The glacial tarn above Plaza Francia was frozen over. I lifted a rock, affixed a woman's name to it, and thrust it toward the tarn. I wanted the rock to shatter the ice and sink to the bottom with my lies. Instead, the rock rasped across the surface, leaving five jagged scratches like claw marks from a human hand.

It was too poetically comic, even for me. I laughed at myself and walked off down the glacier. I was going home to my wife and my life back in Canada. February 2 had been our sixth anniversary. Behind me, the tracks of my retreat had already blown away.

- *No Picnic on Mount Kenya* by Felice Benuzzi
- *Nine-Headed Dragon River: Zen Journals 1969–1982* by Peter Matthiessen
- *The Unbearable Lightness of Being* by Milan Kundera

KUSUM KANGURU SOLO

Our ignorance proved an insuperable handicap from the point of view of material achievement; but from the spiritual point of view, which is of far greater importance to the true mountaineer, it was in the nature of a gift from God. Every step led to new discoveries, and we were continually in a state of amazed admiration and gratitude. It was as though we were living in the beginning of time, before men had begun to give names to things.

—*Felice Benuzzi,* No Picnic on Mount Kenya

APRIL 1990: The Sherpas call the mountain Kusum Kanguru "Three Snow-White Gods" in reference, and deference, to its alabaster-pleated summits: the West, Main, and East. A Canadian trekking guide had pointed out the mountain when I was guiding an ascent of Imja Tse (Island Peak) in the Khumbu region of Nepal. He added that it was on the trekking-peak list, which meant that a permit would be inexpensive.

There was nothing "trekking"-looking about the peak. It looked Peruvian: harrowed ice gullies and snow arêtes sweeping down to the north; to the southwest, steep, stacked tan-and-black rock bands etched to half height with a sapphire line of waterfall ice that led into a snow gully, arcing onto a ramp of snow and rock and more rock and, hopefully, the summit ice-and-snow pleats.

It looked like there *was* a route there.

he southwest face of Kusum Kanguru in 1991.
wasn't climbed till 2013 by Alexander
uchkin and Vyacheslav Ivanov.
arry Blanchard

APRIL 1991: Having said goodbye to my first guests at the airport in Lukla, I had five days free before my next client arrived. I was keen to take a closer look at the southwest side of Kusum Kanguru. I would be soloing. *Could I climb the southwest face by myself?*

APRIL 17: I left for a two-day reconnaissance with Tenzing, my sirdar, the leader of the Sherpa team. Midmorning, we left the heavily trodden track to Nāmche Bāzār and followed the defile of the Thado Koshi River. Swarms of trekkers, porters, and climbers faded away below us.

We were alone. I didn't know if anyone had ever been up there. It was a paradigm shift to suddenly be in Himalayan wilderness. Underfoot, large boulders were overgrown with a three-inch carpet of moss, while invisible waters gurgled beneath. The roar and charge of the river was ten feet to my right, while curtains of water beads fell from the canyon rim twenty feet overhead. The air glowed with water droplets backlit by sun.

We spooked him from the bank, and he bounded from river rock to river rock, vaulting over the open current like an acrobat. *A wolverine!* was my first thought. But no, he had the comically cute bandit's face of a raccoon, thick reddish fur, and a ringed tail. Tenzing blurted, *"Wah donka!"* and pointed, beaming. Then I got it. A red panda! I stopped in my tracks, slack-jawed, eyes as wide as hubcaps. Hopping away with balletic grace, the panda looked back over his shoulder, and then he was gone. Sixty seconds later, I could breathe again.

"Holy crap, Tenzing! That was a red panda!"

He told me that they call them wah donka in the Makalu region, where he was from. His English was pretty good. "Do you see them often?"

"No, not too many."

Two hours farther on, we were cul-de-sacced inside a keyhole of dripping moss-covered overhangs. I understood why so few trekkers ever came up here. We'd been teetering from boulder to boulder, clinging to clumps of yak grass, and mauling banisters of bamboo, all while the Thado Koshi's churning waves roared beneath our heels.

Tenzing shucked his pack and unsheathed his Gurkha-issue kukuri. The sword had a foot-long blade and weighed several pounds. He kept the lobe-shaped cutting edge honed like a razor. In a simple act of woodsmanship, he hacked down an evergreen, bucked the limbs down to handhold size, notched footholds into the trunk, and then leaned the rustic ladder against the cliff.

"I'm sorry I cut down that tree," he said, looking a little bewildered at my concerned face.

"It's okay. It's the only way we're going to get up here."

Above the ladder, stalks of bamboo, eight feet tall and a couple inches in diameter, lay in legion in front of us. I felt like a tortoise trying to find its way through a field of golden wheat. Half of the time, Tenzing had to hack passage with his kukuri. We developed a running joke. I'd say, "Kukuri time," and Tenzing would unsheathe the glittering silver blade.

I was pulling on one tangle like it was an elevator door that wouldn't open when I saw movement six feet to my right: a long part along the spine, with strands of ocher hair falling in heavy, combed lines. I was immediately afraid—the animal was big as an antelope. He glanced back—wide black pupils encircled with a tawny iris, sweeping foot-long horns, and pert, alert ears—and then bolted. I'd just come close to bumping into a Himalayan tahr. Once again, I stood awestruck. Swizzle sticks of bamboo parted in front of my chest; I stood there holding onto them, exhaling a "Wow!"

Eight hours of hard work saw us lost in a maze of grassy granite hummocks immediately below the soaring southwest face of Kusum Kanguru. There was a route. So enticing, but too hard for me alone. I decided to attempt the less steep—more ice- and snow-featured—north face when my next guiding trip was over. Tenzing and I were back in Lukla the next day. I tried to capture it all in my journal alongside an ink sketch of the valley we'd been up. The spine of the cloth-covered book lay flat on the kitchen table of my guest house, or across my thighs in my room, me writing poems or words and drawing by hand from memory or sight and filling a number of pages.

MAY 9: My last client left Lukla. The next day, Tenzing and I would start for the north face of Kusum Kanguru.

I rested and read, finding inspiration and delight in Felice Benuzzi's classic wartime mountaineering memoir, *No Picnic on Mount Kenya*.

An Italian working in the Colonial Services in Abyssinia (modern-day Ethiopia), Benuzzi was taken prisoner of war in 1941 and interned in a British POW Camp near Nanyuki, Kenya. He could see Mt. Kenya from there. To cure his wilting spirit, he and two other inmates organized an escape for the sole purpose of placing the Italian flag on top of Mt. Kenya. The trio hoarded rations for six months and clandestinely made crampons and ice-axes. They "escaped" for eighteen days, eventually placing the flag on Lenana, one of Mt. Kenya's lower peaks, and then "surrendered" back into the camp. Upon hearing of their phenomenal adventure, the British Commandant commuted their twenty-eight-day sentence to solitary confinement down to seven, due to the trio's "sporting effort."

MAY 10: Tenzing hired two porters. We walked from Lukla to Manjo. The next morning, we started up the Kyashar Khola along a fine, empty trail. It was such a contrast to the hordes we'd left marching to Everest Base Camp, or to the defile of the Thado Koshi, where we'd clung to wisps of bamboo for dear life. There were no red pandas or tahr. On the trail lay paddies of yak dung, which our porters collected for their fire.

Having finished *No Picnic on Mount Kenya*, I sat cross-legged in my tent that night reading Peter Matthiessen's *Nine-Headed Dragon River: Zen Journals* 1969–1982. (As I crowd in on sixty-five, it amazes me how much time I've spent sitting and reading in tents, on more than thirty-five expeditions abroad. How much would I have read otherwise, if I'd had the time to do so?) Matthiessen studied under Zen master Tetsugen Bernard Glassman and wrote about him in the book:

> "Such masters are very rare," says Tetsugen with a sigh, comparing Harada with other teachers whose clarity of insight may be unsurpassed, yet whose private weakness—usually drink or women—will disillusion the more idealistic students, and sometimes turn away from Zen those who confuse the teacher with their own notion of a "true" spiritual leader. "They want to dehumanize the teacher so that he reflects some personal deity of their own." Tetsugen smiles. "We try to improve a little, but we are who we are."

At the teahouse where I stayed in Lukla, *dudh*, *chi*, and *chini* (milk, tea, and sugar) emptied from my glass. May 9. Barry Blanchard

MAY 12: Dawn came clear and cold. We shook the frost off. I watched the porters cook tea and ramen noodles in a small, dented, kettlebell-shaped pot charred black from wood smoke but polished to a sheen on the inside. They balanced the pot on three upright tabular stones, feeding a dry-grass fire with twigs and, eventually, yak dung. The dung smelled sweet in the crisp morning air. Tenzing had a kerosene stove, pressure cooker, and several pots, and he was able to boil more water quickly. We filled a thermos with sweet milk tea and gave it to our two young porters. I offered them instant oatmeal, but they weren't keen on it; they did, however, appreciate more boiling water to make more ramen.

The trek up the trail was pleasant. Looking toward the north face of Kusum Kanguru, I began to visualize myself high on the route, climbing.

The steeply flanked V-cut ravine of the Kyashar Khola opened onto the U-shaped, flat-bottomed, glacially eroded valley of the Kyashar Glacier. The horseshoe of the Kyashar Himal cut frozen sawtooths into the blue sky. That magnificent skyline enclosed our hemisphere from Thamserku to Kangtega, Kyashar, and finally enchained the three summits of Kusum Kanguru. White snowfields blazed, aquamarine seracs fronted tumbling glaciers, and long tendrils of snow and ice reached into mottled fans of avalanche debris. Tawny granites glowed up high; around half height, their color aged to slate—this dark rock looked older, weathered. Lower yet, it was matted with burnt-sienna patches of vegetation. And lower yet, the yak grass and low growth melded to a carpet that swept to the valley floor. I was on fire to climb.

Big packs, sun-scorched lips puffy and suppurating, noses scabbed over from sunburn, the two climbers coming down the trail looked like they'd been ridden hard and hung up wet. But they were still smiling, a Brit and a Kiwi jazzed up from their six-day repeat of the Ball–Curtis climb (the famous 1985 north face climb of Kusum Kanguru by British team Tom Curtis and John Ball). They shucked their packs and sat to tell me about the route. I told them of my plans to solo it and maybe go for a direct finish (Ball and Curtis had avoided the direct line due to poor snow conditions). They gave me advice, and then the Brit pointed a question at me: "How do you intend to descend?"

"I don't know. I thought maybe the North Ridge."

"No, that is not the way," the Brit stated a tad impatiently. "You'll want to use the descent that we used. The one that Ball and Curtis used." And he graciously took the time to sketch out the descent route on paper, while pointing out the prominent features in the landscape. It was clear that he doubted my preparation and that he wanted to help keep me safe, in spite of myself.

We arrived at our base camp at 14,370 feet to find that flat tent platforms were already established—as well as the skeleton of a stone kitchen. Twin frozen waterfalls hung a backdrop not 300 feet away; the one on the right still looked to be in shape, climbable. I was tempted, but I was here for Kusum Kanguru. The ice would have to wait. (American climbers Dave Custer and Susan Ruff would climb these routes a decade later, in November 2001.)

I prepared to climb, trimming my pack to seven pitons, two Stoppers, three ice screws, four slings, my light down sleeping bag, a bivy sack, hanging stove, spartan rations, and—against the advice of the Brit and Kiwi—a single 150-foot-long 7 mm rope. They had made a number of rappels of that length with their two ropes tied together, two of those down the front of a serac and "spooky as all get out." I would be making twice as many raps on my one rope folded in half (75 feet).

I sketched Kwangde into my journal. When the sun went down, I retreated to my minute yellow tent to write my first will. I wrote it to my wife, declaring my love for her, as imperfect as it was. *Was I good enough? Did the universe even want me in it?* It felt proper for me to be going up onto the mountain alone to try to answer that.

I sat cross-legged, thinking on how my life had led to this beautiful line in the Himalaya. I needed to see how close to perfection I could come in my alpinism. Could my time in, and learning from, high mountains allow me to climb in control, knowing what the mountain would allow and what it would not? Could I climb alone and climb well and climb free? At the same time, I had also married young because I wanted to be a father who was there for his child, something I had absolutely hungered for when I was young. One hand held my wedding ring; the other gripped my ice-ax. My two hands were tearing me apart.

MAY 13, 1 P.M.: "I will be back in two days," I told Tenzing. Soon I was zigzagging up a grassy slope, looking to the North Ridge of Kusum Kanguru, and thinking about Alex Lowe, who'd soloed the line in 1990. He had had one child at the time, his oldest son. I wondered if he'd chosen the ridge because it was safer, no rockfall, no cornices to come thundering down. Was I feeding a self-deceptive cycle by climbing out on the face, inside the gullies? I'd always survived face climbs, therefore...

But I had to be back in Lukla in five days. I was stronger on ice and snow than on rock. My safety would come with the frost and climbing fast to minimize my exposure. Or so I concluded.

MAY 13, 6 P.M.: Cairns built by the Brit and Kiwi guided me up the moraine. I found a fairly level spot beside a gurgling, proglacial stream and went about constructing a bivy patio. As the evening frost fell onto the mountain, somewhere high on the face a trapped wedge of water froze inward from its periphery. When it became solid ice, it expanded 9 percent—enough to nudge off a large rock. Frost shattering. Gravity grabbed the rock and catapulted it earthward. It hammered into the mountain a dozen times, dislodging more rock, ice, and snow. I heard the barrage before I saw it. The roar was loud and deep. Big rocks. *Could they hit me?*

I panicked and then assured myself that I was far enough out from the face. Bursts of granite shattered against a large ledge in the lower couloir. Yes, they were big, and yes, they had bombarded the route. Crap.

The last rock clattered to a stop. It was over, and quiet, save for the crackling of the creek and my pounding heart. I breathed deeply and then thought about packing up and heading down to camp to get more gear and the 9 mm rope, re-routing myself to the North Ridge.

I stood. The face was absolutely silent. I started hacking—the remnants of a lingering virus—spat out phlegm and then blew streamers of snot from both nostrils. The mountain would freeze deeper and deeper all night, and the face would be safe when I started climbing, I told myself. I'd be well above the freezing level when the day's heat reached its zenith.

I unzipped my bivy sack and slipped into my sleeping bag. Rich clusters of stars shone overhead. I was alone in a bivouac high in the Himalaya. I took it all in for a few moments, spellbound by the universe. Then, I rolled onto my side and went to sleep.

MAY 13, 11 P.M.: My alarmed shrieked. I sputtered and coughed and clawed inside my toque to shut the damn thing off. Instant oatmeal, chocolate, Italian salami, a quart of tea; a quart of water and, new for me, a quart of hot coffee for the caffeine. I swallowed my last twelve-hour Sudafed to suppress my cold symptoms, at least until I got off the face.

I'd studied the bergschrund the day before—it had looked like the right side was the way over. But by headlamp, I saw that the left was the way to go. Spindrifted snow pattered onto my prized dark-blue and black onesie, which Integral Designs in Calgary had made and given to me as a prototype.

Several yard-high petals of snow reached from the 'schrund's lower lip. I gently inserted the picks of my ice tools into the lip, but they cut through the snow's structure. Grabbing my tools by their heads, I wiggle-coaxed the shafts into the fragile veil of snow. Beyond, a gaping mouth yawned, black and hungry. In the fantasy realm of my mind, I was gently easing myself over a film of saliva and seawater. If I were soft and secretive enough, the beast wouldn't awaken. I pressed my crampons down rather than kick them in, easing my torso to the snow to distribute my weight, trying to be as light as a helium balloon.

It was satisfying to feel the upper lip and know that solid snow lay over ancient gray ice. I hauled off and sunk a pick. The resonance of its bite anchored me to the solid, the physically permanent. I stepped from the ethereal veil, scampering away from the beast.

The cadence of my movement was in tempo with my deep breaths. Beyond the reach of my headlamp, the lower couloir vanished to black. I strove to stay close to the upper wall but couldn't always distinguish it in the dark. Two bulges of hoary ice grew in the hemisphere of my headlamp. It felt so good to surmount them efficiently with my pack on, the purple rope snaking off below. I didn't break stride. It was just good, plain, old fun!

MAY 14, 4 A.M.: The sun was just beginning to warm the jagged alabaster skyline between Thamserku and Kangtega. The high edge of the mountain was rising from the realm of the moon, pulled toward the brilliance of the sun. The mountain was the border between worlds, coming to me as I rose toward it.

Above me stood a seventy-foot verglas-streaked wall studded with chunks of protruding rock. In the light of my headlamp, the ice looked like a spider's web laid over the dark stone. The first crux. I reasoned that there was enough ice to climb if I stayed in the thickest veins. Each time, the ice would take a pick in the one and only place hidden in the weave of tin-colored strands. I climbed by intuition.

A long arête of perfectly sculpted snow lay above and to my right, reached by crossing a gully of jade-green ice that lay parallel. The frozen spine was safer from falling rock or avalanche, but the snow was hollow. My tools plummeted through like framing hammers hitting papier-mâché. The gut of the adjacent gully was ice, but it was also where most rockfall—and all avalanches—would funnel. I stuck to the edge of the gully, my tools sunk in the green ice and my feet kicked into crisp snow.

As the angle steepened, I trended left, away from the Ball–Curtis, looking for the direct. I climbed the edge of the green ice but, just like the centerline of a canoe, the gunwales merged at the bow, these gunwales

being arêtes of snow that pinched down my gully, leaving me stuck in a cul-de-sac and having to cross an arête, usually to the left. The crossings were horribly insecure on hollow snow. I took to leaving my pack anchored to an ice screw; I'd climb to the end of my rope, anchor to two screws, and then rappel back to my pack on a friction hitch (to save on weight, I hadn't brought a rappel device). With my pack on my back, I'd prusik back up the rope using a sling to create an ascending hitch (an autoblock).

MAY 14, 9 A.M.: I could feel the warmth of the day. I felt safe, but also tired and dry. I stopped for an hour to brew coffee, rest, rehydrate, and eat.

I climbed away with my pack but soon reverted to going ropelength by ropelength; the snow was crap, and the overall angle of the face steepened from 60 to 70 degrees. Twenty-five hundred feet up the face, the cough suppressant I'd taken quit. I coughed and expelled knots of mustard-colored phlegm.

MAY 14, 4 P.M.: Four thousand feet up, I leaned my head against the mountain and looked down at my frontpoints. They looked like the rounded teeth in an old dog's mouth. I'd have to sharpen them. I coughed and hacked. A long cord of mucus trailed from my mouth onto the hard ice. Thirty feet to my right, a deep fluting of chaotic snow bordered the green ice. Within that swirling structure, I recognized the universe's repeating spiral: the arms of a galaxy, the fronds of a fiddlehead fern, the decreasing chambers of a snail's shell. Below one of the spirals, there looked to be a hollow.

I leaned onto the rope and made a tension traverse to the hole. It could be enlarged to a one-man cave. I sunk my third screw, tied off the rope, and returned to retrieve my pack. No shovel blade. I hacked with my ice tools, raked with my crampons, and scraped with my helmet. At the far end of the hollow, four drips of ice hung but didn't touch the floor. My mind leaped back to Aconcagua and the four small pillars of ice that had arrested me there, how they'd spanned from a black scythe of ice above to the living water below. I looked again: four—damn—and they didn't touch down. I didn't like it. I avoided touching them.

one and off the face, I took a photo and coiled my rope. Soon I'd be down and back in yak stures. Barry Blanchard

Night came. I sat inside my cramped cave, my empty pack blocking the door, the stove hissing away, melting ice. I'd fall into fits of hacking that left me breathless, like the dry heaves from drinking way too much alcohol. Hunks of slime and sugar-cube-sized custard crap came from my lungs, threads of blood drawn in them. Spontaneous episodes of hyperventilation would come over me, and I'd have to claim control of my breathing, which reminded me of my breathing on Everest three years earlier when I'd developed pulmonary edema. Here, at 19,800 feet above sea level, I wondered if I would die before morning. Then snowflakes exploded into the cave, and I didn't understand because it wasn't snowing. It took a full minute for the smell of burned nylon to register. "Oh fuck!"—I'd leaned into the stove and melted a fist-sized hole in my down jacket.

I grieved not having a partner. I needed a partner to help, to evaluate my health against, someone like my mate Kevin Doyle to lean on. Yet I felt him there, like he was sitting beside me. I almost asked him if he'd like cool water this time rather than more hot liquids. I got into my pit and soon found that I coughed less lying on my side or sitting up. I wondered what would be found of me in time.

MAY 15: Dawn came, and I wasn't dead. Going up 1,000 feet sounded a hell of a lot better than making 4,000 feet worth of 75-foot rappels down. I brewed and packed and sharpened my crampons and picks, and then I climbed away. I let the image of my wife force me to do everything well, do everything right. Saw her waking and slowly rising to stand and face the day, like wheat warming to the sun. Traversing the arêtes to gain the ice gullies was horrifyingly insecure—wet sugar balanced on the edge of collapse by diaphanous crusts. At one point, the structure I was on failed. I screamed as I scratched down a yard, my body clenched against the terror of tumbling backward before my sharpened crampons caught. I needed to be down and left. I squandered an hour trying to improvise an anchor before admitting to myself that a bollard carved into the deeper, more solid snow-and-ice matrix would hold.

"COME ON, BARRY! Get it together. Do this for your wife. Do this well. No mistakes," I shouted.

At midday, I stood under a leaning shark's tooth of snow twenty feet high. It scared me. I was anchored to gunmetal ice. I left my pack and eased under the left edge of the tooth, digging and digging to get my picks into ice. Useless snow structures, like a pillar of cantilevered white apple crates, squeezed in on my left, threatening collapse with the lightest touch. I slowly and cautiously threaded the needle and then stepped onto a 35-degree slope. The summit ridge!

I carved a snow bollard, picketed a tool, and sunk a screw into an exposed scrap of blue ice; anchored, I rapped back to get my pack then kicked steps up twenty feet to the summit. Streamers of mist raced between cornices, harbingers of an afternoon storm. I knelt and hacked and spat up green and red. I'd accomplished a new line on a beautiful Himalayan peak, the actualization of a dream. I took one heartbeat of pride, then turned to face my anxiety over the building storm and my imminent need to get down.

Five-day-old footprints from the Brit and the Kiwi pointed off down the North Ridge. The cornices there looked horrible, like a line of capsized hulls waiting on one human nudge to send them into the depths. I started off, praying that I didn't have to go far down the ridgeline. In places, I left the tracks and climbed lower, where I was less likely to have a cornice fail underfoot. I had no partner on the other end of the rope to compensate for that. At one point, I climbed onto an insecure wafer crust of ice above the 5,000-foot drop of the north face. Feeling an impending fall, I hopped to the other side and used the adrenaline to hammer my way up to a perch.

Safe, I stopped and breathed myself down. Clouds tumbled by, and there was a stiff, cold wind blowing out of the south, but there at my feet were the remnants of a bollard! The Brit/Kiwi rappel point! I made two rappels and landed in the growing gray fury of the storm.

MAY 15, 3 P.M.: I couldn't see a thing, couldn't move, felt so very, very small and inconsequential compared to the power the atmosphere was unleashing on the mountain. Shallower ground below me, or so I thought. *Would I have to stay here? When would the storm end? Why the fuck was I up here without a partner?* Then I caught a glimpse of the slopes below leading to a flat-looking col, the head of the tumbling glacier, the next step in my descent. Dull-gray clouds clamped down, and I started downclimbing, facing in, feeling my way with my front points and praying that I didn't step off a cliff or into a crevasse.

The ground shallowed to flat. I turned, fully extending my one ski pole like a blind man's cane to probe the glacier. I neurotically poked my way down into the maelstrom, lunging back from any change in the shadows or teetering of vertigo. I stopped often, and several times had the illusion that I was still moving; twice I toppled onto the snow, even though I had stopped.

The gray darkened toward black, and the wind bit with frostbite on my right flank. I had to get out of the storm. And then in front of me was a snowdrift presenting a yard of vertical. I shucked my pack, sank to my knees, and began gouging with my helmet. Providence had bounded recrystallized snow into a firm yet aerated matrix; by alternately drilling with crampons and scooping with my helmet, I had a one-man cave excavated in an hour. I sealed the door with my pack and quartered my last chunk of sausage into desperately needed stew.

Threads of blood spider-webbed the green shit gurgling up from my lungs, but inside the sanctuary of my cave I was beyond worrying—I knew I'd see the next day. "You won't beat me, you microscopic motherfuckers!" I screamed, protected by the mottled walls of the cave. "I am waking up tomorrow and going down!"

MAY 16: The miracle of a cold, calm, clear dawn. I ran down the broad saddle of the glacier until crevasses, some wide and transverse, began forming in rank. Tiers of seracs squatted menacingly above my head.

I found the Brit/Kiwi anchor at the edge of the glacier and nervously stepped over the edge onto the steep face of the serac. Deep azures swirled with aquamarines and turquoise. The surface was polished to glittering glass by heat and cold, and sculpted as voluptuously as the woman in Rodin's *The Kiss*. Twice I reached the end of my rope to find natural holes in the ice through which I just had to thread the rappel rope. I left my last screw on the final rappel and jogged out of the firing range along a protruding rock buttress.

When I reached the valley floor, I felt Milan Kundera's "unbearable lightness of being": as if this event, and all others, happened just one

Tenzing starts on dinner in the treeless hummocks high above the Thado Koshi River. The track leading to Everest Base Camp is far below. Barry Blanchard time and life had no weight or meaning. The engagement was over. Even though I hadn't performed perfectly, I'd performed well. Several hours of weaving my way down into richer, thicker, luscious air brought me above base camp. Tenzing was burning juniper on a small stone altar. I was a day late. He was praying for me...for me.

I sat on my pack and wept.

🎧 "This Is the Modern World": The Jam

📖 *Darkness Visible: A Memoir of Madness* by William Styron
📖 *The Complete Posthumous Poetry of César Vallejo* by César Vallejo
📖 *One Man's Mountains: Essays and Verses* by Tom Patey
📖 *Iron John: A Book About Men* by Robert Bly
📖 *The Mont Blanc Massif: The 100 Finest Routes* by Gaston Rébuffat

CHAPTER 8 — ASPIRING ALPINIST III

THE RICHARD CRANIUM MEMORIAL ROUTE

While I had been soloing on Kusum Kanguru, my wife had been trekking and sightseeing in Nepal with a girlfriend. I flew home to Canada while they traveled south to spend a month on the Malay Peninsula. I felt a lethargic fatalism; perhaps if I put off confessing my adultery long enough, the problem would resolve itself. I was being cowardly and arrogant—a blaring contrast to the way I practiced alpinism. I felt like a fuck-up.

JUNE 1991: Jon Krakauer, the writer and mountaineer, called. ABC TV had approached him to write six scenarios on extreme sport for a pilot of a series, *The Extreme Edge.*

Jon said, "I told them to film Mark soloing something in the Alps. Mark told them yes, the Frendo Spur on the Aiguille du Midi, but only if they got Jean Afanassieff, a French mountain guide and filmmaker, to organize the shoot, David Breashears to film it, and Barry Blanchard to rig it. They want to shoot July 9 to 18 in Chamonix. Can you be there?"

"Hell yes!" I said. "I'll move heaven and earth, and I will be there." Seeing Mark, climbing with him, making TV, and getting paid to do it—I felt like I'd won something. My first call was to the producer in Los Angeles. I'd be making double my day rate as a guide, plus expenses.

My next call was to Breashears. "It is great to finally talk to you," he said. "I feel that we should have talked before this. Mike Weis speaks highly of you and has given you his stamp of approval." David and Mike

Mark Twight pulling up through the spindrift to get over the bergschrund and plant his picks into the ice of Les Droites. Barry Blanchard were old Colorado climbing buddies. I had learned a ton working with Mike on *K2* (the movie) in 1990. Eventually, we got down to business.

"I want to do an elevator shot of Twight. Can you hang me behind him and raise me?"

"Ya, sure," I said, not really knowing how, but knowing it was possible.

JULY 6: Riding to Calgary on my motorcycle, we had stopped beside the road in Cochrane, Alberta. My wife stepped off the back of the bike and undid her helmet, her face focused with concentration.

"What did Mark mean when he wrote, 'deny, deny, deny'?" she asked. She'd seen a fragment from his last letter sitting on my desk in the basement. My admissions were finally made, several more women. The ground under our marriage fractured again. The vortex that I'd created grabbed me, and I began the inevitable spiral down. In arrogant stupidity, I told her to just get back on the bike. She wouldn't get back on the bike until I told her their names.

JULY 7: David Breashears looked like a college professor when he walked into the boarding area at Logan International Airport. We met there on our way to Chamonix. We started in talking about the project and then about climbing, but soon found greater depth. We shared the instant bond of a recent breakup of his long-term relationship and the tenuousness of my own marriage. He suggested that I read *Darkness Visible* by William Styron. I countered with *The Complete Posthumous Poetry of César Vallejo*. We were surely the two cheeriest guys in the airport.

After landing at Charles de Gaulle Airport, we transferred to a van and started driving. Hours of lavender flowers and mustard fields sped by, and then the Alps grew and we turned for the steep climb to Chamonix. It had been a decade since I'd climbed in Cham, with my friend Kevin Doyle. That trip had set the course of my life. I'd found my calling in the forest there after descending from the north face of Les Droites in 1980. I would be an alpinist.

It was as exciting as hell to be driving back into the valley. Rather than camping illegally by the cemetery like Kevin and I had done for four months, I checked into a three-star hotel. My life was looking up on some fronts.

JULY 11: The téléphérique doors slid open at the Plan de l'Aiguille mid-station. I shadowed Mark as he wove through a gaggle of slow-moving tourists and other climbers. Mark knew exactly where he was going, and he wanted to be there now. We gained the approach trail, extended ski poles, and I raced along hot on his heels. My heart rate ramped up, and my breathing deepened. The grass beside the trail looked radiant and smelled so lush with life. I was climbing with Twight again! (While Mark was living in Chamonix, from 1988 to 1993, he tried to be more "French like," and spelled his name Marc.)

"Did I just put my hand in some Norwegian asshole's shit?" Mark asked. I was above him, the rope still stowed in my pack, as we moved together up moderately difficult granite. He'd reached blindly for a handhold and had indeed sunk his fingers into the recently passed feces of some alpinist.

"Why yes, Doom, you did. Hard for me to tell if it is Norwegian or not." I expected him to rave with rage. Instead, he started laughing and slowly lifted his hand and stepped down to clean it off in a snow patch. I realized that my friend had mellowed since I'd last climbed with him, three years earlier on Mt. Everest.

"You get this," he said at the lower crux of the route. After we tied in, I led up massive blocks of granite beetling like dragons' teeth. Good, clean cracks protected with the only two cams Mark had brought. It was physical, and I worried about him soloing it.

"Oh, don't worry, I'll bring some auto-assurance for that."

"What do you mean?"

"A short chunk of rope and those two cams so I can back-rope myself."

Later, we cramponed up the perfect spine of an ice-and-snow arête. It looked like a brushstroke in a Japanese watercolor. When the arête melded into a granite wall, Mark said, "I think we should head out left here and avoid the *rognon* finish." A *rognon* is French for a rock island in a glacier. Mark pronounced it *rug-nion*.

"It'll take too much time, and we'll miss the last 'phérique from the top of the Midi." Our ascent of the Frendo Spur, which had started at

7,500 feet from the Plan de l'Aiguille téléphérique station, would end at the Aiguille du Midi station at 12,605 feet. The whole of our 9,210-foot descent back to Chamonix would be accomplished by cable car. You have to love climbing in the Alps.

In the heat of the day, we skirted on soggy ice coated in oatmeal snow. The ablated brow of a serac bulged from golden granite. We had to climb the steep tin-colored ice to exit. Mark made for a lone rock protruding from the ice, the size and shape of a Volkswagen Beetle's hood. The instant he stood on it, gravel grated under several tons of pressure, and the rock began sliding into freefall. Within four heartbeats, it was bounding down the ice, gouging destruction like a meteor bouncing across the moon.

I screamed, "ROCK! ROCK! ROCK!" as Mark flattened onto the ice, arms extended, both tools thankfully sunk solidly, and then bicycled his front points in and screamed, "Fuuuuuck!" in a deep, ragged baritone.

I pounded to my friend. When he raised his head from the crook of his arm, I could see an adrenaline hangover in the slack sagging of his eyes.

"Why does all the God action have to happen at the end?" Mark asked.

"I don't know. God hates us?"

"Hate him back—it works for me," we recited in unison and laughed. And then we shook it off and continued to the top. Now, I marvel at how we came to accept such brushes with death, those pats from the Reaper's bony hand. We were both intelligent enough to realize that it was a numbers game. If we played it long enough, our numbers would come up. (We didn't know it then, but within three years, we would both give up soloing; I was thirty-five and Mark thirty-three.)

We made the last 'phérique with a half hour to spare. I had a half baguette stuffed with a foot-long hot dog in one hand and a cold beer in the other. The bun was a sealed unit, and I got to squirt ketchup, mustard, and mayonnaise into it before the dog got stuffed in. Brilliant! No muss, no fuss, and so bloody good.

"Make sure you stand by the window," Mark said as we boarded. "The first couple of drops over the towers are really steep, and the tourists will freak out and scream, and then they'll fart." They did.

Mark drags one of our ropes up the first ascent of the Richard Cranium Memorial route. The sun is up there somewhere. Barry Blanchard

"I've been getting to work on film stuff with the guys in the valley," Mark said. We were back down in Cham, sipping cold beer in the warm sun. I felt the luxurious fatigue of having used my body hard, and I could see that my friend was in the same space.

"How has it been working in French?"

"Good and getting better all the time. I'm speaking the language now, although I'm learning it from guides, and that's bizarre, yet perfect. I just started understanding what they were saying to each other, stuff like, 'My ass is so sore—that guy had me bent over the barrel all night.' Figurative, not literal."

"Did you ask about a courtesy reach-around?"

"Of course," he smiled, "but in kindergarten French. But they got it and laughed, and we bonded. Figuratively, not literally."

"Have you told Raine about the other women?"

He locked his eyes onto mine. "No, how about you?"

"Yes, it came out when she saw the 'deny, deny, deny' line in your last letter. I didn't volunteer it."

"Fuck—sorry, man."

"Don't be. I'm embarrassed because I wasn't strong enough to own up to my actions. Either that or I was just too bloody lazy. Either way, I feel weak and pathetic."

"I don't know that either one of us is ready to be married, not man enough yet. Raine will be home on Friday. She's working through the week in Paris and commuting back here on the weekends. It's the only way we can afford to be here."

JULY 12: I piled into a van with a bunch of our crew. Peter Pilafian would be shooting first camera, plus serve as the director of photography. I'd worked with him on *K2*, and it was good to see him again. In the back of the van sat Marie Hiroz, who would be recording sound. She was also an accomplished climber.

"Why are you wearing such thick clothing?" she asked me outside the Plan de l'Aiguille station, later that afternoon. We'd been filming Mark on the lower part of the route. Neither she nor I were involved in the helicopter shot that was going on. I had on the pile salopettes that I'd worn on Nanga Parbat three years earlier.

"I'm having a challenge staying warm."

"Oh yes, you and Mark climbed the route yesterday. I forgot. I can see how you'd be cold after a big day." The warmth of her smile reached into my chest.

A half hour later, David and I climbed into a Lama helicopter that had the doors off and the back seat out. There were pick points for us to clip our climbing harnesses into, but that was up to us. The pilot powered up and raced directly to the pinnacle that we were to get out on. The Lama was so gutsy he didn't have to spiral to gain altitude. I felt like I was riding an arrow loosed from Odysseus's bow. The pilot put a skid to the tip of the vertiginous dark spire and looked over his shoulder with a "You two can get out now" impatience furrowing his brow. I glanced nervously to David, and he glanced nervously back. I stepped out trembling, like a gun was pointed at my back and a tightrope over Niagara Falls was now underfoot. David didn't look any better when I turned and squatted on the rock and offered him my hand amidst the deafening roar of the rotors.

"Holy crap! These French pilots do not dick around," I yelped as the ship belly-rolled away.

"No!" he said giddily. "That was just wild."

They came back a couple of hours later and we wrapped for the day. Most of the crew, Mark, David, and I sat around enjoying the late-day sun sitting on the grass of the Plan de l'Aiguille. Thierry Renault strode over fresh from a day of guiding. One of the best alpinists in France and known to all as "Turbo" because of his speed, he received effusive welcomes from all the Europeans, kisses on both cheeks from Marie, and hand-pumping *Saluts!* from the men, including Mark, who was trying hard to be European. Soon everyone was bantering happily in French, though they all graciously switched to English when they noted David's and my silence. But he walked away anyway and sat on a rock and looked out over the valley, no doubt trying to untangle the threads of his failed relationship.

"Did you see Breashears walk away?" I asked Mark later.

"Ya, that was powerful." Mark was always keenly aware of theatrics.

Jacques, one of the French guides, solved the elevator shot with a rescue winch that his dad, also a guide, had used in the 1950s. Designed as a backpack, it had cranks like the pedals of a bicycle. Jacques, David, Mark, and I had taken it to a roadside crag down-valley in Servoz to test it. It took some muscle power to run, but David was happy with its smooth motion. At one point, Jacques and I were atop the cliff belaying Mark and David as they climbed to us. Jacques was belaying directly off his anchor with a purple aluminum belay plate.

"Look, it is brilliant. I can take my hands off the belay and roll a cigarette." And he did: the device would pinch off a second's fall automatically.

"Wow, that is brilliant. What is it called?"

"It is a New Alp plaquette, Magic."

I had the first one in Canada.

JULY 14: Mark and I were zipping through Chamonix in "Big Butt," Mark's white 1985 VW Polo MK2 hatchback. We'd wrapped for the day and needed to be at the train station to meet Raine's train from Annecy in three minutes.

Raine stood on the platform, a lion's mane of dirty-blonde hair, large blue eyes, her chiseled jawline framing a bold cleft chin.

"You're late," she spat. I could feel the strain between them.

"I know," Mark said, sidestepping the confrontation with the élan of a matador. He picked up her bag and said, "You know this guy." I reached out my hand and she took it and smiled. I didn't quite know what to do. Her beauty left me tongue-tied.

JULY 15: "Um, ah, Mark, could we do that last bit again?" Peter asked, looking down the steep corner that Mark had just climbed. Peter's requests for retakes got under Mark's skin.

"What 'we,' white man?" Mark spat. "I'm the one who's climbing around without a rope here. You're anchored in."

"Uh, what are you going to do with those?" Peter pointed at the rock shoes Mark had just taken off, to switch to mountain boots for the snow and ice.

"I'm going to throw them off," Mark hissed.

"No, no, you're—" Peter didn't get to finish. Doom stood up and heaved the purple shoes off the mountain one at a time.

Mark's anxiety hit a flash point on the last day of shooting. Peter, Jean, Marie, Jacques, and a couple other members of the mountain crew all stood on a ledge chopped into the route's final ice slopes. Peter was shooting down on Mark coming up the ice; David and I were anchored to the arête far off to the side, shooting across. Then someone on the ledge above Mark moved, sending a softball-sized piece of ice bounding downslope to rake a glancing blow across Mark's face. The hit could have taken him off. He grunted. Everyone froze. Nothing was said for thirty seconds.

"Alright," Mark bellowed. "No one fucking moves until I get up there! No movement at all!" No one did, and we finished the shoot.

Marie invited David and me to a dinner gathering at her friend Laurence's that night. Turbo and a few others were there. Laurence's apartment was compact, like so many things in Europe. But I felt the warmth of welcome as soon as I stepped inside and Marie stated, "Here, you must drink this." She smiled and handed me a flute of champagne, her eyes twinkling. I felt a little lightheaded even before I sipped the champagne.

The food that evening was delicious, and the company so playful, entertaining, and intimate.

"Have you ever bayonetted champagne?" David asked. Dinner was done. He and Turbo ducked into the kitchen, coming back with the biggest knife in the house. Turbo grabbed two unopened bottles of champagne and directed the guests out onto the balcony. He removed the foil-and-wire binding from over the corks, and then, holding one bottle horizontally, slid the back side of the heavy blade down the neck. "POP!" The bottle was instantly decapitated, the cork and the glass ring collaring it cut clean off.

"Bravo!" I exclaimed over everyone's "Ah's!" and laughter, ushering my flute under the bubbling froth.

"Here, let me do one," David said, second bottle in hand. Turbo handed him the knife, and David slid it down the neck of the bottle. "Crunch!" The bottle fractured in a jagged line that spewed champagne like a waterfall. I thrust flutes into the flow, and we all laughed with

David, a graceful dancer in the vertical but so much the clumsy professor in much of his horizontal life.

JULY 16: On my last night in Chamonix, Mark, Marie, and I sat close around a bar table drinking and talking about love, sex, and lust. The air around us was hazy with pheromones. Marie got up to go to the washroom.

"If you don't take her home, I am going to," Mark said.

I leaned toward him and asked, "Why don't we take her to my hotel room together?"

"Whoa! Bubba, you are the coolest guy I know. But I just can't do that right now. I'm getting out of here."

Marie came back and Mark left. She and I went back to my hotel room.

After, I said, "I'm married. I'm going to have to tell my wife."

"That is your problem," Marie said as she buttoned her shirt.

JULY 21: My wife said she was going to visit her sister, and then she'd move out. In a defiant act of hollow bravado, I packed her things into

cardboard boxes and stacked them by the back door. It was as if my vaulting ego had suspended me over the shattered plane of our marriage. That illusion was the last I would know for a very long time.

I didn't realize that I was actually falling—bound for the bottom. Darkness and pain, hours alone in an empty, hollow husk of a house. I'd been left behind. I wanted her back desperately, demanded her back defiantly; I begged and I shouted. She moved farther away. Sleep arrived only when I was totally exhausted from climbing, or bleary-eyed from staying awake writing, drawing, and reading. My dreams scared me.

SEPTEMBER 9: I flew to Zürich to meet Jim Scott, a client I'd guided in the Khumbu four months earlier. We were in Europe to realize Jim's dream of climbing the north face of the Eiger. The weather sucked. Eventually, on our first attempt, Jim said to me, "You only get to the Hinterstoisser Traverse for the first time once in your life. I'd like to lead this." He did, taking us across this infamous "point of no return" halfway up the wall. Soon after, a storm mugged us, and I led us back to Don Whillans's rappel point, which I'd read about in Tom Patey's *One Man's Mountains.*

We were encrusted in icicles and matted with snow when I opened the Stollenloch, an old wooden door onto a short tunnel intersecting the spiral of the rack-and-pinion railway inside the mountain. A train was heading up the tunnel, all of twenty-five feet away. I had the bizarre experience of locking eyes with a passing Japanese tourist, and I saw shock arrest his being as he shouted inaudibly at me and pointed.

I thought I had read somewhere that there was enough room to retreat down the tunnel and press up against the wall if a train came—but I wasn't sure. Three hundred feet above us, a couple of guys were retreating from the North Pillar, a steep route up and right of Jim and me. I shouted my question to them. After some attempts, a reply came in German-accented English: "I don't know, but I have read that there is enough room."

"He must have read the same book I did," I said to Jim.

We took to timing the trains to establish the schedule and be able to run into the tunnel during the longest gap between them, hoping that

lark, picks sunk in the ice, concentrating and
oming up to my belay. Barry Blanchard

what the Germans and I had read was true. But there was no rhyme or reason to their coming and going. Finally, Jim said, "Fuck it." And he sprinted into the tunnel as the end of an upbound train rumbled by. I ran in after him. We were five minutes into our jog when we saw the light of an approaching train.

"Shit!" I spat. We shucked our packs and pasted them—and ourselves—flat to the wall. I breathed out hard as the unopposable momentum of the train rattled by one foot behind my back. And then it was gone, and Jim and I were cackling like hyenas and back to jogging down the track.

The weather was going to be poor for a while, but it was better—climbable—over in Chamonix. I convinced Jim that we should head over there. When I called Mark, he invited us to stay at his place, as he would be going to Switzerland to climb with Marie.

"Wow, really?"

"Yes, we've been hanging out together since you left."

"Hanging out, as in 'hanging out'?"

"Uh, ya."

"Well...I guess that I didn't imagine I'd be hearing that," I said. "It's okay that you stole my girlfriend."

"You weren't here, man, and I needed to climb with her, and she needed me."

"It's another thing that we have in common."

Mark started laughing and said, "Indeed, yes indeed. I'm going to hand you to Marie—she can describe how to get to Cham."

"Surprise!" she said playfully, and then she started laughing, and so did I.

"You must put your car on the train," Marie said. And then she told us how to drive to Kandersteg, on the north side of the Bernese Alps, drive onto the car train, and emerge from a nine-mile tunnel at Goppenstein on the south side. Jim and I got such a kick out of the novelty of driving our car onto the train.

Mark's house was the last one at the end of the road in Le Lavancher, a hamlet above Chamonix. While Jim went to meet up with an old friend who happened to be in Chamonix, Mark and I went to the Yeti Bar in Argentière and got into the beers.

"I told Raine everything. She knows about Marie."

"Holy crap, man—how is it going?"

"Intense and hard. I need to decide which woman I want to be with."

"Men have made harder decisions in this life."

"Yes, but maybe it won't be Raine or Marie."

"Huh, I hadn't considered that," I said. "Think long and hard, man. To the bottom of your soul. You do not want to be where I'm at. Climbing is the only time that I don't think about her, and I climb as much as I can because I need to get away from the vortex of my grief. I get out of it only for the minutes of a lead when I can't think of anything else—can't think of her. Sleep quit working. I'm afraid of my dreams. It hurts, brother."

Mark sat beside me on a bench. His blue eyes stayed fixed on mine. The sheen of a tear glittered below each, and it felt good to know how much he cared about me, loved me. He counseled the knife—perhaps the only tool he knew how to use at the time. *Cut away and rebuild, stronger and better.*

"I think this would all have been easier for you and me if we had had fathers," I said. I handed him my copy of Robert Bly's *Iron John: A Book About Men*. The book had helped me see the wound my absent father had left on me. I railed against Mark's father, and mine. More beer, and Mark cried in confusion over his father and my condemnation of them for not being there for us. Mark's emotions ran deep, and his heart was huge, but so much of the world would never see that beneath his Dr. Doom persona. You had to spend time with him, engage him, and then he'd hold nothing back.

We were well liquored when we left the Yeti at 2 a.m. A series of bright-orange road pylons *thwapped* under Big Butt's front bumper, and Mark couldn't correct, so they disappeared like a row of carrots being sucked into the ground by the Goofy Gophers in a Looney Tunes cartoon.

SEPTEMBER 11: Jim and I climbed a route on the Aiguille de Praz Torrent. The next day, he caught me on an uphill run to Lac Blanc, which left him beaming. I'd outpaced him early, and then fell into analyzing my marriage. My pace slowed. Jim was ten years older than me, and he was slathered in sweat but grinning when he tapped me on the calf. "Huh!" I blurted, and cranked up my pace and left him again, which was an asshole thing to do, but it's what I did.

We drove back, put our car on the train again, and made another attempt on the Eiger. This time, the storm mauled us at Death Bivouac; getting us back across the eight sideways ropelengths of the Second Ice Field was definitely a test of my alpine-guiding skills.

OCTOBER 3: Mark would be flying to Nepal on October 7; my flight home was on October 8. We had four days to climb in Chamonix. Mark chose the northwest face of Les Droites. It had been eleven years since Kevin Doyle and I had climbed the Jackson-Shea, on the north face. Gaston Rébuffat's *The Mont Blanc Massif: The 100 Finest Routes* placed it at the ninety-ninth hardest, and the route had demanded everything that Kevin and I had learned about climbing. It was the route that sealed my destiny as an alpinist. The seminal ascent of my life.

When we started packing, Mark asked, a little incredulously, "Is that all of the clothing you're taking?" I'd laid out neoprene socks, long underwear, and the brand-spanking-new purple-and-pink Mammut guide's pants that I'd bought in Grindelwald; an underwear shirt, pile shirt, and fleece pullover; plus, my black Mountain Equipment Co-op Bush Pilot down jacket to pull on over it all.

"Ya, I think that will be enough."

"I've got an extra layer and shells for my top and bottom."

"We're going to be moving; we'll be warm."

"What if it rains?"

"It's not supposed to rain, is it?"

"No, but what if it does?"

"I guess I'll suffer. I'm good at that."

The Téléphérique des Grands Montets had shut down on October 1. Mark and I walked from the valley floor. It was nice to be clomping along behind him. The last of the summer's greenery was already wilting to brown, peeking from mist being dispatched out ahead of a cold front.

The Argentière basin looked like chalk in the oblique cast of the autumnal sun. One inch of winter snow crunched underfoot, the first snows that would stay. Ours were the only footprints. In the summer

The north face of Les Droites back in 1980, eleven years earlier. Kevin Doyle

months, the glacier would have been crawling with people. By dusk, we were sitting inside the winter room of the Refuge d'Argentière brewing tea and cooking dinner.

OCTOBER 4: When Mark and I crunched away from the hut before dawn, I caught an echo of myself and Kevin eleven years and twenty-one days earlier in our Peter Storm sweaters descending the selfsame slopes on our way to the north face. Kevin and Mark were two of my closest friends, men whom I loved unconditionally, although I had yet to gain the depth of heart to tell them.

Mark strode across the glacier like his ass was on fire. I caught him up, and we were soon pondering the puzzle of the bergschrund. Much of it had been stretched open by the summer's heat; it lay agape, a long, linear maw leading to the bowels of the glacier. Dawn revealed a singular keyhole passage. A dense brow of last winter's snow arced over Mark as he gently eased his feet into the fragile meringue that had drifted over the slot during last week's storm. A constant stream of spindrift hissed into the keyhole and onto Mark's shoulders. Then he could reach the dirty, old ice of the face, which he swung into briskly and powerfully with his right tool. It bit deep, and he knew he could no longer fall into the 'schrund. "Ya!" he shouted, and then I was paying out rope quickly as he charged up the slope above.

When I got to him, I untied from one of the ropes. We climbed 1,000 feet of steepening snow and ice, me dragging the yellow rope, him dragging the green. Some 1,500 feet to our right, the sun had ignited the bronze granite falling from the Col de la Verte, and I swear that I could feel some of the reflected heat radiating onto my right flank.

Mark and I breathed hard, toiling through shadow and frost. We'd swap the lead every couple hundred feet to share the trail-breaking, and I would pant out one of the Diceman's dirty nursery rhymes every time I passed Mark; we would laugh, and our laughter lightened the exposure of our situation. It would have taken but one rock to bound down the slope and hit us in the head, and we would have rocketed down the face to disappear into the bergschrund, forever. But Les Droites was splendidly frozen, and we marched on with deliberate force and execution.

The thin strand of tin-gray ice Mark had spotted snaked up the snow-encrusted wall like tinsel. The crux was one foot wide, several inches thick, and vertical. My lead. I'd painted the shafts of my tools flat black and labeled the left one "Fear" and the right one "Love." I synched my wrist loops and began tapping my way up, trying to intuit where the ice was thickest and most attached to the underlying rock. I investigated any opportunity to place protection; I had a Stopper and a Knifeblade piton in when Love let me down. The pick broke, leaving one inch of metal embedded in the ice.

"Ah fuck, Doom! I just broke a pick. Watch me, man."

"I'm with you, Bubba."

There was the possibility of a nut placement right of my shoulder, and so I hacked away ice with the shorn pick. I couldn't break it any further, so I swung hard. A nut slotted in, and I buried it with blunt blows from the broken pick. Then I clipped the yellow rope in and yelled to Mark to take my weight. My spare pick was in my pack, and I fished it out and replaced it.

Twelve feet higher, after I broke Fear's pick, I completely lost it, screaming a blue streak of profanity as I smacked the useless tool against the unalterable granite. Breaking Fear had ruptured my stress threshold, and I was no longer able to contain my rage. However, the violence of my tantrum nearly took me off, which was enough for me to bring it all back in and find a way to deal. The echoes of my last curse oscillated away, and then there was the raging of my breath as I fought to stabilize my weight between Love's pick and my four crampon points. I got in a piece and hauled up one of Mark's tools to finish the pitch. I lowered it back to him.

Mark arrived, and I filed Fear's broken pick into something usable.

"How come your picks didn't break in that shit?"

"Grivel made them for me. They're Mark-proof."

"You don't even have a spare pick, do you?" I knew the answer.

Mark gave me the pouty-lipped, dismissive *phew* of the French, and said, "I think the route doglegs right here. Give me the small Blades."

"You've got everything."

"No, the small Blades are on your right, at the back."

"Well dropkick me in the butt—so they are, buddy, so they are."

In that small exchange lay the difference between Mark and me.

He never relaxed. It wasn't because he couldn't; it was because he willed himself not to. It was war all the time up there for him, yet he still found beauty, the kind only warriors see.

I was different. By then, I'd spent so much time climbing that my relationship with the mountains had evolved into something almost spousal. Much of the time I was jovial, then something would go wrong, and I'd get pissy, or I'd snap like I had done fifty feet below. Every so often, I'd feel the deeper weave of the universe and become euphoric.

I found it hard to pay out the ropes quickly enough. Mark danced over the thin ice with a mastery that previously I had only seen in Kevin Doyle. I pushed myself to follow as quickly, and I was breathing hard when I reached Mark's belay.

"You're...climbing...as well...as Kevin...does...when...he's...fit," I panted.

"Wow, shit, you're kidding?"

"No, man, you've become an animal of the wall. You belong up here."

"Thanks, Bubba."

I ran out of ice at dusk and anchored. Overhanging granite thrust out above me as night approached, the glacier below dimming from chalk to slate while above the sky darkened. I didn't know if we'd get off the face. I felt hunted.

"I get this?" Mark asked, pulling his jaw back incredulously, "Okay—give me the rack."

He powered over the granite bulge, blue sparks grating from his crampons. His breathing deepened. "Watch me," he said, and then he pressed up and blew out and was gone.

I seconded by headlamp, the cold and the dark wrapping around me like arms sweeping from behind, pulling. The world constricted to the yard-wide circle of my headlamp. And then I manteled over the top, and there was Mark's wry smile of partial victory.

"That was an incredible lead, my friend."

"Thanks, Bubba." And he handed me the last of our cold water with a final slice of oily sausage.

I pulled a shovel blade from my pack and began attaching it to one of my ice tools.

"Yo, Bubba, what are you doing?"

"Getting ready to bivy. We're going to bivy here, aren't we?"

"Blanch, we're in Chamonix—we can't sleep here. The Couvercle Refuge is about 3,500 feet down complete with blankets and beds, and that's where we're going. Besides, I've got this descent totally rehearsed, with rap anchors in place and everything ready. To quote The Jam, 'This is the modern world.'"

I followed Mark down the southwest side of Les Droites. He told me that he'd done the descent a couple of years earlier with Philippe Mohr, one of the few French climbers who Mark had formed a true partnership with. Philippe had died on the Aiguille Sans Nom a year later. Mark became somber, and I knew that he was feeling Philippe's presence. He became quiet, more precise, and more effective. I followed him gently.

---

alfway up and we are finding the way and I'm
ptimistic enough to smile at the camera.
1ark Twight

Midnight. We bedded down in the Refuge du Couvercle. For the second time in eleven years, I was sheltered by a roof that had protected climbers since alpinism's beginnings. Some, like Mark and me, were here now; others, gone.

OCTOBER 5: The rising sun brought rebirth and optimism, and Mark led us down the Mer de Glace. Near the terminus, he took us up the eastern lateral moraine onto a hiking trail, and we walked right to his front door. I felt light and alive, like our route had led me into the light and out of the dark, even though I knew the darkness would inevitably return.

Mark and I stood at either side of the stairs leading down to the restaurant l'Atmosphère, and both of us swept extended arms inviting Raine, dressed to the nines, to head down the stairs first. Mark smiled when we both raised our gaze.

Mark and Raine knew the two brothers who owned the restaurant. We were immediately ushered to one of the best tables, where our first bottle of wine was already open.

"Raine, would you order for me?" I asked.

"It will be my pleasure, Barry." I loved the way she said, *"Et pour monsieur,"* to the waiter and nodded to me before they fell into consultation.

"...and then Bubba broke his pick, and it was like...." Mark was describing the route in detail for Raine, with me throwing in adjuncts, and he was doing it so well and with such animation that it was hard for me to know that they faced colossal challenges in their two-year-old marriage. They looked to be deeply in love.

As Mark grinned and continued, I realized how beautiful the two of them were, and then I became aware of other eyes in the room looking at the three of us. We were in the prime of life, having a marvelous time, thoroughly enjoying each other's company.

"Have you ever bayonetted champagne?" I asked. Half a dozen bottles of Moët later, the restaurant was closing. We laughed our way back to Big Butt. Mark gunned the VW over a foot-high granite parking block, and then somehow steered us home. When I came to, Mark and Raine had gone to the airport in Geneva. Mark's gloves hung around

I'm getting high on the Richard Cranium Memorial Route as the light of day fades away. Mark Twight the woodstove like a string of black prayer flags, and I sighed and said, "Oh well—he'll figure it out over there." Then I went for water, gallons of water.

Mark named our line on Les Droites "the Richard Cranium Memorial Route." In the years since, several French climbers have asked me, "Who was this Richard Cranium?" "Dick" is short for Richard," I'd explain to them, "and cranium means "head." The "dickhead" route was the place we were at in our marriages, and a way of thinking that we were trying to bury. That always gets a hearty laugh out of the French. One of my French buddies wiped his eyes after he'd finished laughing and said, "Barry, it is hard to be an angel all the time."

🎧 "Folsom Prison Blues": Johnny Cash
🎧 "The Bottle Let Me Down": Merle Haggard
🎧 "Wicked Game": Chris Isaak
🎧 "Censor": Skinny Puppy

📖 *The Roominghouse Madrigals* by Charles Bukowski

CHAPTER 9 — THE CELL I

HEART

I like to draw and often sketch in a journal. I designed my ice-ax/heart/feather tattoo and often record what I see and think. One day I drew an image based on native pictographs that I meditated on in Alberta. It was of the left side of a man's body with only half of his heart intact. So much of the time I felt like this—half a man with half a heart—yet I wanted like hell to be a full man with a full heart.

I read and I wrote, and I drew, and I climbed; some of the time, I drank, but that scared me. The bottle seemed bottomless, its blackness absolute.

OCTOBER 25, 1991: I was having a nightmare in which Mark walked into my room and said that he'd blown his head off. I was groggy. I asked if it was him, and he took my left hand in his. I could see narrowly that he was wearing climbing clothes; his anorak was orange, but inside out; his head was hooded, and there was black. I began to argue with him, "You do not have to go into death." I asked him why, and he said that it was just too hard. I was terrified that this was real. My hand outstretched, I told him that he could stay here with me. He turned to me and screamed, "No! They won't allow it; they won't allow anything but forward thought." His face was inflating.

I woke up. My heart pounded and throbbed. Sleep wouldn't come again until I was numb. I cracked open *The Roominghouse Madrigals* by

My design for the tattoo on my left forearm: a Grivel ice-ax, noting alpinism; a full heart for a full life; and a bald eagle feather, powerful Indigenous medicine and a writing tool. Barry Blanchard

Charles Bukowski and put it down four hours later, having folded over the corner on a dozen pages to mark poems to read again. I slept for two hours, then got up and went rock climbing with Troy Kirwan, my buddy and fellow guide. I led more than my share so that I wouldn't think about my soon-to-be ex-wife.

OCTOBER 31: Alone in the condo, I loaded *Paris, Texas* in the video player for the twelfth time in a half dozen years. There was a drum-roll tap on the door. Troy and Shell burst in wearing costumes. They'd been to a rental shop in Calgary. Shell was a spider with the requisite eight arms, which she displayed by raising hers to fan out three extra arms on both her left and right sides. Troy was a swashbuckling pirate.

"We've got an Elvis suit for you!" the spider said, beaming.

"You are not sitting here by yourself, buddy. You are coming to a Halloween party with us," growled the pirate. I went upstairs and changed into The King.

It was quite a scene. "Look at all those tongues," Troy nudged me and winked. Strawberry blonde, blue eyes, and a striking smile. Christine was dressed up as a mouse with a Red Army hat and tongues sticking out all over her.

I walked over and said in my best Elvis, "Uh-huh-huh...howdy, ma'am." She smiled and said, "Well hello, Elvis. Can you guess who I am?"

"Uh...no, ma'am—you got me."

"Come on, think hard."

"Uh...I'm coming up blank."

"Mousy Tongue! I'm Mao Tse-Tung."

We danced. I learned that Christine lived in Banff, although I already recognized her from the Nepalese emporium where she'd worked. Hers was a beauty that a guy couldn't forget. She taught swimming and was in a relationship. I could sense it was headed for the rocks.

NOVEMBER: I guided, I rode my motorcycle, I clung to my climbing. It kept me going up, toward light, toward the surface. My psychiatrist guided me to the conclusion that my wife had moved on. She was seeing another man. The condo was rented out from under me. I moved to #6, Shady Lawn Motel (now defunct), Dead Man's Flats, Alberta. One of my climbing buddies, Jo-Jo, called my minute cabin "four sheets of plywood with a roof." I thought of it as "The Cell."

Raine had taken to calling me when her nights turned terrible. Looking back, I think that she knew Mark was leaving even before the words were said and their stuff was split, boxed, and moved into separate places. We would talk long, often with quiet pauses, the line crackling over, or under, the Atlantic—however the hell it got to me in 1991. We were the two left behind.

"The Italians say that during a breakup, there is a knife between you, and one is holding the handle while the other holds the blade," she said.

"That explains some of the pain."

"I know, Barrel, I know." We cared for each other, took care of each other.

DECEMBER 11: I hit the answering-machine playback button on one of my first days in The Cell. "Barry, it's Mike Weis. I need to talk to you, man. Don't make any plans to go to the Himalaya this spring. There's a big climbing picture coming down the pike, and it's going to get the green light. Call me."

"Holy crap!" shot through my brain. I dialed Mike in Colorado.

"It's called *Cliffhanger* and it's going to be produced by Carolco and Sylvester Stallone will star."

"Rocky?" I blurted.

"Ya, Rocky. I've spent the last three months flying all over the world looking at mountain ranges. It's been wild, man, a private jet and champagne and caviar and shit. Renny Harlin, the director, likes the artistic look of the Dolomites in Northern Italy, even though the story takes place in Rocky Mountain National Park in Colorado."

"Whoa, the Dolomites don't look like the Rockies."

"Ya, I know, but who gives a shit? The audience definitely won't know the difference. We'll be in Cortina d'Ampezzo for a couple of months in the spring. I want you on my rigging team. Can you be there?"

"Hell, yes. I'm there for you, boss, but don't the Dolomites get a lot of thunderstorms in the spring?"

"I told them that—that we'd be better off in the fall—but they said, 'It's okay—we'll tough it out.' That statement is going to end up costing them money, I can guarantee you. They also need climbing doubles for Stallone. Could you send the production office in LA some shirtless shots of you?" Mike laid on a convincing Schwarzenegger: "Pump it up." If you get chosen to double, you'd have to be in LA in January to start training. Could you do that?"

"Is that a trick question? Hell ya, I could."

It was as exciting as all get out to think that I could double for Stallone—I felt like I'd been catapulted from the basement to the penthouse. I got Pat Morrow, an accomplished photographer and friend from Canmore, to shoot me posing like a body builder, got the photos developed quick, and Fed-Ex'd them to the *Cliffhanger* production office in Santa Monica.

"What about Christine?" Troy asked. "The gal with all those tongues?" Having just handed divorce papers to my wife on my behalf, he hoped I would get on with my life.

"She's seeing a guy."

"Shell did some research. That guy's moving to Nelson, and Christine isn't going with him."

I signed up for Christine's stroke-improvement class, which helped my swimming a lot. Eventually, we had a dinner date, and then another, and another.

In November Mark had soloed the north face of Kusum Kanguru and had been able to rappel the face; a couple of Spanish climbers had retreated down it several days earlier, leaving an ice screw on every rappel.

"That must have been one hell of a lot of ice screws."

"You know it. I didn't count them, just clipped them and kept rapping."

"I've been talking with Raine a lot."

"I know—she told me. I'm glad you're there for each other. She's going to need you more."

"She's helped me."

"Cool, that's cool."

Mark had got out the knife, cut Raine and Marie away, and moved in with a gal that he'd met in Kathmandu. He'd also quit drinking; he worried about getting drunk and calling his wife.

The phone became a lifeline between Raine and me. We used it often. "Barrel, I'm going to Seattle for Christmas to stay with my parents. I'd love to come do some ice climbing with you. Do you think that's possible?" Raine asked from the far side of the Atlantic.

"God, I would love that—when can you come?"

I called Mark the next day: "Raine is coming up to go ice climbing, and I think that we could end up sleeping with each other."

"Whatever you two need to do, man. It's okay."

A lion's mane of straw-colored hair walked through the arrivals gate in Calgary, and I felt so very special to be the man that Raine smiled at and came to and hugged and kissed. Her arms felt strong, and she smelled like lavender and rain, and I trembled within her embrace. We got her bags and went out to my car.

"It's beautiful, Barrel." I'd handed her an ink drawing of my red heart pierced by a Grivel Super Courmayeur ice-ax. Underlying it and crossing the axis of the ax lay a real bald-eagle feather. "The full heart is for a full life," she said. "The ice-ax is your alpinism, and the eagle feather is your Métis heritage."

"I want to believe that the eagle feather is taken from a live eagle, which is no small trick. You need to dig a pit to stand in and cover it with boughs. Then hold a wounded pigeon above the pit. When the eagle hits the bait, you reach up and grab its tail feathers. It's a living feather. Also, a writing tool—I want to be a writer," I said.

I took Raine to the Lido Café, a 1960s-themed diner in Calgary. We sat in a booth enjoying grilled-cheese sandwiches and milkshakes while I plugged quarters into the wall-mounted jukebox: "Folsom Prison Blues" by the man in black—Johnny Cash—and "The Bottle Let Me Down" by Hag—Merle Haggard. That evening, after dinner with Kevin and Yolande, the four of us headed to the King Eddy to hear live blues. I danced with Raine and held her close.

The Cell was small. My gear ate up three of the bedroom walls, and my desk the other. My bed sat in the main room, which was also the kitchenette. One more door led into the bathroom. I hugged Raine powerfully, gave her a kiss on the lips, and got ready to sleep on the floor.

"Barrel, you could sleep in the bed with me. We just can't do anything—I don't think that I'm ready to be your lover."

"There is no way in hell I'll be able to sleep in bed beside you, my dear. This will be better. I'll get some sleep this way."

DECEMBER 29: The Professor Falls, 920 feet WI 4, was big and blue. We scampered up it, enjoying the quality and colors of the ice.

"Good God, girl, how can you climb with those puny front points? They look like baby bunny ears sticking up from your white toe caps."

"They are short, aren't they? Yours are way longer."

"I like a lot of front point."

"These are Mark hand-me-downs, just like all my stuff."

"He wasn't doing you any favors with those crampons."

"No shit."

I placed a tanned leather cord over Raine's head. Its beaded leather pouch was the size of a box of matches, and it lay between her breasts. "It's a medicine pouch. It's for protection. You need to fill it with talismans."

"How will I know what to put in it?"

"You'll know when you find them—they'll speak to you. And this is for your hair." I handed her a beaded floral hairclip backed with smoked leather and pinned through with a hand-carved wooden needle.

"It's beautiful, Barrel—I love it!" She sniffed it and smiled radiantly. "It smells like beef jerky!"

We were in the Banff Trading Post, a business that had been in Shell's family since the pioneering Banff legend Norman Luxton went to the till one day in 1961, took out the cash, and said to his employee—Shell's father—"It's yours on one condition: whatever the Stoney bring, you have to buy it all." Then, he walked out the door. The Stoney were Nakoda Indians whose reservation sits between Calgary and Canmore. The long talks on the phone twined with our words as we were getting closer and closer.

Shell and Troy lived in the basement suite of her prodigious family home on Kootenay Avenue, one of Banff's more affluent streets. Troy had invited Raine and me to dinner and to spend the night so that we

In The Cell with my fresh tattoo, medicine pouch, Andy Parkin's painting of Everest, and ski and climbing gear. Barry Blanchard would be that much closer to Polar Circus—the climb we were planning for the next day.

Later, I lay naked on the bed and watched her reach and unsnap her black bodysuit. "I'll be back in a minute, lover." She walked away to the bathroom. I jumped up and wriggled into the bodysuit and snapped it tight, then lay back in a starfish position. Raine laughed and laughed. Then I took it off.

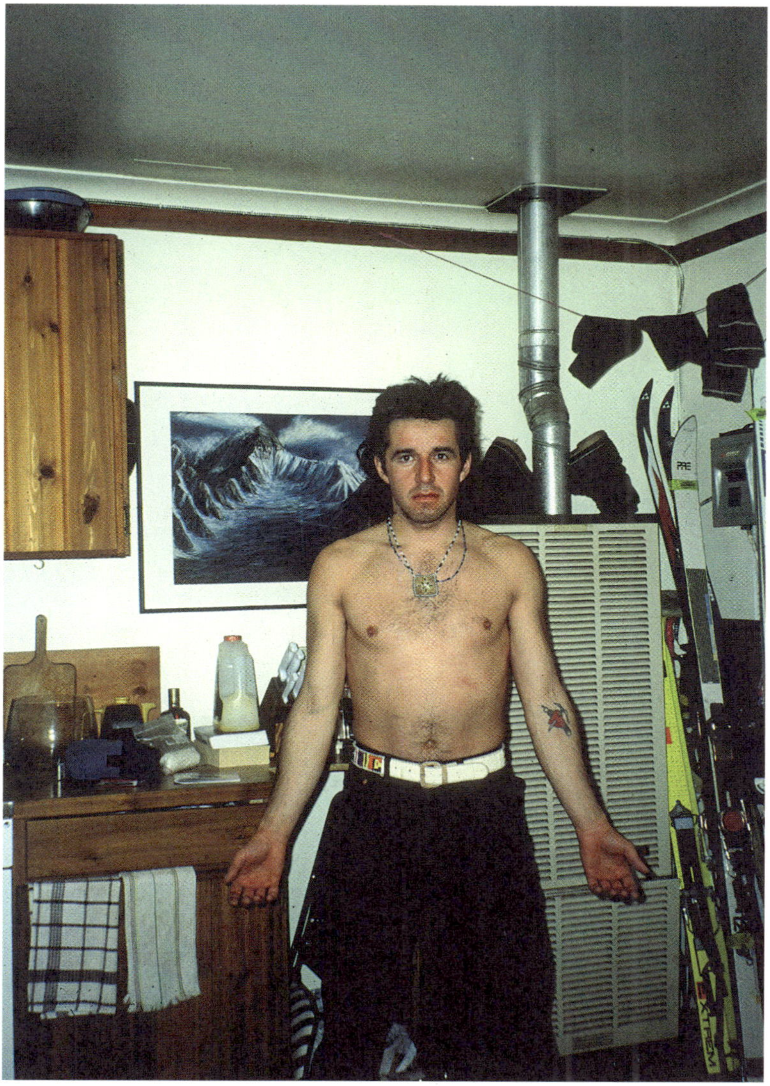

DECEMBER 30: Polar Circus, 2,300 feet WI 5, proved to be a long one. We were rappelling by headlamp when, at one station, the rap lines refused to pull. Wind and snow swirled in the sky, and I was shivering. "Fuck, I guess I'm going back up." I spat. "Give me a hug and a kiss." Raine did, and then I laughed, looking down to her white plastic toe caps, where she'd drawn bunny faces with a black felt pen to go with her bunny-ear front points.

"Are we going to make it home?" Raine asked. Snow crowded onto the windshield of my Toyota Tercel station wagon like we were underwater driving through a school of silverfish. I hit the high beams, and the windshield flashed into a video game, with hundreds of bright particles assailing us.

"Whoa!" Raine exclaimed. I clicked back to the low beams, rolled down my window, and looked to the shoulder. I paralleled it to keep the car on the road. Then there was an eerie red light ahead, and Raine spooked: "Huh, Barrel. Look out!" I eased onto the brakes.

"Cool, this is good. We can ride this trucker's taillights. He can see way more from up there," I said.

We got home late. I put on Chris Isaak's *Heart Shaped World*, and we made love. When "Wicked Game" came on, we were lying naked on our backs, my right palm on top of her left, heat accumulating there. Tears welled up. I felt good; I felt loved.

"I love you, Raine."

"I love you too, Barrel."

The next week I was walking back from guiding Louise Falls at the back of Lake Louise with Chris, a client from New York City who was a fine climber and a good guy. "Screw it. I'm going to put the plane ticket on my credit card and go see her in Seattle this weekend," I told him.

"Sounds impetuous...but good impetuous, from the heart. You should go, man."

I sat reclined in the chair of Dermagraphics Tattoo in Seattle. The needle buzzed, and I felt the incisive pain of it stabbing into my forearm 1,500 times per minute. It was uncomfortable, but Raine was holding my right hand and looking into my eyes. I was calm.

"How does that look?" The tattoo artist asked. I had my living eagle feather, heart, and ice-ax, but the heart's right lobe looked to be a shallower red.

"Can you add more red in there?" I pointed.

"I can try." He put the needle back in, but it made that part of my heart a shade deeper. It has aged as a shadow, like a nearly healed bruise.

Monday, I flew home. Later that week, Raine flew back to France. We had shared two perfect weekends. It felt tremendous to have touched and been touched, to lie in bed after the frenetic rush of lust had passed and then calmed to tenderness. I felt my heart, and my heart felt whole.

Raine encouraged me to keep going, even as she knew something ugly and cynical was growing inside her, something she didn't want me to see. She knew she'd need time before she could be in another relationship. She told me not to wait for her.

I wrote to Mark, telling him that Raine and I had connected and that it had been a beautiful thing. He wrote back on a Skinny Puppy postcard of the song "Censor," and I had to chuckle: it depicted a man's hateful face parted in two by a caduceus, too similar to Half-Man Half-Heart. He wrote that he knew it would happen. He felt no shock or surprise. Years later, when he and I were both in our second marriages, we mulled it over and he admitted that it had hurt him.

"But you gave me your blessing."

"Ya! That's because I didn't think that you two would actually do it!"

"I'm sorry for hurting you. It is not why we did it. I love Raine, and you know I love you."

"I know, but I cut her away."

"That seems sad, man."

"It is—really, really sad. And I live with that."

🎧 "Low Self Opinion": Henry Rollins
🎧 "Straight to You": Nick Cave and the Bad Seeds

CHAPTER 10 — THE CELL II

CLIFFHANGER

MARCH 1992: Mike Weis had assembled an American all-star rigging crew for *Cliffhanger*. A dozen great American climbers and me, the lone Canadian. I checked into the Hotel Alaska in Cortina d'Ampezzo. My room was twice as big as The Cell.

Our contracts were based on a six-day workweek, and I was making four times what I would as a guide. Monday would be my first day on the job. As I prepared my stuff on Sunday night, I realized that I'd left a suit bag, stuffed to the seams with clothing, sitting back in The Cell. My buddy Brad was staying there while I was gone. I phoned him and got him to unpack it and tell me what I'd left.

"Your bloody underwear are here, Blanchard. You're going to have to buy some briefs."

I was also short the belt for my guide pants. When I walked into the hotel breakfast room the next morning wearing the black leather belt with white snakeskin inserts and a silver horseshoe buckle that I'd bought cheap in Argentina, David Breashears said, "Oh, Barry, you look so Hollywood!"

"Ah, why thanks, David. Not by intent. Have you got any extra underwear?"

Mike inaugurated our rigger's meeting and introduced the four Italian mountain guides who would be working with us: Marcello Caminetti, Ferruccio Svaluto Moreolo, Oswald Santin, and Christoph Hainz. They were mountain people, climbers, compact and powerful

ne helicopter carrying the spinning broken
assis of a second one on the set of *Cliffhanger*.
ur team anchored and set the broken chassis
to drop by one-foot increments.
rry Blanchard

to a man, with squat fingers and climbing clothes that had felt the scrub of limestone.

Kevin Powell was a paramedic, climber, and photographer from Southern California, brought on to keep our crew healthy and repaired. Kevin's promotional shtick was, "Say no to Rowell and yes to Powell" contrasting himself to Galen Rowell, the hugely successful climbing photographer.

The California climber Dave Schultz and I spray-painted hundreds of carabiners pink to mark them for our department. We'd laid out another fifty onto a sheet of plywood to spray when Mike walked by and heard me ask Dave, "How was it doing The Nose and The Salathé?" Dave had enchained them both on El Capitan in a day with Peter Croft.

"It was amazing. Seven thousand feet of granite and no gobies!" Dave exclaimed, thrusting toward me the backs of his hands, which were enviously free of the near-unavoidable scabs and cuts that accumulate from jamming cracks rich with razor-sharp crystals.

"Ya, but Schultz has been doing so much climbing that the backs of his hands have callused to rhino hide," Mike said. "You could take a knife to them and cut for minutes before you'd get any blood." Mike reached and pinched the back of Dave's left hand below his trigger finger, the site of maximum pressure in a hand jam. Dave offered me his right, smiling. It felt like I was pinching the bottom of my heel.

"How long did it take?" I asked.

"Eighteen hours."

"Wow—how did you manage that?" I'd taken three and a half days each, a week in total, to climb each of the routes in 1981.

"We simuled almost everything." (Simul-climbing is where both the leader and the second climb with a fixed amount of rope between them, the leader placing protection and clipping the rope to it. If either climber falls, it is likely they will pull the other off; both will then fall until they counterweight each other on a piece of protection.)

"How did you adjust the rope between you?"

"The bottom guy runs the rope through a Grigri on his harness; it's easy to take in and let out rope."

"You'd tie a knot in the end of the rope, right?"

"Fuck no! That bastard would get caught too much," Schultz challenged, and then added, "And I cut a half-moon into the feed side of the Grigri, so it pays out smoother." He enjoyed the shock on my face.

Our rigging crew had a week to prepare before the first and second units arrived. Our Mountain Safety/Rigging Department would also be responsible for loading and unloading helicopters. I got the job of preparing a helicopter safety briefing to present to the cast. My first of many trips to the La Cooperativa di Cortina, this time for poster board and felt pens. They had underwear! And belts!

A week later, the big guy walked into a conference room in the Hotel Alaska. Sylvester Stallone wore a baseball cap, plaid jacket, jeans, and boots. He wasn't tall, 5′8″, but he was broad and solid, 195 pounds of hard-edged muscle. He and producer Tony Munafo did a bunch of hellos, handshakes, and kisses with the cast.

Mike emceed our meeting. Soon Bobby Gaines was going over clothing and food for the mountains. Bob had doubled as Captain James T. Kirk in *Star Trek V*, and he ran the Vertical Adventures Rock Climbing School in SoCal. He had also spent time at Stallone's house teaching him to climb on a climbing wall built in Stallone's personal gym. "The guy is a serious bodybuilder," Bob had told us. "But he's kind of freaked out by heights and he doesn't really dig climbing." Bob deferred to Stallone, offering both his palms like he was passing a rugby ball and saying "And Sly knows a lot about nutrition and what is best to eat in the cold."

"Ya, ya," Stallone started, "Carbohydrates are important for a base—you need carbohydrates." We all listened like we'd been given audience with a prince. In my mind, we were: *Rocky* and *Rocky II* were great movies. I had started running seriously after seeing *Rocky*.

The next day, we leaped into the grind of making a Hollywood movie; for us, it meant long hours at a diversity of rigging jobs in numerous locations. Bob McDougall—a world-class kayaker who was taking a break from his work at Patagonia, the clothing company—and I spent a week scaling loose rock off a cliff above the Cristallo ski area: walk around to the top, rap down with a crowbar, hammer, and rock bar, and bash off choss, under which was usually more choss. We rode the lift, and then skied down to work. At the end of every day, when we all got back, we'd have our rigger's meeting.

"Mike, man, we could spend the rest of our lives on that cliff and eventually level it to a flat field of stone. There is no end to the looseness," McDougal said.

"We have to get it all off," Mike replied. "They want to have the whole first unit there, a hundred people, makeup artists, caterers, women in high heels. If any of them get hit by so much as a pebble, we'll get crucified."

"What about making some chain-link umbrellas that we can pull over them between takes?" Kevin Donald suggested. And so were born the "deflector shields": awnings of baseball backstop that we pulled into position on industrial carpet coasters and pivoted overhead to protect cast and crew.

A huge plywood dance floor was constructed below the Cristallo Cliff, where the famous publicity-poster shot of Stallone hanging by one arm in a singlet and tight black shorts was taken. Sylvester used a stepladder to get into position five feet above the plywood, clinging to a letterbox-sized positive handhold that Schultz had spent two days sculpting into the rock with a power chisel.

Two of the world's best rock climbers, Ron Kauk and Wolfgang Güllich, had been hired as climbing doubles for Stallone. I missed the cut (not cut enough?). Ron and Wolfgang traveled to LA in January to start training; before their first meeting with Stallone's people, they agreed between themselves not to do anabolic steroids to gain muscle mass.

"And that was a good thing," Ron told me. "Pretty much the first thing we got asked was, 'So, are you willing to go on the juice?' We said no and hit the gym with Sly's trainer, eating a lot of meat and lifting a couple times a day. Wolfgang starts getting bigger and bigger, but my native blood just had me gaining a spare tire. You know, brother, the make-it-through-the-winter gene."

"I hear you, brother. I still had my reserves when I came down from Rakaposhi in '84. All my muscles were gone, but I could still grab love handles."

"Ya. I don't know if I'm going to be doing any doubling for Sly, but he likes me and set me up to double some for Michael Rooker on climbing

Ron Kauk and Wolfgang Güllich doubling for Michael Rooker and Sylvester Stallone in costume and hamming it up. Barry Blanchard stuff that Raleigh Collins can't do." Raleigh was a Southern Californian who'd been hired as a climbing double for the actor Michael Rooker, who would play Stallone's fellow climbing ranger.

Both Ron and Wolfgang looked like rock gods, with long manes of black hair falling past their shoulders. A week later, I got into the hotel's elevator and there they stood, shorn down to business cuts to match Stallone's hair.

"Uh, Wolfgang? Ron?" I acted like I didn't recognize them.

"Ya, you're really fucking funny, man," Ron spat. He was not happy with his new do.

Making mountain-climbing movies works fine until the helicopters can't fly because of mountain weather. Then, the units run to "cover shots" (indoor locations that that can be driven to) that the director might use in the final edit. When those get used up, it becomes a game of show up for call, hump the pooch until 2 p.m.—the time that the

insurance company recognizes as a minimum—and then stay out of production's sight until they wrap the day.

The uphill running around Cortina is fabulous. I'd change on weather days and run for an hour or more through the snow, sleet, or rain. I was striding back from a longer run as Ron Kauk and Daniella, an Italian gal he'd started seeing, walked hand and hand in the rain, their Gore-Tex hoods drawn. As I strode by, Ron lunged all wild-eyed, giving me a double thumbs-up and a "Yes! Barry, yes!" It felt good to be cheered on by this rock legend.

Ron was one of three Indigenous North Americans working on the picture. I was another. And Perry Beckham, with whom I'd worked on *K2*, was the third. Perry and I spent a lot of our days off climbing together, getting to be better friends. He got me going on cappuccino—"cappers," as he called them. Until then, my thirty-third year, I hadn't drunk hard alcohol or coffee. My time in Cortina changed all of that.

Perry and I were sitting in the hotel lobby enjoying our cappers when he leaned over holding open a copy of *Climbing* magazine and said, "Alex is a fucking psycho, man. He's a fucking psycho." There was a picture of Alex Lowe hanging from one ax embedded in a truncated dagger of ice the size of his chest. He looked like Stallone did hanging onto the chipped letterbox in his movie-poster hero pose, except Alex was way off the deck in Provo Canyon, Utah, clinging to an insanely fragile ice feature. The picture had been taken by Mark Francis Twight. It pulled at my heartstrings. I wanted to be there with them. Mark had named the route "Prophet on a Stick."

Renny Harlin, the director, was a loose cannon of Viking lineage who stood a broad-shouldered six-foot-plus, with a blond mane hacksawed at mid-spine, full beard, and bottomed-out baritone. He was prone to stepping over our safety lines and marching toward the edge of a cliff as if acceleration due to gravity, 32ft/sec/sec, was merely an opinion. At one point, Kevin Donald had to run out and tackle him before he walked onto a cornice! A lot of the crew had become complacent with mountain hazards and commonly stepped over our safety barriers. We were forced to default to the human shield; we would stand in line between the crew and the edge. It was frustrating, but not as frustrating, or as funny, as the day we learned that we couldn't get to work because one of our Bell 204 helicopters had been sequestered to fly Renny's golden retriever to first unit to calm his nerves, while the other 204 was en route to Austria to pick up a gal Stallone had a date with that night.

Then the ceiling dropped, the peaks disappeared, and out of sheer boredom, while on standby at the airstrip, Brooke Sandahl—a 5.13 climber from Bend, Oregon, and a partner in the climbing-equipment manufacturer Metolius Climbing—grabbed an old railway tie dripping with creosote and comically imitated a caber toss. That was it, game on. The riggers spent the rest of the day seeing who could toss the tie the farthest, and it was poetically correct that it was McDougal who was crowned the "King Tosser." Eight grown men exhausted, their astronomically expensive mountain clothing stained in creosote, all laughed at the various gut-busting techniques of tossing the caber. *Boys will be boys.*

Christoph Hainz was one of the strongest climbers in the Dolomites and a no-BS mountain man. Summing up his experience to date on *Cliffhanger*, he told Perry and me, "This is not my job." And he waved it away with his powerful right hand. He and I spent all day drilling one-inch-wide by yard-deep holes into the flat limestone on top of Sass Pordoi. We were working with Perry to establish a halo of anchor points for the jib arm—a mast with a forty-foot crane arm. Each hole took three hours. Christoph and I traded off on the heavy industrial drill and the hand pump we used to suck out the pulverized limestone dust. If the dust didn't get extracted every three minutes, the bit would seize.

Back in Cortina, I walked into our Sunday night rigger's meeting. There, the climbing legends Earl Wiggins and Jim "The Bird" Bridwell looked like they'd been in a brawl, with cuts on their faces and black eyes. They'd been drinking and driving in the small late-model Fiat Jim had bought; a tight turn during a heated discussion slammed them into a rock wall, and they'd both gone through the windshield. The story took time to tell, and during the telling I reflected on the fact that the Coloradans on our crew were wild-ass wild men, and that there was a spectrum to their wildness. At the merely wild end were Tom Ruwitch, Doug Snively, and Doug Neithercut. Tom had climbed The Nose on

El Capitan in 1967 when he was sixteen. Wilder yet were Mike Weis, Paul Sibley, Kevin Donald, and The Bird.

But the wildest of them all was Earl, a guy that they called the "Single-Celled Animal." I'd asked Mike why, and he said, "Because a single-celled animal doesn't have any fear. Earl was born without fear." Earl grinned wide, and Mike continued, describing Earl's first ascent of the parallel-sided sandstone fissure Supercrack of the Desert, near Moab, Utah. "He led it on Hexentrics, none of which would have held squat. If he'd fallen, he would have hit the deck and it would have been forever, but Earl didn't think about that because he can't—he's the Single-Celled Animal."

Earl and I had hit it off playing eight ball in the hotel bar, where we often unwound over beer and missed shots. He couldn't break the rack during our first week in Cortina, because, he said, of an "ice pick to the ribs."

"What do you mean?"

"I got an ice pick to the ribs last week in a bar in California."

"How?" I asked incredulously.

"Disagreement with another patron."

"You were in a bar fight?"

"Yes—lucky the guy just hit a rib."

"Fuck, Earl, let me look at it."

Red, hot to the touch, bloated, and tender.

"It's infected, man—you have to get on some antibiotics." I had to badger him into going to see Kevin Powell, which was weird because Earl's own dad had been a doctor. The antibiotics worked.

Earl and Jim finished their car-crash story to amazed grins, head wags, eyes downcast in disbelief, and nervous chuckling. Mike summed up: "You will be at work tomorrow." The gravity of that thumped down into our meeting like a judge's gavel. Everyone was caught off guard, especially Earl and Jim.

Earl stuttered a bit, "Oh-oh, ya, Mike, we'll be at work tomorrow." Hard-ass love between wild-ass men.

Monday morning, I headed out with the first unit to the top of the 9,300-foot peak of Lagazuoi. Stallone was running toward the cliff edge, and our Mountain Safety had once again been thinned to a human shield. I was stationed close to the video monitor while Renny, the director of photography, and Stallone reviewed the scene. The back of Sly's upper arm framed one side of the shot.

"Nice triceps shot," Stallone said in Rocky's voice.

Later, Sly had to stand near the top of a vertical ladder at the cliff edge while acting out talking on a walkie and throwing a bag of money into the rotor of a hovering helicopter. His safety got reduced to my tying a piece of webbing around his ankle and securing it to a hidden cable with a quicklink. "It's going to hurt like hell if he actually goes over the edge," I thought, imagining the poor guy hanging upside down by his ankle, the webbing biting his flesh like barbed wire.

It was strange to be on my knees tying the webbing around Sly's ankle while Renny talked to him, the makeup artist powdered his face, and the wardrobe guy tucked his T-shirt back under his vest. Sly was oblivious to everyone except Renny. Stallone got into position, and I twisted the quicklink closed around the webbing; I could feel the vibration of fear in his ankle—he was truly afraid of heights.

We did a number of takes, and then Sly dropped the radio and grabbed the ladder and shouted, "Hey, Mike! Mike, this thing came undone."

"What thing, Sly?"

"The safety thing."

"Holy shit, c'mon, Barry—let's go."

The big guy was right: the quicklink had vibrated open 1/8″ during all the takes, and the webbing had lined up perfectly to escape it, like a letter through a mail slot.

"Holy fuck, Sly, you're right," Mike gasped.

"Ya, I know. I saw it and I knew that I wasn't moving a muscle."

"Barry will crank it up with pliers, and then we'll tape it shut."

"Ya, Mike, do that. I was fucking freaking out."

As I worked, I could feel the honest quivering of terror in him. His leg was as hard as stone yet trembling, like in an earthquake. Mike and I walked away, the first assistant director bellowed, "AND ACTION!" and Sly went cool as a cucumber. We got the shot and moved on.

The Torre Divise are twin towers that stand 100 feet apart, cleaved by an impressive 500-foot-deep chasm. That was where a female character would plummet to her death in the opening scene, when the buckle to her climbing harness tore apart. It was ludicrous to have the overbuilt metal buckle pull apart like putty; the production had already allotted money to settle the lawsuit that would entail from the harness manufacturer. The filming and stunts required an impressive build of two ten-foot-tall metal towers on either side of the chasm. Tom Ruwitch and I were gleefully yanking as hard as we could on a 3:1 pulley, trying to get the first rope strung across to lie flat, when the Wall Hauler pulley gave a loud "POP!" and the rope's purple sheath tore open to reveal the pristine white core strands beneath, like flayed flesh exposing tendon.

"Holy crap!" Tom blurted.

"Shit," I replied.

When we inspected the Wall Hauler, we saw we'd bent it.

"Never underestimate a 3:1," I observed.

"What are we going to tell Mike?" Tom asked.

"The truth—that we screwed up. He'll probably tell us not to do it again and to explain it to the rest of the riggers. Then he'll tell us to get another rope from our stores. It's kind of like a Styrofoam-cup dispenser

on these features: Something gets broken, and you just pull out another and a new one plops down to take its place."

Later that day, Earl and I were helping Perry tension the first of three steel cables between the towers when I stepped into the coil of spare cable lying on the ground.

"Get out of the bight," Earl said.

"What?"

"Get out of the bight, man." And he pointed to my feet, planted on the wrong side of the cable.

"Oh, okay." I stepped out. "What's the big deal?"

Earl, who'd spent the last decade installing high-tension powerlines, said, "Let me tell you a story about the bight." He lit a cigarette.

"One night, I'd thrown a spiral clamp out of the back of my truck, into the thrash pile, because it was worn. My foreman comes along, looks at it, and thinks, 'Earl is throwing out a good clamp.' And the asshole hangs it back in my truck. The next day, I'm 100 feet up a pole and I suck 13,000 pounds of tension on one side of the line, and 13,000 on the other, then I step up into the bight and the worn clamp blows and the line hits me in the waist, scrapes up my gut and tears all the muscles in my back, cuts my throat open, and flips me upside down."

"Holy fuck."

"Ya, I end up hanging by my feet with blood flowing into my eyes."

"Then what happened?"

"Took me two hours to get to the ground, where they picked me up, then six months in the hospital."

I haven't stepped into a bight since.

MAY 1992: The thunderstorms came in, and with them more down days. I was back on top of Lagazuoi. Dark masses of cloud tumbled over the peak, and our horizon contracted to a half mile. Clusters of snow the size of fallen ash leaves hurtled through the air. Renny Harlin walked away from the set toward the cliff edge.

"Barry! Get out there and watch that guy," Kevin pointed. I hurried out and stood eight feet from Renny.

"They sent me out here to keep you safe. Sorry, man."

"It's okay. What do you think the weather is going to do?"

Dave Schultz, Bob McDougall, and Oswald Santin gleefully launching into the nascent sport of jib-arm jumping. Barry Blanchard

"I think it's building. It's probably going to get worse."

My radio squawked, "Mountain Safety, Barry Blanchard."

"This is Barry."

"Could you ask Mr. Harlin if he needs anything? Anything from craft service?" It was Renny's personal assistant. But Renny looked annoyed and said, "I told her I don't eat today." Renny was obviously trying to maintain some shape under the pressure of eighteen-plus-hour days. I got back on the radio: "He doesn't seem to be wasting away out here. He tells me he's fine." That bought him five minutes of quiet to stand and look into the storm. Then he said, "Okay, let's go back and try to get something." The weather got worse.

Late in the month, the second unit was filming the opening scene on the Torre Divise. Lightning struck, and the whole crew took a jolt to the central nervous system and dropped like they'd been KO'ed. Everybody, forty people, to the ground. Steve Danton, the first assistant director, ended up face-down in a puddle, and was only saved by Mike getting it together enough to grab his collar and yank his face out of the water.

Earl staggered to his feet, the damp gray air crackling with charge, and sprinted to the far side of the 100-foot-square summit plateau, thinking that anywhere other than where he was had to be safer. An incendiary surge of white light exploded and knocked him on his ass for the second time. He sprang up and sprinted back. By the third strike, he was back at the near edge, where grown men whimpered and makeup artists bawled and clutched at crucifixes. The lightning vaulted Earl over the edge.

"I thought, 'This is it,'" he told me that night over beers and billiards, "and that it wasn't actually going to hurt because I was already plank stiff and numb from the electricity." One body length down, he landed on the only ledge for 500 feet. "I realized that God was trying to tell me something, so I stayed put," Earl recalled.

When Kevin Powell returned to the States, Mike got Dr. Kurt Papenfus, from Snowmass, Colorado, to take over the care of our crew. At the time, Kurt was Hunter S. Thompson's personal physician, and he told me how Hunter had invited him to his home/shooting range, the Owl Farm, in Woody Creek, Colorado, just before Kurt got married.

The broken chassis of a helicopter—purchased from a heli graveyard, then painted and labeled for the picture—about to get lifted to the location. The fight scene between the hero and villain of *Cliffhanger* took place on the bottom of the upside-down chassis. Barry Blanchard

"I get there, and Hunter hands me his personal .44 and says, 'You get to bust six caps, kid, my wedding gift to you.'" One would expect that any physician thus feted by the progenitor of gonzo journalism would favor the prescription pad. We came to refer to our doctor as Kurt "Pop-a-Few."

The Torre Divise boys were in a lot of pain. When Kurt dispensed several little white pills into Mike's palm, Mike said, "Oh, no, I'm a child of the sixties. I've conducted exhaustive research into the effects of pharmaceuticals, and I can tell you this is nowhere near enough." Mike curled his fingers in a give-me gesture; Kurt rained more pills down.

Mike had me accompanying Allan, the middle-aged plate photographer, to shoot the backgrounds that other scenes would be projected onto. He was a charming man who took the time to educate me on the finer points of single-malt scotch.

Allan just wasn't the man to don a harness and go over the edge, so the production hired Ace Kvale, an American ex-pat professional skier and photographer who lived in Verbier, Switzerland. Ace had published a lot of pictures of Mark Twight climbing. It was great to go to work with him.

The south face of the Marmolada is impressive: 2,600 feet high, two miles wide, and comprised of immaculate limestone. The Bird, Ace, and I were happily rigging and shooting plates 150 feet down the wall when a frantic call came over the radio from the first unit some thirty miles away. Renny had commandeered a helicopter, and he and Sly were flying halfway across the Dolomites to check out the final smooching scene between the hero and heroine on our summit.

"You okay here?" I asked Ace.

"Happy as a clam man, happy as a clam." He stood on an aluminum rigging platform with the big plate camera anchored and pointed down the sheer wall. Bird and I being the only Mountain Safety people within a thirty-mile radius, we jugged the lines like our asses were on fire. I guided the ship onto the summit glacier; snow turbined up, and I kept the door closed while the rotor wound down.

"Hi, Sly. My name's Barry, and I'll be your mountain safety." I grabbed the big guy's hand, and he held on tight, with an honest 3,000 feet to the pastures below. His green lizard-skin cowboy boots offered about as much purchase on the snow as roller skates on greased glass.

"Ya, ya. Barry, I remember you—ya, I'll hold onto your hand." Sly has a very strong grip.

Bird, away from the landing and blocking the immense south face, got to deal with Renny, the Viking, who marched right out to the edge. As the Viking talked a nervous Sly through the "Kiss," Bird and I formed a human shield against the drop, both of us knowing that the first thing we'd do if either of them stumbled would be to twist at the hip and shout, *"¡Olé!"*

Then they climbed back into the ship, in their sunglasses and leather jackets, and lifted off. Panicking PAs barked at us over the radio until we assured them that the star and director were safe, and then it all got quiet again on top of that magnificent limestone wall. The Bird sat on his pack and lit a cigarette.

It had been some of the only contact I'd had with Sly since our initial safety briefing, over three months earlier, when I'd hoped to instill a healthy fear of the helicopter rotor in him. The next day, I was bringing in one of the 204s onto a snow landing we'd been using for over a month. I put my back to the wind and lifted a piece of orange flagging tape overhead to give the pilot a wind direction, and then the thump and blast

Mountain riggers setting up the penultimate punch-out between the hero, Stallone, and the villain, John Lithgow. The story takes place in the Colorado Rockies, but we shot in the Italian Dolomites. Barry Blanchard of the rotor got me squatting, ready to open the side door once the ship had settled and the pilot made eye contact and gave me a nod. The skids touched down; the machine's weight settling onto them pried them a foot wider, just like on every other snow landing. Then the Bearpaws—the large plastic plates attached to the back of helicopter landing skids for use on snow—dropped through the snow and the helicopter bellied-out with a *crunch*. The pilot yanked on the collective and twisted the throttle open. The 4,600-pound ship, plus 1,500 pounds of cargo, leaped eight feet into the air, bucked fore and aft like a horse, and then stalled and smacked back down, burying its belly in the snow.

"Holy fuck," I gasped.

It took us awhile to dig the ship out. Brooke said to me, "Man, that was so cool that you crept toward the ship when it went nuts. McDougal and I saw the rotor—it came this close to the ground." He stacked his palms, the right one two feet over his left. "It would have cut you in half if you'd run away."

"Ya," Bobby McD added, grinning, "We would have been splattered with Barry. Would have been washing you out of our clothes for months!"

It had been another eighteen-hour day. I sat drinking green-bottled Belgian beer on the edge of my bed, mind numb, staring at Italian MTV, when Henry Rollins mugged my attention with his aggressive voice and powerful singing of "Low Self Opinion." It was the first I'd heard of him; likewise, Nick Cave and the Bad Seeds, who followed with "Straight to You." I slashed their names down; they would become two of the most poignant artists in my life for the next decade.

MID-JUNE 1992: The first unit and half of our rigging crew took off to the studio in Rome. The rest of us remained in the Dolomites to continue shooting stunts. It was all so peaceful again. The ringing of cell phones ceased, as did the growing mounds of cigarette butts and crumpled coffee cups dispersed across the trampled snow, all picked up by the lower castes of Hollywood culture. New snow fell, shafts of fresh sunlight sliced through the overcast, and the mountains shone with radiance and superiority, just as they had back when Hannibal crossed.

It was while being bathed in such light that Dave Schultz divined jib-arm jumping. Dave anchored the arm at its full reach, 90 degrees to the cliff edge on Ponta dei Lastoi. I doubled and redoubled a climbing rope, and then tied monster knots at both ends. With one knot anchored into the end of the jib, the other clipped into your harness, you walked along the edge until the rope cluster came tight, about thirty-five feet, and jumped off into 800 feet of exposure. Your stomach would rise to your mouth, and the wind would scream as the world blurred, and your guts collided against your spine when you bottomed out the arc to swoop up into weightlessness.

Oswald, one of our Italian guides, was gripped out of his tree. However, all the North Americans had taken the plunge (some couldn't get enough), which meant that he had to, too. "I am scaring! I am scaring!" he shouted at the edge. He screamed for the full two minutes of swinging.

The second unit was shooting the finale punch-up between the hero and the villain with the stunt performers. Bobby Gaines and I were working with them. One of the ADs was walking around the set looking at guys' legs.

"Barry, you look like you have muscular legs," she said. "May I see them?"

Is this a trick question? I thought, but said, "Sure, what's up?"

"We got a shot request from the director. Renny wants a POV of Gabe's [Stallone's character's] feet stepping up to the edge of the cliff for the opening scene." She circled my exposed legs, looking, and then concluded, "Yes, you have very muscular legs."

"Why, thank you."

"You can double for Sly."

"What's involved?"

"Simple: you just have to step up to the edge of the cliff and hold for a beat. We'll shave your legs from the knee down, and makeup will put Sudden Tan on to get them brown, like Sly's."

Shaved and tanned, I stepped to the lip and held my position. Two takes later, we had it in the can. The second unit director said, "Let's have some fun." Bobby held me by the waist and lowered my feet into the top of the frame, and I executed an en pointe ballet *brisé*—a scissor step—before Bobby lifted me back out of frame. We heard that got everyone howling when they viewed the daily rushes.

Cliffhanger was released a year later. My mother, Paulette, and three of her matronly sisters saw it at a matinee in Regina, Saskatchewan. When my feet came on screen, all four jumped up, yelling and cheering, scaring the hell out of the other moviegoers. My mother still considers my foot doubling for Sylvester Stallone to be the high-water mark of my career.

Gervasutti's Climbs by Giusto Gervasutti

CHAPTER 11 — THE CELL III

ELUSIVE HAPPINESS

Giusto Gervasutti, one of the progenitors of alpinism, was a searcher who sought meaning in the high, austere peaks of the Alps. His beautiful autobiography, Scalate Nelle Alpi (Gervasutti's Climbs), *was published in Italian in 1945, the year before he died in a rappelling accident. (He and Giuseppe Gagliardone were retreating in the face of a storm, from an attempt on the pillar on Mont Blanc du Tacul that now bears his name, when their ropes hung up. Gervasutti climbed back up, cleared a jammed knot, and belayed Gagliardone down to a ledge. He then lost control of his rappel.*

> *For myself I prefer an unattainable happiness, always near, always elusive: the prize which vanishes every time one grasps it, to give way to another, still harder, still more distant. The moments when the heart really overflows with happiness come when the sense of life is heightened by tension and struggle—the actual moments of conquest, or more often of defeat, and not the dead moments when victory has been achieved."*

—Giusto Gervasutti, Gervasutti's Climbs

1990, Barry Kenneth Blanchard sitting sidesaddle on the Honda 750 Four that was gifted to him by his father, Norman Kenneth Blanchard. Barry Blanchard

JULY 1992: When *Cliffhanger* was done, I was ready to leave Hollywood and get back to climbing mountains. I got a ride to Briançon, just inside the French border, with a gal from Cortina who'd finished working with craft service on the movie and was meeting up with her boyfriend. I rented a car there.

After enjoying the first decent cheeseburger I'd had in over four months, I barreled toward Chamonix. When I pulled into Raine's driveway and rushed up to see her, it was clear that a shift had taken place since she'd spent a couple of nights in my room in Cortina a month and half before. It was like her arm was out and her palm braced in a "stop" against my chest. She told me that she needed time away from being my lover, from being anyone's lover.

"I just want to dance and have fun, Barrel," she said. I slept in the living room.

JULY 7, 1992: The forecast was good for today and into the late afternoon on the day following; then there'd be thunderstorms. I was on fire to climb. Raine wanted to get up high, too. We decided on the Gervasutti Pillar, hopped onto the téléphérique, and whisked up to the Cosmiques Hut at nearly 12,000 feet. An hour before dawn, Raine and I crunched off across the Vallée Blanche glacier toward one of the finest alpine rock routes in the world: 800 meters of superb granite, almost all of it in the intermediate range of 5.6 to 5.8, with one wide crack of 5.10. That crack rasped some skin off my left ankle; blood dripped into my low-cut rock shoe. Higher up, I kicked steps into snow and left faint traces of red on the coarse crystals.

The forecast was right. The golden granite dimmed to gray; feldspar crystals no longer twinkled in sunlight. It began to rain. Two Swiss mountain guides, the only other souls on the route, caught us up. The four of us huddled against the wall, rushing into rain gear and pulling on mountain boots.

"We're in trouble, aren't we, Barrel?" Raine's sea-blue eyes were anxious.

"Yep, this is fucked, but going up is a lot better option than going down. We gotta move, though."

"I'm ready." And then she rested her gloved hand on my shoulder, "I'm glad I'm here with you. I trust you. We'll be okay."

Raine on the golden granite of the Gervasutti Pillar in the early morning light, the bicolor 100-meter rope she'd just bought me as a gift tied into her harness. Barry Blanchard

Our sprint over the summit of Mont Blanc du Tacul at midnight remains my most immediate experience with lightning—and I'm the first to admit that I've had far too many. I felt hunted, and that scared the hell out of me. Raine and I staggered through the raging heart of the storm. The absolute-white explosions of light were simultaneous with the tearing thunder. My lungs shook. I felt the pressure of the hits reverberate against my heart. Snow raged on the wind and accumulated into the silhouettes of the Swiss guides' headlong plunge steps down the normal route. Steep snow overlying a glacier was such a contrast to immaculate

granite we'd climbed up. Eventually, the snow erased even that trail of breadcrumbs.

"Barrel, your ice-ax is crackling!" And then another explosion of blinding white light. Balls of electric blue shot across the black surface of the glacier and rolled away to darkness, save for one hazy white light.

I ran my finger over the shattered plastic ferrule of my tool. St. Elmo had broken it with his fire where I had strapped it—inverted, spike to the air—onto my pack. Raine had seen the bright-blue finger touch it. We found our way to the Cosmiques Hut, where the custodians, worried about us, were waiting with the light on at 2 a.m.

We survived that, but the next day, back down in the valley, friction began to fly between Raine and me, especially after I contacted Mark. So much of him was still in her. The timing was wrong; I wasn't right for her. Could I ever have been right for the woman who'd been married to one of my closest friends? I'd thought so, but I'd deluded myself. The Gervasutti was the last big climb that Raine and I did together.

Mark and I laid plans for the Cordier Pillar on the Grands Charmoz, but only after I consulted Gilles Claret-Tournier, my oracle at Cham. I'd known him for over a decade and always sought his advice before big routes. As usual, he handed me spun gold: "Barry, the first four pitches are usually wet. You should go higher up the Glacier des Nantillons and traverse back onto the route above the wet rock."

JULY 17: Mark and I charged from the Plan de l'Aiguille station. Water flowing from the Blaitière Glacier had frozen onto the trail overnight; a twenty-foot-wide plate of ice gleamed as if freshly polished by a Zamboni. The ice held a couple of degrees of grade; a slip would send you rocketing off a deadly drop. A couple of British climbers—so obviously British, in Berghaus jackets and National Health Service glasses—knelt there, strapping on crampons.

"Are you ready for this?" Mark's eyes were piercing and determined.

"What are you going to do, man?"

"Watch," and he pranced across the ice, leaping from dry rock to dry rock like a ballet dancer. Then he touched down on the trail on the far side and was gone.

"Right, then—what route are you two off for?" one Brit challenged.

"The Cordier," I said, and then started leaping from rock to rock.

"Well, we'll be right behind you," he asserted, obviously pissed at being passed.

It was one of those days when the rope felt like a living thing tying Mark to me. We flew up the route. At one offwidth, Mark

By midday, the clouds are descending toward Raine and me on the Gervasutti Pillar. Barry Blanchard wrapped his powerful hands onto one side of the crack and laybacked with his feet pasted to the other. It was an inspiring display of brawn. I tried to imitate his speed, but I didn't feel secure enough and I slotted my arm into the crack to chickenwing like I'd learned in Yosemite. I climbed the pitch slower than Mark, then ran my lead out to the end of the ropes.

"I don't think it makes sense to go past the established anchors," he admonished. "It's faster to take the easy belays and change up more often."

"Okay, Doom. I'll stop where I'm supposed to."

My friend Stevie Haston had spoken the truth when I'd asked him about the Cordier: "The stone on the top was better than Yosemite." Perfect bronze and golden granite, it could have come from the mountains of my mind. By afternoon, Mark and I were striding down the Glacier des Nantillons. We'd be making the 'phérique with time to spare. As we rounded below the route, we saw that the Brits had been caught up in a cluster with several other parties, halfway up.

My ticket home was out of Rome. Mike Weis let me stay in his hotel room. He and Dave Schultz were flying to Sardinia for their weekend off from studio work for *Cliffhanger*. They'd taken to free diving into sea caves to see how far they could go. (This is what happens when a wild-ass Coloradan gets away with a wild-ass Californian.)

I enjoyed a final dinner out with David Breashears and a couple of gals from *Cliffhanger*. The Roman summer night was warm, and I was dressed well in clothes that fit, right down to new Calvin Klein briefs. The red wine was fine, and the night felt gentle and soft, like I was floating in warm Mediterranean water.

My last night on Hollywood's dime was in the Hyatt Grand Central, NYC. I had a pocket full of per diem and a trolley full of duffels. I tipped the bellman well, more when he bought me a six-pack of cold Stellas. The best way from the Calgary International Airport back to Dead Man's Flats was a $100 taxi ride. I walked back into The Cell. My bed at the Hyatt had covered more square footage.

AUGUST 18: I went alone to the south face of Mt. Yamnuska. I started with Red Shirt. It went well, so I jogged down the back side and across the face to Forbidden Corner, 5.9, 1,000 feet. Precision, breath, flow, I moved well, had the endurance to figure out the hard parts, the discipline to calm my mind.

When I return to the route, three decades later, I can't believe that I climbed the loose flake on the eighth pitch without a rope. It is completely detached and lies to the wall like several hard-shelled briefcases balanced end to end. An ancient piton nailed into the topmost crack holds the stack together with compressive force. I'm always nervous there, always trying to press down, never pull out. Someone is going to pull those flakes off one day. I'm just glad it wasn't me at age thirty-three.

I mentioned my free solo on Forbidden, the hardest and most serious on rock in my career, to Jeff Marshall, the preeminent free soloist on Rockies rock at the time. I was chuffed with myself when I said, "I soloed Forbidden, Jeff. I hear you soloed it, too."

"Ya, I did that about a year ago, Blanch."

"What did you think?"

"It was a nice warm-down after soloing the Kahl Wall," he grinned massively. (Kahl Wall is a 5.10a, 900 feet, and also located on Yamnuska.)

"Fuck you, Junior." I used my old nickname for him. Kevin Doyle and I had given it to him in the 1980s because he is just a pup.

"Ha-ha-ha. Touché, Blanch, Touché!"

OCTOBER 9: I drove to Seattle to meet with Jon Krakauer, Steve Swenson, and Greg Child. I was interested in climbing K2. Steve and Greg had climbed its North Ridge in 1990, and Jon was a friend and a source of good advice. When I was adamant on climbing in alpine style, Jon said, "I'd be happy to get to the top of K2 in any style."

Reinhold Messner had named the Southwest Pillar of K2 "The Magic Line." As I pored over pictures of the second highest peak on Earth, I saw why: it was a beautiful, bold black staircase that led from the Negrotto Col at nearly 21,000 feet to the sky. Everything else on the south face looked white and skiable. The Magic Line was abrupt, technical, an alpinist's route. I felt the warrior inside me rise. I mailed my application to climb it to the Pakistani Embassy in Ottawa.

DECEMBER 16: I soloed The Trans-Canada Iceway, a 650-foot WI 4 gully on Mt. Rundle. I started by headlamp, pounding my mountain bike four miles along the Riverside Trail. The route was superb but required hours of traveling through huge avalanche country. Much of my safety came from the lack of snowpack. My family's history sifted around in my mind. We are the Métis, born from Scottish and French fur traders and Indigenous women. Our culture predates the formation of Canada, and I am well aware of how Canada marginalized the Métis after the Riel Rebellion of 1885. How my grandfather had been born and raised on a road allowance, some of the only unwanted land available to the Métis. I've spent much of my life not feeling good enough. Late in the afternoon, I was striding through the forest back to my bike when an overwhelming sadness ambushed me, and I thumped to my ass on the frozen moss and wept.

"I'm not good enough. Still not good enough." And as I said it, I knew that I needed to learn more about where I came from. The answer lay in my family's history in Saskatchewan. Over the last thirty-three years, I have made dozens of trips back to my family's homeland in the Qu'Appelle River Valley. My ancestors and knowledge keepers have taught me that we are good enough, I am good enough.

JANUARY 1993: Scott Backes and Mark Twight came to the Rockies to ice climb. They'd endured a week of −25°F at the Rampart Creek Wilderness Hostel when I met them at the Rose & Crown pub in Banff.

"I got the permit for the Magic Line on K2 for this summer."

The metaphorical gauntlet clanged onto the table between us and lit a bronze flame in their eyes. The Magic Line was at work; the three of us were already picturing ourselves ascending it.

Mark and I picked up Jim Elzinga and drove into the Ghost River. We climbed Malignant Mushroom, WI 5, 180 feet, and talked about K2. Jimmy wanted to go but later confided that he wouldn't be able to keep up with a professional climber like Twight. (Though it turned out that Mark couldn't come after all.) We drove out of the Ghost, changed into city clothes, and carried on to the Rose & Crown. Jimmy left after a couple of beers.

I'm loving the immaculate granite on the Cordier Pillar. The Grands Charmoz with the Glacier des Nantillons below. Mark Twight

It didn't take long for Mark and me to get to the other topic at hand. We talked through my involvement with Raine and his with Marie, then moved on to the rest of our love lives. I pictured Raine, Mark, and me sitting down to dinner a little over a year earlier. Everything had shifted. I felt like one of the dinner plates that we'd shared had cracked into three pieces. We were being pulled apart. Three different trajectories.

And then, once again, I needed climbing partners. Mark and Scott couldn't join me on K2. Troy Kirwan, one of my best friends, signed on, even though he'd only been to moderate altitude. Peter Arbic (PA) also agreed to join us. Along with Ward Robinson, he and I had established The Wild Thing on the northeast face of Mt. Chephren over four days in the winter of 1987. It took me five different attempts to eventually climb this route (I wrote about three of those attempts in *The Calling*). In '89, with Jim Elzinga, PA had set the highest point reached on the South Spur of Nuptse: 25,000 feet. The South Spur of Nuptse was one of the Himalaya's greatest challenges.

"Hell ya—I'll go, Bubba," PA said. He and Troy went back to guiding heli-skiing in British Columbia's interior ranges while I stayed in the Rockies to climb and guide ice and prepare for my Ski Guide exam.

Like a lot of mountain guides, I come to the profession with a singular passion for climbing. If I was given a week off in winter, and the alpine wasn't in condition, I'd go ice climbing every day. If I got a second week off, I'd ice climb for thirteen days, and on the fourteenth I'd go ski touring. For many in my association, the passions are reversed: they are skiers first, climbers second. Membership in the Association of Canadian Mountain Guides is heavily weighted toward skiing, largely because the mechanized ski industry—backcountry skiing out of snow-cats and helicopters—is by far the largest and most lucrative segment of Canadian guiding.

I had passed the climbing side of my exams first time; skiing was another story. It was the third day of my Ski Guide exam, and I knew full well that I'd failed the day before when I screwed up a dangerous lead down a frozen snow surface in the trees. I should have taken the skis off and cut steps; instead, I persisted in sideslipping down what was essentially ice. It would have been so easy to have someone slide out of control and break a leg.

"I'm out of here. I'm going to ski out Mountain Creek," I challenged Danny Griffith in the Sorcerer Lodge, a backcountry ski hut in the Selkirk Mountains.

"You can't ski out Mountain Creek!" Danny gasped. He'd been a teammate of mine on the West Ridge of Everest in 1986, and we'd worked together several times. Danny was a friend but also the exam leader.

"Like hell I can't. It goes all the way to the highway."

"No, you just can't leave the exam like that. We helicoptered in here, for Christ's sake! You can't even get down there."

"Bullshit, I can't. It's goddamned skiing terrain. I'd be hiking on it in the summertime. Of course I can get down there."

"Okay, okay, but I think you need to stay on the exam. There's still a lot you can learn from the next five days."

It was good advice. I stayed and I failed, but I did learn more about guiding on skis. Troy Kirwan was on the exam and passed. He became a mountain guide after acing all his exams first go. A guy I'd mentored in the Rockies and St. Elias was now more qualified than me; it was a funny type of inversion.

After they'd been together for three years, Shell had left Troy for another guide. That winter and spring, Troy and I played the field hard and climbed hard. He became the lead gun, willing to risk massively if it meant forgetting about her for a while. It was a pattern we learned to exploit—whichever member of our crew was going through a breakup got the sharp end. This yielded some brilliant leads.

FEBRUARY 1993: Troy, Grant Statham (aka "Whipper"), and I crunched up to Amadeus, a WI 4+ in the Kananaskis that rarely forms to the ground. For the first time, a slender pillar of ice had touched down! But it was about the size of my thigh where it rested on a pedestal the size of a truck tire. The blue-hued ice thickened to the size of my torso within a body length, then it hung free for thirty feet before touching the rock. It was beautiful, but fragile and dangerous. The three of us just stood looking at it, and then Troy said, "If this was France, we'd climb that thing." His jaw was set—I'd seen it before. He tied in and tapped his way up masterfully. A beautiful, bold, and totally engaging lead. My buddy climbing at his best.

In May, I pulled open the front door of The Cell. My head felt like fuzz, and my teeth like they had little fisherman's knit sweaters pulled over them. Troy and I had shut down the bars in Banff again, and I'd driven my motorcycle twenty miles home to Dead Man's Flats. A spruce bough was snagged between the front forks of the Honda, and I had no idea how it got there. I had to wrap both hands around it and jerk hard to rip it free.

"You've been drinking too much, Blanchard," I said to the bike.

Agate Lines: Area
"King of the Road": Roger Miller

THE MAGIC LINE

To walk up the Baltoro Glacier is to pass under the Earth's ultimate expression of the word "mountain." The bold golden turrets of the Trango and Uli Biaho towers; the shark's tooth of Paiju Peak; Masherbrum's tusk thrust so high into thin air; the squat bulwark of Muztagh Tower, where Martin Boysen so famously got his knee stuck in a crack; the 7,000-foot granite ramparts of Cathedral Spire, which had yet to see an ascent—each day brought into view another mountain, each commanding awe and igniting desire in my soul. The whole time, we were walking toward the Shining Wall, the west face of Gasherbrum IV, a perfect, chiseled pyramid of pale, glowing marble, where, in 1985, Voytek Kurtyka and Robert Schauer made the greatest alpine-style ascent of the twentieth century.

JUNE 3, 1994: Peter, Troy, and I flew to Toronto and boarded a Pakistan International Airlines (PIA) flight for Lahore. With Michele Sinclair, a longtime client, and Lisa Willemse, Troy's girlfriend, we were a party of five, which met the numbers required for our expedition's permit for K2. PIA had given us double our allotted baggage allowance, and we had been good to them, getting a picture of the three of us wearing their T-shirts in *The Globe and Mail*, one of Canada's national newspapers. Chris Dafoe was their Western Canada arts correspondent; we'd sat together on the jury of the Banff Mountain Film Festival six months

he Magic Line, dividing shadow on the west
.ce of K2 from sunlight on the south face of K2.
arry Blanchard

earlier. He was happy to branch out and write an "adventure" piece for the paper.

JUNE 9: Our liaison officer, Captain Imran Ullah Khan, arrived at Flashman's Hotel in Rawalpindi. He was medium height and dashing, with a chevron mustache and round burnt-umber eyes, and his English was impeccable. He had just sat down in a chair in my room when the gents from the carpet house that I'd been doing black-market currency exchanges with since 1984 showed up. Imran turned a blind eye as I walked them to a different room to swap greenbacks for rupees.

We'd been in Rawalpindi for six days, and I was more than ready to leave. I wanted to be in base camp. When I thought about how many times I'd had that exact wish, the answer was seven—once for each of my expeditions to Asia. With each day in the lowland heat, my doubt and fear compounded. Was what we were attempting ridiculous? Three men, 12,000 feet of technical climbing up the second highest peak on the planet—the earth's boldest thrust into thin air. A storm could trap us up high...or could it? Is there any mountain that can't be retreated down through the teeth of a storm?

The five us were sitting around in my hotel room. "My confidence is failing," I admitted. "I don't know if we can do this thing—maybe it's just too much." There was a long, breathless pause, and then Peter leveled his deep-brown eyes on me.

"Don't get psyched out, Bubba. We are some of the best climbers in Canada. We will get our chance." Then he described to Michele and Lisa precisely why, listing some of our ascents, some of the peaks we'd been on in the Himalaya. I sipped my Murree beer and gazed off into my life, my heart heavy with anxiety.

In the morning, we would be flying to Skardu. I knew that I would gain strength there; my resolve would return with motion toward the mountain. K2, a mutinous black pyramid hovering above the atmospheric haze, which I'd glimpsed nine years earlier from high on Rakaposhi. It looked like something not of the earth. When people asked me if I'd be going to K2, I'd always replied, "No—that one scares me." I'd held that fear for seven years...and the last twenty-four hours.

JUNE 10: A jet to Skardu; jeeps to Askole. There, we met our two sirdars and ninety porters, twenty of whom were "breadmen" carrying atta (flour) to make chapattis to feed all the porters on our eight-day trek into K2 Base Camp. Every day or two, some of the breadmen left us to walk back to Askole, their loads of atta having been consumed.

JUNE 13: We began walking up-valley toward the Baltoro Glacier, toward K2. One day later, I sat cross-legged in soft ash-colored sand on the banks of the Domurdo River pressing ridges into the sand with the soles of my hiking boots. I watched 300 porters from several expeditions—our 90 included—queue up to get into the man basket that would ferry them across the charging mud-colored water on a suspended cable. The basket ferried two porters at a time, and it took long minutes to send it to and fro. I'd been sitting in the sand since 8 a.m. It was now 11:48, and I wondered if there would be enough time in the day to get our porters across. I rose to stretch my aching knees.

Lisa came striding over, beaming, and presented a half dozen small reddish stones. She'd been collecting them on the hillside with Imran and Peter. "Imran says that they are low-grade rubies!"

"They look like raisins."

Imran walked up, held his palm open, and jerked his head for me to choose one. I picked the finest—a pea-sized multi-plated ball glinting ruby red. Imran turned abruptly and strode away, letting me know that it was a gift without telling me so. I pulled out the beaded medicine pouch that I wore around my neck and added Imran's ruby to my talisman: a lock of Raine's hair, a sliver of bark from an ancient spruce I'd ski-toured by that winter, a metal pendant Christine had made me.... I wondered if the ruby would hurt when it pressed into my sternum. I knew that it would protect me. I sat down cross-legged again. The swollen Domurdo raged on.

Peter and Imran took to disappearing whenever our porters took longer breaks. They'd walk back conspiratorially, often giggling.

"Looks like Sneaky Pete's found a sidekick," Troy said, grinning at me.

"Satan's consorts. Man, I couldn't smoke dope up here—it would destroy me."

"Ya, but you don't smoke it down low either."

"I figure I've got more than enough challenges in my life with beer, red wine, and scotch."

"Amen, brother, amen."

JUNE 18: We stood at Concordia, where the massive Baltoro and Godwin-Austen glaciers meet. My heart surged at the sight of the broad, imperial pyramid of K2. The Magic Line sat dead center, cleaving sunlight from shade in the morning light, a striking series of rock steps and ridges, each gaining thousands of feet and penultimately merging with the West Ridge. Legions of ice penitentes stood in rank and file on the surface of the Godwin-Austen Glacier. Several wide, medial moraines had laid roads of black between the glowing pickets of ice.

JUNE 20: We marched up one of the black roads and arrived at Base Camp. The Strip. The tents of four other expeditions looked like colorful shirts hung along a clothesline. Their teams were two, three, and four times the size of ours. In the space between the Swedish and the Canadian/American teams, we set up six tents and began constructing a cooking shelter from a waist-high ring of rock, bamboo, and leaky Pakistani Army tarps. Our cook, Karim Khan, was younger than all of us. Troy and I had taken to calling him "our teenage son." He'd been adamant about hauling in four porter-loads of atta.

"Karim must have a starvation complex," I'd said to Troy back in Skardu. "He gets freaked out when I suggest that we're taking too much atta. There's fear in his eyes."

"Well, we'll be able to sit on all of the bags of atta," Troy proclaimed when we put the finishing touches to our roof. Our cooking structure would have done the inhabitants of Gilligan's Island proud. A cyclonic gust roared down The Strip, violently flapping all the tents in its way. Our shelter imploded, and the Pak Army tarps ballooned, crumpled, and charged off down-glacier like trampled newsprint down a windy city street. We ran after them, joined by Dan Culver in our mad, hypoxic scamper. A hell of a nice guy, he helped us reconstruct and reinforce our shelter. Three years earlier, Dan had become the fifth Canadian to climb Mt. Everest. He, Dr. John Haigh, and our buddy and fellow guide Jim

Peter Arbic, Lisa Willemse, Michele Sinclair, and Troy Kirwan hang on tight to the line, crossing a swollen river en route to K2. Barry Blanchard

Haberl were the Canadians on the seven-person Canadian/American team led by Stacy Allison, the first American woman to climb Mt. Everest.

Troy, Pete, and I were anxious to see Jim. We called him "The All-Canadian Boy" because he was so earnest. Jim always tried to do the right thing. I remembered a conversation we'd had about relationships and marriage in Peru six years earlier. "Monogamy is the ONLY way," Jim had told me and, as always, I'd felt his commitment and belief. Now he was sitting in our cook shelter sipping tea and telling us how a Slovenian climber, Boštjan Kekec, had died five days earlier trying to escape from Camp 4, high on the Abruzzi Ridge, during a storm.

"In a half dozen expeditions over here, I've never been on a peak where people are dying," I said. Pete, Troy, Jim, and I all stared into the milky surface of our tea. Mountaineering wasn't worth dying for, yet I also knew that I would push very hard to get what I wanted. When death placed a bony hand on my shoulder, I would be afraid, but I would also fight and eventually pray. I knew that, too.

Pete hung our beer bags in Karim's cook tent, where we hoped they wouldn't freeze. We looked forward to having twenty quarts of beer in three weeks' time. Pete also set about making a barrelful of apricot wine. It was good to see him get so much use out of his chemistry PhD.

Viki Grošelj was a very accomplished Slovenian alpinist, and his English was perfect. "We want to climb the Magic Line in alpine style," I told him over tea in their large mess tent.

"Ah, the fucking Magic Line," he said dismissively. I was shocked. He continued, "Messner made such a big deal of that line, then didn't actually try it himself! Slovenians went there and wasted a whole expedition on it. I think that it is too hard...but I am done with K2. I want to get home and get back to coaching my son's soccer team. They've made the finals in their division." He looked up toward the mountain. "I am more proud of that than I am of this fucking K2...be very careful up there. Promise me you will."

JUNE 29: Pete, Troy, and I climbed onto the De Filippi Glacier footing the south face of K2. The next day, we started up the broad couloir leading to the Negrotto Col, the objective of our reconnaissance and acclimatization trip.

"This slope is the endless pig of misery," Troy gasped and leaned on his ice tools, their shafts sunk into the softening slop. The three of us stood at 21,700 feet, the sun pounding heat into our backs. Our crampon points balled up with snow mush, and each of us had to arrest slips when our front points sliced through the increasingly structureless snow. The slope was 50 degrees and 3,000 feet long. We caved into the smothering heat and breathlessness four-fifths of the way to the col and pitched our two tiny tents against a rock band that bordered the gully.

JUNE 30, LATE AFTERNOON: I kicked my crampons into hardening slop. The sun had swung off the endless slope of misery, and the snow immediately firmed to meringue. My mind felt light, like a wisp of smoke, and I felt good—free to climb higher and higher, yet slower and slower. Troy and Pete followed in my footsteps. Two hundred feet above, at the Negrotto Col, I could see the flattened remnants of tents fluttering like dead leaves. We turned around, retrieved our tents from the night before, and downclimbed the endless slope of misery. It was too long to rappel with our minimal gear. Downclimbing it was torturous.

"I'm never climbing that slope in the day again," Pete declared.

"Hallelujah, brother," Troy said. "Next time, we'll go at night."

We descended to The Strip, where a sixth expedition had showed up: a team led by the British mountain guide Roger Payne that included his Kiwi wife, Julie-Ann Clyma, and fellow Brits Victor Saunders, Alan Hinkes, and their doctor and base camp manager, Caroline.

JULY 4, 10 P.M.: Pete, Troy, and I left Base Camp. Ten hours later, we climbed into the Negrotto Col and pitched our tents to rest and sleep through the heat of the day. Pete excavated a Slovenian bible and vintage 1970s ice-ax from crushed tents layered archaeologically into the snow.

Later that day, up higher on the climb, I spat, "The rock is good! I wish the siege climbers had cleaned these goddamned caving ladders!" as I threw the aluminum rungs aside so that I could get at the incut edges of rock behind.

We had fun that day. Climbed 1,300 feet higher than the col on good stone, snapping goofy pictures of ourselves eating our preferred high-altitude food—beef jerky—while holding a sponsor's sport bar wrapper lower and askew: "Real men eat jerky!" We rappelled, packed up our camp, and downclimbed the endless slope through the night. Physically, it hurt to be repeating the same repetitive kicks, and always there was the concern of a slip and fall, which ground away at our vigilance with a monotony that pushed us to complacency. Then my foot would slip or break through the snow, and I'd get slapped back to reality by the pounding of my heart and cold clouds of expletives expelled by my gasping lungs.

JULY 5: We walked into Base Camp at dawn. Karim ushered us into the eating shelter for black tea with milk and sugar and deep-fried parathas. I laid on peanut butter and jam, and crunched into the delicious crisp bread, then another with a fried egg, and then another....

"We'll be ready to go for it with the next weather window," I said, wiping peanut oil off my greasy lips.

"Ya, Bubba. We should give it a go. I think we're acclimatized enough. It would be nice to get more than four days of climbable weather in a row, though, and we haven't seen that," Pete said.

"We need the wind out of China again," Troy observed. Having a north wind was one of the harbingers we'd identified; it was a mantra spoken up and down The Strip: "Wind out of China, wind out of China."

Our Can/Am friends had occupied their high camp on the Abruzzi Ridge the day before. Later that day, over the radio, we heard Phil Powers announce that he was on top. "What in the wide world of sports is a hick from Wyoming doing on top of K2?" I shouted into the radio.

"Enjoying the view, friend, enjoying the view."

An hour later, we learned that Jim and Dan were the first Canadians to stand on top of K2! We laughed and hooted and high-fived. Later, Dan fell while descending. He fell to his death. The mood on The Strip plummeted, as concern mounted for those still high on the peak. The mountain had fallen into storm.

The next day we walked up The Strip. Seven teams camped along it now, plus one more below, at the junction of the Savoia and Godwin-Austen glaciers, trying to climb the West Ridge. Well over a hundred people. We'd been getting to know everyone; we were part of a small town divided into barrios, yet all part of the amalgamated community. Dan's death forced a grave pause on us all.

JULY 7: We walked out again, this time with Phil Powers. Jim and his teammate John Petroske had been too exhausted to descend the day before. More storms, more steps. Jim fell into each of our arms and cried. He didn't have to be strong anymore; we would be strong for him. We walked our friends back to their base camp.

Their cook tapped Dan's name into an aluminum pot lid using a piton and ice hammer.

JULY 11: We stood solemnly as prayers were recited in English and Urdu and Dan's name was added to the too many already clustered around the Gilkey Memorial. This man-high beehive of stone piled onto some of the only non-glaciated bedrock footing K2 bears dozens of memorials (including names pounded into metal plates and pot lids) and pictures of those who lost their lives on the mountain since 1953. As we walked back into camp, the wind screamed, our shelter flapped violently and then imploded, and for the second time we sprinted after the tarps. This time, Dan was not running with us. I knelt on a captured tarp and heaved and sighed, choking back tears.

JULY 12: The Can/Am team walked away. K2 was enshrouded in storm. I still wanted to climb it.

JULY 13 AND 14: We charged to the Negrotto Col only to be mugged by a storm. We cached a lot of our gear below the endless pig of misery.

"I don't think we're going to see the six days of climbable weather that we need to get up this thing and down the Abruzzi," Pete said. It was the forty-third day of our expedition; the twenty-fifth that we'd been on or below the mountain.

"I can't face the endless slope of misery again," Troy spat. He'd had a hard night there haunted by headaches and Cheyne-Stokes breathing. The deep ventilations followed by periods of apnea were a sign that he wasn't acclimatizing as well as Pete and me. Pete was worried that if Troy got acute mountain sickness on the Magic Line, we wouldn't be able to get him down.

"I think we should switch to the Kukuczka/Piotrowski," Pete suggested. "It has a lot more snow climbing on it low down, and I think we'd be able to get up it in three days. If Troy needs to come down, we'll be able to climb down with him. We won't have to rappel." (Jerzy Kukuczka and Tadeusz Piotrowski had established their route up the South Face in the summer of 1986. Kukuczka spent a day surmounting a 5.9 pitch at 26,900 feet.)

"Guys, we came here to climb the Magic Line," I challenged.

"If we go for that, it will just be you and me," Pete replied.

"I'll be okay, you guys, added Troy. "I'm still keen to try—came all the way over here to try. But I think what Pete is saying makes sense." I looked into his blue eyes for ten heartbeats and said, "Okay, I'll buy that, buddy," and then put my hand on his shoulder.

"We could retrieve our stuff from the bottom of the endless slope of misery and then traverse over and re-cache it, even in this weather," Troy suggested.

"Good idea, man," Pete replied. And we moved our cache from the Magic Line over to the Kukuczka/Piotrowski, a little over a half mile to the east and 1,400 feet higher.

JULY 21: We got a twelve-hour break in the storm and were able to move our cache 1,300 feet higher up the Kukuczka/Piotrowski. Back in camp, I looked back to the crevasse holding our cache and said, "If the winds flip, it's going to get buried."

"No, I think it's fine," Peter stated.

"Not if the winds change."

"The winds aren't going to flip. It won't get buried, or I'm not a heli-guide."

A hello at my tent door, I unzipped it, and there was Anatoli Boukreev, who looked like Dolph Lundgren, sounded like him too. He was part of the five-man Northlight Expedition composed of the Australian Andrew Lock and the Germans Reinmar Joswig, Peter Metzger, and Ernst Eberhardt. Anatoli was from Kazakhstan, and he sat in my tent vestibule pitching me, in his Thorlike voice, on the opportunities to heli-ski in his home country.

"Anatoli, you need to talk to Troy and Peter. They guide heli-skiing—I don't."

"But you are Mountain Guide of Canada?"

"Yes, but I'm a strange one. I spend my winters ice climbing and ski touring."

"Hmmm. I like to ice climb. Ice climbing is good."

"I hear you, brother." The next day we got a brief window, and when I fixed my binoculars on our cache, I could see that it was buried.

"Pete, the wind's flipped. Our cache is buried."

"Ya, I can see that. I'm glad we marked it, but it's going to take some digging to retrieve it."

The storms continued, and we fell into the rhythm of getting up, eating breakfast, and then cruising The Strip. Morning tea with the Dutch Internationals who included in their numbers Jeff Lakes and Tim Styles, both guys we knew back in Canada. Lunchtime tea with the Swedes because they had the best food and nicest dining tent. High tea with the Brits (but of course), where I enjoyed flirting with the exuberant

Troy and Pete stacked up some rocks as a route marker on the south face of K2. It wasn't miserable the entire time we were there. Barry Blanchard

Caroline. One day I walked into their camp with Roger Payne and saw his wife, Julie-Ann, toweling off her hair.

"You won't recognize me, Roger—I'm clean!"

"Ah yes, but I've seen you clean before, my dear," he cracked.

I laughed heartily as Roger beamed.

After tea, it was back to our tents to read, write, listen to music, fester...and wait for climbable weather. Strange to know that so many other souls were doing the same, lying in their sleeping bags trying to stay warm as the sun dropped beyond the cement-gray sky somewhere. I began to catalog the different sounds that various forms of snow made when they hit the fly of my tent.

All the liaison officers were captains in the Pakistani Army or policemen, and they had their own clique with a separate visiting schedule. Their communication lines included Broad Peak Base Camp, several hours back down the Godwin-Austen and K2 glaciers. Word had rocketed through their grapevine when a Korean expedition showed up there with a dog in tow. The Pakistani liaison officers took the dog for a mascot and that made them happy. The next day, however, all were confounded, confused, and disgusted when the Koreans smacked the dog in

the head with a rock, singed its hair off over an MSR stove, and promptly cooked and ate it.

JULY 22: We got invited to the Base Camp Olympics, as organized by Reinmar, Peter, and Ernst, the Germans on Anatoli's team. Pete, Troy, and I got trounced in all the athletic events—stuff like underhand lobbing a palm-sized rock to knock a softball-sized rock off a six-pack sized rock sitting fifteen feet away. Then it came to the a cappella singing event, in which the three of us nailed "King of the Road" and our only medals—an accomplishment given that the Catalonians had marched in, arm in arm and two rows deep, singing their national anthem. Our medals? Three pieces of German fruitcake. Delicious! Far better than any gold or silver.

JULY 26: "It's not ideal," Troy said, "no wind out of China, but I think we should go for it." It was the fifty-fourth day of our expedition and the thirty-sixth day we'd been living on, or below, K2. Mostly below K2, but the weather was opening up.

JULY 27: We crunched out of Base Camp before dawn. The large, planar slopes of the east arm of the De Filippi Glacier were so much nicer to climb than the crevasse-riddled western arm that led to the endless slope of misery. We walked up on our crampons, avoiding the few crevasses and staying to the high ground, safer from the threat of triggering a windslab avalanche.

Our cache was buried under six feet of snow and took us over an hour to dig out. Then, we climbed higher onto the razor's edge of the Kukuczka/Piotrowski spur; cutting from the south face of K2 at a right angle, it granted us a fine white line to follow. We dug tent platforms at 20,000 feet.

JULY 28: 700 feet of chaotically tumbling glacier and evil blue seracs stood above our heads, and it felt—beneath the lethal finality of all that tumbling ice—like we'd been unhooded and flipped to face the sky in a guillotine. Thousands of cubic yards leaned out over our heads creeping, toward the point of catastrophic collapse.

"Fuck, man, we can't climb up through that shit. I'm scared just standing here," I said.

Morning time: Peter Arbic kicking steps up the south face of K2, the Magic Line to the left, the Kukuczka/Piotrowski spur straight ahead.
Barry Blanchard

"It looks like a good place to get crushed," Troy panted.

"I think we should hightail it over to the South Spur. Jean Afanassieff and Yannick Seigneur went across here in 1981. I bet we can be across in less than an hour."

"Won't the Catalonians be pissed if we poach their route?" Pete asked.

"I don't know. I think they're still fixing rope below. This could be our chance to climb K2. If I was in their shoes, I wouldn't hold it against them coming onto our route in alpine style. It's not like it's a new route. Česen soloed it '86, as we all know."

"It makes a lot more sense than spending a day climbing up through that crap," Troy said, nodding up toward the tumbling chaos.

It was amazing how quickly we could scamper horizontally, scared shitless, relative to what we could manage going straight up. We got across the 700-yard traverse, from the Kukuczka/Piotrowski to the South Spur farther east, and out from under the scythe of seracs in just thirty minutes! I kicked steps to the arête of the South Spur, it being our eastern horizon, and when I crested it, I saw two of the Catalonians busily fixing rope not more than 150 feet above. We yelled and waved, and they did the same in reply, undoubtedly wondering where in the hell we'd come from. Troy, Pete, and I continued on our merry alpine way, making

sure not to come within an arm's length of their fixed line. Passing Jordi and Jordi, we exchanged goofy grins and a lot of "Okays." We spoke little Catalan, and they, little English.

We labored on. Troy began to fall off the pace, but he kept coming, never quit pushing himself upright from the heads of his axes and taking another series of steps before folding forward to breathe and breathe.

At the day's end, we found the dark portal of a crevasse and stepped inside. It was cold but comfortable. We flattened out a floor with shovel blades screwed into the heads of our ice-axes and set up our tent. Troy had a horrible night, suffering from a constant headache. His eyes looked haunted and hollow, the flesh of his face heavy and sagging.

"I can't keep going up," he said, tears falling from his blue eyes. The only other time I'd seen him cry was when Shell had left him. His heart was broken then; now it was breaking again. "You guys should keep going. I can get down from here if the Catalonians will let me use their ropes."

I radioed the Catalans, and it was a bit of a scramble to get Josep, their leader, whose English was perfect, on the other end. I posed our request, and his reply was immediate.

"Yes, of course! Troy can use our ropes—you have our full permission. He can stay in our camps if necessary. We will help Troy however we can."

Handshakes and hugs, platitudes and tears. Troy started down toward the Catalans' fixed lines; Pete and I climbed up. Soon Troy was small, and then he disappeared from our view.

Hard, hot work. Pete and I took turns breaking trail, weaving left and right, trying to read the snow for wind slabs. It was a fine line between our fear of avalanche and our need for good, supportive footing.

At 25,000 feet, it simply began to hurt. I forced myself to continue kicking steps until I had to stop and slump over and breathe. I was so grateful for each time I stepped aside to do this and Peter played through, dogged, determined, tough as nails. It then felt good to push myself to catch up and play through for him, to shoulder my fair share.

"No wind out of China," he said as he took over.

Late in the day, fog hissed into our world, and the frost bit instantaneously. We rushed into more layers, knowing that we could lose fingers and toes to the cutting, metallic cold. At 26,000 feet, our day was done, and we pitched in against some exposed rock. Finally, we got into the tent—where I'd wanted to be for the last hour. Feathers of frost reached from the inside walls already. My crampon straps had frozen into crusty bands of iron, and for the first time in my career I could not get them undone. Pete had to help me.

JULY 30: Pete and I climbed onto the shoulder of the Abruzzi Ridge. Six climbers were ahead of us, moving toward the Bottleneck. We knew that we knew them all, we just didn't know exactly who was who. My crampons bit into snow as firm as Dover chalk, but my balance was off. It felt like I'd be easy to push over—hell, it felt like I was pushing myself over! Fatigue folded me at the waist and pushed my chin onto my chest, and then I'd erect my spine and look up, to expand my lungs and breathe. A midlevel cloud was advancing from the east, as flat as the flight deck on an aircraft carrier.

"This-just-isn't-in-control-enough," I gasped.

"Ya, I'm thinking that we need to go down," Pete replied. Thus was our decision made, most of it communicated through body language and what we could see of each other's eyes through our goggles.

"God, those guys must be doing better than us," I gasped, looking into the Bottleneck and seeing six climbers.

"No, Bubba, I don't think that they are. We've been gaining on them for the last hour."

"How can they keep going if they feel like I do?"

"They're taking their chance, I guess," Pete said, and then he turned around and started heading for the Abruzzi. Dark clouds sailed in from the east. Pete and I marched down and down through wind, snow, fog. We'd made our oxygenless, alpine-style attempt and we'd been beaten. Now we told ourselves that we just wanted to get up K2, and to that end we cached our packs at Camp III, about halfway up, for another attempt. I anchored mine out from the camp on a wind-scoured edge where I reasoned it would not be buried by snow, while Pete left his inside the Brits' snow cave.

Late that afternoon, Pete and I walked away from the Abruzzi toward The Strip. Troy's green, blue, and pink suit grew from the gray. He was crying again, so happy to see us and it was so good to feel the love of his hug.

That evening, we learned that Anatoli, Andrew, Peter, and Reinmar had made the top, as had the Swede Daniel Bidner and his Danish teammate, Rafael Jensen. The next morning, we learned that Peter, Reinmar, and Daniel had been lost on the descent, dead. *Fuck, bloody fucking hell.* K2 shrouded itself in a cloak of storm that day, and it was just as well, as I couldn't stomach looking at the goddamned peak.

JULY 31: Rafael was frostbitten. Andrew helped him down to 25,300 feet, where Victor Saunders and Alan Hinkes abandoned their climb to take over Rafael's care and descent. Julie-Ann Clyma and Roger Payne nursed him through the night at Camp III, then got him to the base of the Abruzzi the next day. Pretty much everyone on The Strip helped carry Rafael, in a litter, back to Base Camp. Communally, it meant so much to help Rafael, who was four years younger than me, off the mountain. He was evacuated by helicopter a few days later. Daniel, Peter, and Reinmar's names got pounded into pot lids and

added to the Gilkey Memorial. Adding Boštjan and Dan, there were five men dead that season, frozen into the flanks of K2, somewhere. The storms continued.

The Swedes were leaving and giving away much of their remaining food. Pete stepped beaming into our kitchen shelter, lovingly holding a hank of ham.

"It's prosciutto!" he announced.

The next morning, Troy and I were up early slicing the prosciutto a quarter-inch thick and frying it in Kareem's treasured frying pan, then we'd wolf it down, tears of culinary glee twinkling in our eyes. It tasted so bloody, bloody good!

"What in the fuck are you two doing?" Pete exclaimed upon entering the shelter.

"Pete! Man!" I exclaimed. "It tastes like bacon!"

"Ya, Pete, you've got to try some, man." Troy smiled like the Cheshire Cat, his lips glimmering with grease.

"Ah, fuck," Pete sighed. "I can't even get mad at you two because you're just plain ignorant." Troy and I were stunned, arrested mid-chomp. Pete continued, "That ham was lovingly cured by old Italian men for two years. It's meant to be sliced diaphanously thin and wrapped tenderly around melon balls." More stupefied silence from Troy and me.

"Ya, Pete, but it tastes like BACON!" I finally infused.

"Ya, Pete, BACON! I mean, BACON!" Troy added.

"I'm climbing with plebeians," Pete concluded, and then exited in disgust.

We swirled into a vortex of waiting for good weather. Days became weeks, and our visiting schedule granted structure to our days, as did reading, writing, drawing, and spending time in our tents. Breakfast, lunch, and dinner became important punctuations in time, each day dragging to dusk, and the dark, and the cold, and the hope that the next day would dawn clear. *Please.*

I carved a pipe from a tree bough our porters had left behind and then spent several hours burning a draw hole into the bowl and stem with a piece of wire that I heated red-hot again and again. It looked good

Pete on the way to the Negrotto Col, the Godwin-Austen Glacier merging with the Baltoro Glacier at Concordia behind him. Barry Blanchard once I'd carved four sacred directions into the bowl and linear patterns into the stem. I handed the pipe to Imran, who held it in admiration as I turned and walked away.

Caroline, the Brits' doctor, and I sat in our shelter one afternoon talking, laughing, getting closer, eventually touching, and instantly feeling heat. I kissed her, and she kissed me back with a soft, warm, and open mouth. I pulled her toward me, scraping my knees over the gravel and sand that tops the deep-gray ice of the Godwin-Austen Glacier. We eventually took it to my tent, where I plugged *Agate Lines*, the Area album, into my Walkman and turned up the speakers. We made love all afternoon.

"Why did you only bring six condoms?"

"I didn't think that I'd be getting laid a lot when I came to K2."

"Silly bugger, I guess we'll have to start pulling out and praying, hadn't we?"

"Yes, I guess we shall. Shall we start?"

"Yes, please."

It was so amazing to have a girlfriend in Base Camp. Several days later, she and I fell asleep spooning in my tent, and then it was time for her to head back to her tent. She leaned over and kissed me on the neck from behind and it felt so good and soft and heartwarmingly tender.

The next morning, I was reading when I heard Troy say "Howdy" to somebody.

"Yes, good morning, do you know where I might find Dr. Caroline?"

"Ya, she's with the British expedition. Up there, the big, blue square tent. Who's asking?"

"Oh, I'm her other half."

Holy crap! My heart rate spiked. Caroline had told me about the relationship she'd ended *before* coming, how K2 was part of her path to freedom. I sat stone still. Her "other half" continued up The Strip, while Troy crunched over to my tent.

"Holy crap, Bubba! Did you hear that?"

"Ya, shit!"

He crawled in all giddy and giggling. High romance and intrigue in the Karakoram!

"Did you know that sweet Caroline had a boyfriend?" he asked me.

"No, she told me that she'd broken it off before coming here, but it was not what he wanted. She didn't think he'd be able to get to her up here."

"Well, somehow he's showed up."

Troy and I crawled out of my tent, and we could see Caroline a football field away, sitting and facing her other half, three feet of weighty thin air separating them like a no-man's-land.

"That looks heavy."

"Ya, a 'Dear John' recited in person rather than read alone. Poor guy—I have no idea how he managed to get up here."

Caroline came to my tent a couple of hours later.

"He borrowed money and somehow managed to get attached to a trekking group that's back down in Concordia. I told him again that it's over, that I'm involved with someone."

"That's tough news to hear after such a long trip."

"Yes, he's upset, but I told him back in Britain, and I told him that I didn't want to see him over here—or anywhere. He's going to stay a couple of days then leave. My team doesn't want him here because he doesn't have a permit. He can have my tent, and I'll stay down here with you."

"Whatever you need, darling."

A day and a half later, Caroline's ex walked away down the glacier. I had to feel sorry for the guy. Such a long way to come to have your dreams denied. He looked small as he hiked away.

Troy, Pete, and I were sitting in our cook shelter, talking about the first ascent of The Wild Thing on the northeast face of Mt. Chephren back in the Canadian Rockies. It was one of the finest alpine climbs of my life. Suddenly Pete leveled his brown eyes on mine and then slapped me with an insult: "I don't know why Ward and I even took you along." Tension had been building between us since we'd descended from the mountain, and I didn't know what to say.

"Fuck, man!" I burst out. "I don't know what I've done to piss you off, but if there's something that I'm doing that I can change, please let me know."

Pete's stare was glacial. "Humpff," he grunted, and then got up and walked out.

"Fuck," Troy said. "I think that guy has joined the Brits. I'm going to talk to him."

Troy caught Pete heading up to the Brits' base camp.

"PA," he said, "I don't know what the fuck your problem with Bubba is, but you've got to lay off of him." Twenty-four years would pass before I talked to Pete about what had happened on K2. We should have done better with that. Bottom line, we simply weren't on the same page with how much we were willing to risk to get up the Magic Line. Specifically, I was willing to go for it again even after Troy had had such a hard time with the altitude. Pete had shared a tent with Troy at the Negrotto Col and seen him throw up everything, even hot chocolate. He'd also listened to Troy's Cheyne-Stokes breathing through the night. Pete feared that if we went for it, Troy might have gotten deathly ill, and we wouldn't have been able to get him down. The promise he'd made to Troy's mother to bring her son home safely weighed on him. I'd pushed to start our last attempt as soon as the storm had ended, even while Pete quoted a letter he held in his hand from "Uncle" Timmy Auger, a mentor to the three of us and the head of public safety for Banff National Park at the time. Timmy was also a mountain guide and highly accomplished climber, one of the few Canadians mentioned in Warren Harding's classic book, *Downward Bound: A Mad! Guide to Rock Climbing*.

"Timmy's urging us to practice a bit of patience and to let the storm snow settle," Pete said. We should have talked about it all back then, but Pete and I could both be assholes, and we seemed willing to sweep it under the rug.

Pete had another kind of experience while were out there. On one of his walks up the glacier he discovered human remains melting out of the glacier 1,200 feet above The Strip. We soon deduced from the remnants of clothing swaddling the bones—a red-plaid lumberjack shirt, an Eddie Bauer down jacket—that it was likely Art Gilkey, a member of the Third American Karakoram Expedition. On August 7, 1953, Art collapsed in front of a tent while considering a summit attempt with seven of his team members. Doctor Charles Houston diagnosed thrombophlebitis—a blood clot in the leg. The team aborted their summit attempt and started

Julie-Ann Clyma, Roger Payne, and Victor Saunders, members of the British expedition, inspect the likely remains of Art Gilkey, lost on K2 in 1953. Roger made sure that the remains were boxed up and shipped back to the UK. Peter Arbic

to organize a descent for Gilkey. Bad weather set in and held them at bay until August 10, by which time Gilkey was displaying symptoms of pulmonary edema. While lowering Gilkey in an improvised stretcher, the team, except for the last man—Peter Schoening—started to slide down the mountainside out of control. Schoening was able to arrest the group's slide with his ice-ax. This superhuman feat has since been called, simply, "The Belay on K2." Continuing down, the team reached their Camp VII. Gilkey was anchored to the slope while the camp was restored. Some muffled cries were heard from Gilkey, but when the team returned, Gilkey had slid away and was lost.

Roger Payne showed up and took charge, as was his character. "We need to collect the remains, box them up, and take them back to Britain for analysis. If it is indeed Art Gilkey, which I think it has to be, his family will have to decide how to put his remains to rest," Roger said. Who could argue with the right thing to do? Later that year, Bob Bates, a member of the 1953 expedition, flew to the UK and affirmed that it was indeed Art. Bob still had that same jacket they had all gotten for their trip in 1953.

AUGUST 13: The weather cleared later in the day, but committing to climbing almost seemed an inconvenience...it would interrupt cappuccino with the Dutch Internationals at 9, midday tea with the Brits, and another afternoon of passion and languor with Caroline. Be that as it may, the three of us shot up to Camp II on the Abruzzi, 23,310 feet, the next day. Our twelve-hour window of weather slammed shut, the wind howled again, and snow amassed. Troy and I descended. Pete, with the Brits, battled on to Camp III, where six feet of snow had buried their snow cave and collapsed its roof.

AUGUST 20: "I was able to get my pack, Bubba, but yours was at the other end of a wind slab that I just didn't want to risk crossing," Pete said when he descended with the Brits.

"Fair enough, man, fair enough."

The Brits walked away from K2 the next day. I kissed and hugged Caroline, hoping to see her again in Rawalpindi.

AUGUST 22: The wind shifted to blow out of China. The sky cleared, and K2 looked beautiful. I still wanted to climb it.

"I'm done, man," Troy stated. "I'm not doing well with the altitude. I'm just here to support you guys now. I'm not going back up there."

"I'm still exhausted," Pete said. "I'd like to think that I'm Superman, but I'm not. I won't be ready to go back up for at least three days."

"Our porters are coming in five days. That won't leave us enough time. I still want to get up this thing—I'll go by myself," I said.

The next morning, I started toward the Abruzzi. After I left, Imran said to Troy, "You can't let this happen. He can't go by himself—it is not right."

Troy caught me up and said, "Bubba, we came here to climb K2, and the three of us failed. Our team failed. I don't want you to go back up there by yourself, buddy—it just isn't right."

His sea-blue eyes did not waver.

"Okay, man, let's head back to Base Camp and get ready to go home."

"Ya, buddy, let's go home."

AUGUST 26: Our porters showed up. We'd been living on The Strip for sixty-eight days. Storms had worn us down. Death had made us weep, forced the three of us to evaluate the worth of climbing K2 against the value of life. That evaluation would change over the decades. The people of The Strip had buoyed us up, become our community, but time eroded us. So many days of waking to snow pelting the skin of my tent, to the roar of the wind raking K2's mutinous ridges, slowly chiseling off pieces of the mountain. Funny to be your own prisoner in a cell with an open door.

SEPTEMBER 10: We landed in Calgary. We'd been gone for 100 days. Two days later, I was back into a full guiding schedule.

Everest: Kangshung Face by Stephen Venables

CHAPTER 13 — HOLDING ON

THE KANGSHUNG FACE

I sign a post card to the Vice President of the United States
Snow pelts my tent softly
Catherine sits in her tent twenty feet away
I think that all that really matters
is my will to conduct a summit day
—all the cold days—
properly
To not lose any fingers or toes
and have enough strength to climb to the summit
without an O_2 *bottle*
Strength to write
Strength to cook
Discipline to survive the Arctic cold
Now I'll read until lunch.
—"Summit Day and All the Days," *April 8, 1994, base camp*

OCTOBER 6, 1993: "The Kangshung. Isn't that an expensive place to go?" I asked.

"Yes, but Vaseline is kicking in $250,000 US. That will give us a good budget." David Breashears was calling to invite me to join an expedition to the Kangshung Face of Mt. Everest.

"Vaseline?"

limbing some steep ice on the Kangshung Face, ith barbed wire and a broken heart that I'd rawn on my helmet. It was three years after ıy first divorce. Steve Swenson

"It'll be Steve Swenson, Alex Lowe, and Sandy Hill Pittman—Alex is on contract to guide Sandy—and there will be four climbing Sherpas, a cook and kitchen boy, and a great young gal, Catherine, who I've been working with at WGBH. (David had been finishing his Frontline documentary *Red Flag Over Tibet*, at that PBS station in Boston.)

"She will be our base camp manager, but I really need her along to help me log video. Sandy is married, and Catherine is engaged...so, hands off!"

"Who, me?"

"Yes, you, my friend. No hanky-panky."

"I'm sure I can keep my hands to myself. Especially given the Vaseline."

"We'll be producing a series of shorts for the *Today Show*, 'Dispatches from Everest.' Sandy Hill Pittman will be climbing with us and host the dispatches. She's married to Bob Pittman, the guy who started MTV. Sandy is a serious mountaineer and was before she met Bob. She's trying to climb the Seven Summits. We'll be on the route that Steve Venables put up in 1988. I know it isn't alpine style. All that aside, I see this as your chance to get up Everest, man. It would be great for your career."

That climb had been established by Stephen Venables, Ed Webster, Robert Anderson, and Paul Teare. I bought a copy of Venables's *Everest: Kangshung Face*. He made the Kangshung sound totally reasonable. I shelved my alpine ideals and said yes to David.

"'Mr. Blanchard's last expedition to China caused much negative coverage in the Canadian press. We do not feel that Mr. Blanchard will be content climbing in China at this time.' That's what the letter says." Back on the phone with David, I read the missive from the Chinese consulate in Vancouver. "They're still pissed about the interview I did with Jan Wong in Beijing in 1988"—the one in which I'd voiced my frustrations with the Chinese Mountaineering Association.

"Don't worry—I'll get a letter of invitation for you from the Tibetan Mountaineering Association, and you can pick up your visa in Kathmandu. The Chinese consulates and embassy in Canada will be none the wiser."

MARCH 18, 1994: The heat outside the Tribhuvan International Airport in Kathmandu was oppressive. I'd been in Kath for one week. I'd gotten very drunk barhopping in the Thamel district the night before. I was dehydrated, drained, deracinated.

"I bought you all a bunch of bottled water, but I drank it sitting on the curb, waiting for you to arrive. I'm so hungover. Sorry," I said to my bright-eyed teammates, David, Sandy, Catherine, Alex, and Steve. They all did a double take, save for Catherine, who grinned slyly.

Along with Wongchhu Sherpa, our sirdar and trekking agent; Kaji, Phinjo, and Tenzing, our climbing Sherpas; Chyangba Sherpa, our cook (who'd been my cook in Nepal in 1990); and Nowang, our base camp Sherpa, we were the Vaseline Research Everest Expedition '94.

Vaseline Research had provided hundreds of logo patches in a half dozen different sizes to unmistakably brand our expedition. Sandy graciously handed me a pair of tighty whitey men's briefs with a large Vaseline Research patch sewn on the crotch! Lots of laughter, especially when I pulled the underwear onto my head.

Timberland was our official clothing sponsor. David had Wild Things of North Conway, New Hampshire, sew us up one-piece climbing suits that were then labeled Timberland. These onesies had been designed by John Bouchard, one of the best American alpinists of all time. Thirty years later, Steve and I still climb in them.

On paper, I was second in command; in reality, the prospect of telling Alex or Steve what to do felt pretentious and dumb. We called Alex "The Fiend" because of his Galahadlike abilities and cardio capacity to rival the cross-country skier Bjørn Dæhlie's. Steve had climbed K2 without supplemental oxygen and made the second ascent of the north face of Mt. Alberta.

In Kathmandu, I worked with the Sherpas for seven days to make sure David's stash of tents were all in good repair, the mountain stoves ran like clocks, all of our food had been bought, etc.

Gerry Kent, my client and friend, was in the third of five years that he; his wife, Lorna; and their five children, then ages six to fourteen, were spending with the United Mission to Nepal. Gerry and Lorna had made the move to Kathmandu from Cranbrook, BC, after I'd guided him in the Khumbu in the spring of 1991. Our expedition had another week to spend in the city; the Kents had us over to celebrate my birthday. I would be turning thirty-five a week later.

"We call it the Canadian gravity-filtration system," Gerry said, smiling. He was showing Steve, an engineer who specialized in wastewater-management systems, the pail they poured water into. It sat on the highest shelf of a closet. Clear tubing led to a filter—the same type that I had in my small hand pump—two shelves down. Then more tubing led from the filter to a catchment container on the floor.

"You just keep the top pail full of Kathmandu's finest...that isn't actually all that fine...and let gravity do the work!"

"How do you handle sewage?" Steve asked.

"Water is in short supply," Gerry said, "We have a saying, 'If it's brown, flush it down. If it's yellow, let it mellow.'"

"That would be a good saying for Seattle to adopt," Steve stated.

Later that evening, Gerry's youngest, Rachel, sat on her dad's lap and wrapped her thin arms around his thick, powerful neck. Paternal love calmed Gerry's whole being; it looked so blessed to me. The next day Steve, Alex, and I picked up Gerry and two of his sons—Stephen and Ian—plus Stephen's friend Jon, to take them climbing.

MARCH 23: Balaju is a small cliff located on the edge of Kathmandu at the foot of the Nagarjun Forest Reserve. There were several dozen rock climbs up to eighty feet. The lot of us gleefully pulled onto the stone, enjoying the fundamental fun of rock climbing. Gerry had told Ian, the youngest, that we'd be climbing too hard for him. Ian sat anxiously on a rock and watched the older boys crank with some of the best mountain climbers in the world. Alex walked over to Ian.

"Do you want to climb?"

"Sure!"

"Which route?"

"That one!" Ian pointed to an easier route, one with a magnificent jug handhold halfway up. Alex checked Ian's belay setup and then floated up the route. He was the best all-around climber in North America at the time, probably in the world. Alex belayed Ian from the top, and when the young guy grabbed the jug, he turned to all of us and beamed a thousand-watt smile.

"The Fiend": Alex Lowe cranking off twenty pull-ups grasping the edge of a house en route the Kangshung. Barry Blanchard

"Way to go, Ian!" Alex bellowed. "You got this, partner!"

Later, Alex, Steve, and I ran up 2,500 feet to the Jamacho Gumba, a small monastery atop the Nagarjun Forest. Heat and sweat. The T-shirt that Raine had painted religious iconography on for me was damn near translucent when I finally caught up to Alex and Steve on top. Steve was a serious runner, and Alex pretty much needed to be in constant motion for all his waking hours.

"C'mon, let's get a pyramid going," Alex said. He grabbed an iron bar above his head and did five pull-ups. Steve and I followed suit in sets of five, ten, fifteen. We both dropped out before twenty. Alex kept going to thirty. "I know, I know," he panted. "I'm a freak."

Over dinner at the Tibet Guest House, Catherine told us about her day. "They're rascals and scallywags," she exclaimed. We'd all had responsibilities for our final four days in Kathmandu. Hers had been to get three tailors who sat at sewing machines on the floor of their shop to stitch logos onto our clothing and kit. "The two men start drinking at

noon, and I have to be on them like a fat kid on Smarties to keep them going. They're sussed by midafternoon, and it's mostly the adolescent apprentice who does the work."

David had been right. Catherine had spunk. She seemed to be warming to me.

MARCH 24: We drove from Kathmandu and walked over the Sino-Nepal Friendship Bridge with the frothy clay-colored Bhote Koshi River charging below. Our stuff was loaded into Chinese trucks and Land Cruisers in Zhangmu, China's border town and our bed for the night.

Soon Alex found the outer roofbeam of a house, grabbed it, and started knocking off pull-ups, much to the amazement of our cook, Chyangba, and a young Tibetan mother and her two daughters. A couple sets of thirty. "I'm a freak," he reminded us.

"No man, you're a fiend," I said. "You are THE Fiend!"

Catherine and I walked the streets of Zhangmu after dinner, her hand in mine and darkness falling as attraction rose. "I want to kiss you," she urged, turning to face me and pressing up against me.

"No, we can't do this in public. This is China."

"What do you mean?"

"Big Brother is watching, and he has little sense of humor—even less so of romance."

"Oh, come on..."

And as if on cue, a young Chinese man walked by and cautioned us with a shake of his head, "No, no. This is not safe."

We retreated to our hotel, where I told Catherine that my feelings for her were more affectionate than sexual. She went off to bed.

MARCH 25: Mark Twight and I had been in Xêgar, high on the Tibetan Plateau, 14,200 feet above sea level, six and a half years earlier. Now, here I was again, six years later with a new team. At dinner that night in our hotel, I did a double take on spotting a spectacled, combed-over, Chinese Don Rickles–looking guy; on seeing me, his jaw dropped, too. Then, a big smile cracked his face, and he was up and coming over.

"Mr. Zhang!" I blurted, stumbling up from my chair to shake my old liaison officer's hand. Through our interpreter, the young and earnest

Mr. Tang, Mr. Zhang apologized for the "service" he'd provided as LO to my 1988 expedition.

"He says," Mr. Tang started, "that it had been his first time being a liaison officer and he didn't know the job. He has been a liaison officer every season since then and now provides excellent services."

"Please tell Mr. Zhang that I am glad to hear that and that it is good to see him."

Mr. Tang introduced Mr. Zhang to our present LO, Mr. Jolla. The three of them chatted away in Mandarin, occasionally looking my way and nodding and smiling, which told me that Mr. Zhang was sharing the good and saving the bad for a private session later, probably over cigarettes.

"Wow!" I exclaimed to my teammates after Mr. Zhang had walked away. "I just got an apology from a CMA representative. Will miracles never cease?" But the hotel was still cold and there were still turd stalagmites growing in the toilets. Some things hadn't changed.

Later in the night, there was a soft tapping on my door. "I'm f-in freezing!" Catherine explained. "Can I sleep with you?" Very soon after, my feelings for her changed.

MARCH 26: We drove to Kharta, 12,100 feet above sea level. My body loved the drop in altitude. The air felt thicker; moss, shrubs, and bracken were uncasing from the winter snows. Curious Tibetans watched, enraptured, as we unpacked the three transport trucks that held our gear. I loved being around Tibetans again, had fun joking with the teenagers who looked, to me, so much like the Tusken Raiders in *Star Wars* but without the wrapped faces. Like the Raiders, you couldn't turn your back on them. And that's exactly what Sandy did that night.

"A Nikon camera and the $10,000 US that she always travels with," Alex told us the next morning.

"Ten-fucking-thousand US dollars?" I blurted.

"Yes, she always travels with a stack of a hundred hundreds. She left the money and the camera in the vestibule of her tent. Someone reached in and grabbed them."

"Wow," Steve commented. "That could set one of these Tibetans up for life."

"Just another day of guiding Mrs. Pittman," Alex said with a grin.

MARCH 27: Loads were weighed and numbered; porters and yaks hired; 150 burdens allotted. David somehow convinced Mr. Jolla and Mr. Tang to stay behind in Kharta, at the end of the road, which was sad, as Mr. Tang was a genuinely nice and honest man who was eager to be involved. He also had a passion for English literature, and I had enjoyed talking to him about Hemingway.

MARCH 28: We began an enchanting trek through the Tibetan highlands, looking to cross the Langma La, a 17,684-foot-high pass leading to the Kama Chu, the river that we'd follow to its source—the Kangshung Glacier and the east face of Mt. Everest. This shortcut would make our trek one week rather than two; it also meant we wouldn't experience the Kama Valley and its giant juniper trees and rhododendrons, nor would we come to know that the Kama Valley is one of the most sacred places in Tibet, a *beyul*.

MARCH 29: My thirty-fifth birthday. Chyangba baked me a birthday cake! Catherine and I snuck away to pursue our romance. We thought that we'd gotten away with something until we walked back into camp to our Tibetan porters, men and women, holding their hands over their mouths and giggling at us.

APRIL 2: We camped in a meadow beside the Kangshung Glacier. The burlap-colored moss underfoot was as thick and robust as a woven welcome mat. The American Expeditions to the Kangshung had camped there in 1981 and 1983. In 1981, the legendary Austrian climber and filmmaker Kurt Diemberger had handed David Breashears the camera, saying, "I've climbed Everest before. Why don't you give it a go?" David's career as a filmmaker started then and there.

To the south, across the glacier, the north ridge of Pethangtse was beautiful perfection: bronze granite laced with pearl-white snow and aquamarine ice rising in knife-edged steps to a symmetrical alpine horn. I immediately wanted to climb it and then continue to the glowing wall of Chomo Lönzo, 25,600 feet. I knew from my first jaw-dropping glance that the three peaks and faces on the Tibetan side of Chomo

The flattened remains of our base camp after the wind blast from a very large avalanche roared through, wreaking havoc.
Barry Blanchard

Lönzo are some of the greatest alpine challenges on Earth. I longed to be in that beauty, even knowing the price it would demand and the mortal fear that a storm could bring. Up-valley, the white slopes of the Kangshung draped a pyramid from Everest's south summit, with two massive mastodon trunks of crevasse- and serac-wrinkled glacier hanging low, then disappearing over terra-cotta-striped buttresses of steep black rock.

Our route lay up the left-hand trunk. North of the right-hand trunk, the Trinity Gullies gouged three deep, dark open wounds in Everest's albino flesh.

"I want to place our base camp on the Kangshung Glacier," David had said before we left. "It'll save us days and untold tens of thousands of calories not having to walk back and forth miles over that rubbly glacier."

"Sounds good."

"I think we'll be far enough out from the face to be safe from avalanches."

"You've been there, man. I believe you."

APRIL 3: We walked onto the Kangshung Glacier. Several miles up, we chose our base camp site, about a mile and a half from the face on top of the Kangshung Glacier. Our loads were piled, and arrangements made to tip our porters. We paid their wages to the Tibet Mountaineering Association; some smaller portion of that made it to the porters. Alex, Steve, and I stood guard over our gear while David and Wong Chu, our sirdar, doled out monies. Something wasn't right in the eyes of some of our hundred-plus porters. A mosh pit of shoving and escalating curses broke out.

"David, David!" Alex yelled, pointing at the growing mob. "Can you do something David?" I could feel my ire rising.

A couple men were now wrestling, with others who supported one or the other man coming in to push and grab like a hockey brawl. I lost it and strode down and grabbed both combatants by their shoulders and ripped them apart.

"That is A-FUCKING-nough!" I bellowed. Both sides spun in shock at the rage of the sahib. "Any of you fuckers want some of this, I'm right fucking here! Right fucking now!" I screamed, hunched in a fighting stance and pivoting to face all. Then Kaji, a silverback of a Sherpa, ran in holding a gleaming kukuri overhead in one hand and an ice-ax in the other, looking like an angry god. For whatever reason, it worked. The pugilistic porters turned and chilled and walked away.

APRIL 4: We set up our base camp: a kitchen tent and a dining tent complete with tables and chairs. It felt like being on trek in Nepal. Sandy and David set up the satellite phone so that Sandy could dictate articles for *People* magazine to her secretary back in the States. Dean & DeLuca, the upscale grocers from NYC, had sent twenty loads of exotic foods. Sandy supervised Chyangba's preparation of pork knuckles that night; soon after, the Sherpas started calling pork "Sandy meat."

"I like trying to see how far I can push my Nikes," Alex said, smiling. He, Steve, David, Sandy, and I had all carried to a cache at the base of the Kangshung Face. Alex stood in foot-deep snow in his trainers, smiling. The rest of us wore plastic mountaineering boots bound tight in gaiters...and we had dry feet. Our Sherpas would not go onto the mountain until after the puja ceremony, which was scheduled for the next day.

"I believe in all of this," Alex said as we listened to the prayers Tenzing was reading from cloth and woodblock bound scripts. *Khatas*, ceremonial white-silk scarves, hung around our necks. They had been blessed by a lama. On cue from Tenzing, we had thrown handfuls of *tsampa* (roasted barley flour) onto the prayer-flag-strewn stone altar the Sherpas had constructed.

"I keep all my khatas and the knotted red strings that the lamas have blessed at home in Bozeman," Alex added. I'd brought sweetgrass,

Alex Lowe: "I'd rather be down here wishing I was up there than up there wishing I was down here." Barry Blanchard the sacred incense of the West, that my friend Shell had given me, asking that it be burned with the juniper during the puja.

APRIL 5, 3 A.M.: I got dressed inside my tent at Base Camp. I crawled out and looked at my thermometer: 30°F. My altimeter told me I was at 17,815 feet. The summit of Everest was 11,214 feet above me. Alex and I marched away by headlamp.

"Oh well, this is *Everesting*," he said, when we got to the first slabs of steeper rock. He wrapped his hands around the sun-bleached fixed ropes left in place by a Chilean expedition two years before and manhandled his way up.

It snowed all the next day.

APRIL 14: Steve and I faced the steepest passage thus far: an overhanging wall of pale-green serac ice split by a black crack one foot wide. I was determined not to use the Chilean fixed rope. I combined ice climbing and offwidthing skills to get up what Steve labeled "the fissure Blanchard," because I got my crampon stuck in the crack at one point.

It felt good to crank and climb hard, get my pulse hammering and push toward the edge of a fall. That intensity is some of what I've always loved about alpinism; it felt fulfilling to have Steve cheering me on. Then I stepped over the edge of control. Reaching high, I started a long, brand-spanking-new, stainless-steel-coated ice screw; right from the first turn, it whined with resistance against the dense glacial ice. I slotted my ice-ax pick into the screw's eye and reefed, adding leverage. The screw shrieked like a banshee; to my amazement, and fearful concern, the tube bent several degrees. If I fell, I'd go twenty-five feet before hitting snow-covered rock. The twisting got harder, but the screw gave one last scream and, somehow, set secure against the ice. I clipped my weight into it. Free climbing became aid climbing.

Steve and I fixed rope to the site of our first camp that day, 20,000 feet. The steepest climbing was now below us. The Kangshung lay back as a wide glacial ramp above, sliced through with crevasses and seracs. We were on the mastodon's trunk. But then we had to rappel down and expose ourselves to the gun barrel of Big Al—a multistory-building-high serac that calved thousands of tons of blue ice on a regular basis. I'd read about Big Al in Stephen Venables's book. The higher I got on the Kangshung, the more I began to think that he had written his book just to justify the crazy risks he and his team had taken!

We stood at the elbow of our route, the most exposed place to be, when the air exploded with the telltale booming of a serac collapse. Massive slabs of blue ice were falling into the billowing cloud of their footings, which were already being pulverized. The chaos looked like a building being demolished with explosives.

"Avalanche! Avalanche! Avalanche!" I screamed. But there was no place to go, nowhere to hide. Steve and I grabbed our anchor lines and hung like marionettes as the air reverberated thunder and the roiling, billowing white mass charged toward us. Car-sized chunks of solid blue ice bounded from the cloud and exploded high on the flanks of Big Al's gully, the gully that we were tethered to!

Steve calmly looked and then leaned his shoulder in quietly, believing in something. And then we got smacked by the wind blast and were plastered cello-string-tight to our lanyards as chunks of snow and fragments of ice pummeled us from inside a flow that felt like a massive sandblaster. It rumbled off and diminished to the hiss and clatter of the trailing pieces, and then all was quiet.

"Holy fuck! Are you okay?" I asked, shaking off the white plaster.

"Ya, ya. I'm okay. How about you?"

"I think I'm good, but that was fucking terrifying. Did you see the chunks of blue ice shooting out of it?"

"I did," said Steve.

"Man, I thought that was it. I thought we were going to be hit."

"Most of the flow passed below us. I think we're okay here."

"Unless it goes bigger."

"I'm hoping it can't do that."

"I'm beginning to not like this fucking place," I concluded.

We got snow each week, sometimes as much as a foot overnight. On those events, we'd let Everest sit for a day or two. It was wonderful to spend downtime with Catherine.

APRIL 24: We established a high point of 23,000 feet. Alex, Steve, and I all came off the mountain, while David and Sandy went up.

"That was a hard day, Esteeb," Alex said. "We should eat for an hour and a half."

"You're right," Steve replied. I loved the way they judged their days by how long they should eat. A really hard day would demand two hours of eating! Alex and Steve had been on numerous expeditions together, and Alex confided to me that he wouldn't go to the Himalaya without his "Esteeb," as the Sherpas pronounced his name.

APRIL 25: The field gun went off and slapped me awake with the first light of dawn. I knew immediately that it was more than the usual crash-and-roar of the avalanches raining down from the Kangshung/Lhotse horseshoe. The roar grew. I snapped upright, punching my arms from the sarcophagus of my sleeping bag.

I held my breath for three beats of my heart. Then the hurricane hit. The air exploded and my tent flattened me violently, like plastic blister-wrapped onto meat. I screamed and pounded my forearms into the surge. Opening my hands, I saw the tent fabric being sluiced through my fingers like seawater. Something hard bent my left trigger finger back. The ongoing roar swallowed my scream. I laid my elbows into the torrent and took more hits from the harder chunks. The big chunks were coming; we'd be buried. Then the onslaught diminished, the tent wall relaxed, and it all hissed away.

I ripped at the zipper of my limp, broken tent.

"Catherine! Catherine! Are you okay? Catherine!"

"Yes, yes. I think so." I scrambled to her tent. Broken tent poles, everything scattered, pulverized snow as fine as ash blanketing everything. I yarded the tent zipper open. She crawled out, crying. We wrapped our arms around each other and held on.

The Sherpas were up and staggering around. From down the glacier, Steve was walking toward us.

"Steve, are you okay?" I shouted.

"Yes, I'm okay. I got rolled down the glacier inside my tent! It was like being in the Maytag, with all my books and ghetto blaster bouncing around me."

Base Camp was flattened. Our kitchen and dining tents were gone. Chyangba had taken a flying ketchup bottle, or so he claimed, to the

I'm on the left with Steve, Sandy, Catherine, and Alex, eating everything in sight in the cook tent. Yum. David Breashears head. He had a blue egg growing four fingers above his right eye, but otherwise his brain was still on the job.

The highest serac in the world sits just below the summit of Mt. Everest on the Kangshung Face. I believe ice collapsing from it had caused the avalanche, which had run three linear miles down the Kangshung, gathering snowmass, rock, and ice, and accelerating through the Trinity Gullies before hammering onto the glacier and inundating us with a blast of air traveling 100-plus mph. The avalanche was exceptionally massive. By my guess, one of the largest known to man: size 5, 110,000 tons, large enough to destroy a village.

The glacier's southern flank, which had been brown and black the day before, was now plastered white for five miles. Most of our supplies had been blown within a mile. Nowang found one of our plastic washbasins three miles away.

We told David about the avalanche on our morning radio call. He, Sandy, and the climbing Sherpas descended. We spent the rest of the day, and the following several, moving our base camp back to the moss meadow of David's 1981 trip.

APRIL 26: Catherine and I moved into a spacious Himalayan Hotel tent. Our relationship was no longer clandestine, which evoked some judgment from Alex, who had strict views on monogamy. But he was

also a man of the world and accepted the fact that Catherine (with her fiancé back home none the wiser) and I were making tentative plans for a future together. He was soon back to joking with her like a big brother and accommodating her requests that he pull his long johns up to his nipple line and assume his comedic role of "Captain Pee-Pee Whacker."

Built like a linebacker, Kaji Sherpa was one of the biggest and strongest Sherpas I'd known. As we set about relocating our base camp, he was carefully walking toward me, coming down-glacier as I headed back up, on plates of shattered rock that wobbled atop the glacier like a fallen slate roof. His forehead was beaded with sweat below his taut tumpline. He was carrying a double load—200 pounds!—across the treacherous footing. Any stumble or misjudgment would hold consequence. He'd pick the load up, walk through the minefield of mishap for several hundred feet, put the load down and rest for a minute or two, and then pick it back up. It was the most incredible combination of strength, balance, and calculated walking that I'd ever seen. No Westerner, not even Alex, could do what I was witnessing.

"Kaji, you're an animal," I said when we met.

"Oh no!" he beamed, smacking his lips, "Me lazy boy! Make one carry, not two." I bowed to the better man.

MAY 4: Alex hadn't even attempted sleep; he'd stayed up all night, noisily flapping through the pages of *Time* magazine, his headlamp on, eyes flared and darting, jaw jutted and set. I knew the look: I'd seen it in Mark Twight, Kevin Doyle, and myself. We all had hungry jackals inside us. Alex was practiced at hiding his, but it was there, and it hadn't been getting enough to eat. Snow had continued to fall and to be scoured from the south and north sides of Everest's broad pyramid. The westerlies either sublimated it over a mile-long plume or dumped it onto the Kangshung. As we climbed, Alex thrashed a trough through waist-deep powder. I felt his fear like static electricity on the rope I held for him.

We were at 25,000 feet, fixing rope toward the South Col, where we hoped to place our third camp. Even that depth of snow could be stable, yet intuitively I didn't trust it. I expected to see the lightning crack of a slab shoot out from under Alex; it would be a final scythe strike from the Reaper. We were totally exposed. Alex reached the end of the slope, and then he cracked.

"Fuck! Fuck! Fuck! I just did something that I promised my wife I wouldn't do!" Kaji and I climbed up to him.

"I'll try for a bit," I said.

"There's just too much snow."

I plowed into it and then hesitated like I was choking with the excavation of each new step. Snow is the hardest face of the mountain to know and to judge. Rock and ice are relatively solid, but within the wedding-cake whiteness of snow, layers of death can all too easily hide. I couldn't—wouldn't—take another step. I descended to Alex and Kaji.

"It's just too fucking dangerous."

"I'll get on the radio to David," Alex replied.

Kaji did a double take. "No, we can go. Kaji will go." And he plowed into my track, pushing into the virgin snow with powerful thrusts of his knees and sweeping strokes from his arms.

"No, Kaji, no. It is too much risk avalanche," I said in pidgin English. "Heavy danger coming. We must go down." The snow needed time to settle. Alex, meanwhile, wanted to be home with his family in Bozeman, Montana. David had been feeling increasingly nervous about the route ever since he and I had remotely triggered a two-foot-deep slab avalanche while descending from our first carry to Camp II. Black had sliced through white; it had all fractured into a checkerboard, and then churned into a roaring chaos that charged away. We stood breathless until I screamed, "Rotten fucking cocksucker!"

We got him on the radio. "If the two professional mountain guides on our expedition judge it to be too dangerous, I am calling our attempt off. We are going to retreat and clean our equipment from the mountain," David said from Camp I. Steve was in Base Camp and not included in the call. He was outraged that he hadn't been involved in a team decision. Back at Camp I, we had a radio conference. David offered to support Steve and me in a two-man alpine-style attempt, but knowing the amount of snow sitting up there, Steve and I concluded that we'd need Alex. Alex felt that he couldn't abandon Sandy, even after she released him of his obligation to guide her on the Kangshung.

Meanwhile, Chyangba told us in his giddy, happy voice that two thieves from Kharta had come in the night. Nawang, an ex-Gurkha, had spent most of the day tracking them, and marched them back to Base Camp at the point of his gleaming Gurkha-issue kukuri. Our Sherpas tied them up and suggested, over the radio, that they rub hot chilis on their penises as punishment, an act that David kiboshed in favor of just letting them go. The Sherpas reveled in the telling, laughing and laughing. David worried about us all getting killed back down in Kharta.

MAY 9: We held a team meeting. Alex and Sandy wanted to travel to the north side of Everest, to the Rongbuk, and join an American expedition run by Steve's longtime friend Eric Simonson. Steve hesitated to abandon our expedition, but had heard me assure David that, as deputy leader, I wouldn't be quitting our expedition, an act of loyalty that I knew David appreciated. Sandy, Alex, and Steve thus left for the Rongbuk, while David, Catherine, and the Sherpas and I stayed to strip our gear off the Kangshung.

Seventy loads carried by seventy Tibetans with names like Chong Dorje, Tungdu, Tsonang, Tsering, all hailing from a dozen villages: Moyan, Cho Dung, Tashi Gong... We walked back through Rakba, Lhatse. In Kharta, we met Mr. Zhang once again and learned that the Tibetans had stolen his clothes. We loaded into a couple of trucks and several Land Cruisers and were back in Kathmandu after a few long days on the road. A few days later, Alex and Sandy were back, too.

"Sandy pretty much pissed off Eric Simonson from the get-go," Alex told me. "She came on as the rich American, and that rubbed Eric the wrong way. We went out to Lhasa and got our own permit. By the time we got back into the Rongbuk, we were out of time with the season and out of goodwill with Simonson. And now here we are."

Sandy had checked herself and Alex into the Yak and Yeti, one of Kathmandu's few five-star hotels. On our last night in town, she hosted a party for our team. It was extravagant, with food and drink and the traditional Tibetan ceremonial tent she'd bought in Lhasa pitched on the lawn. Alex was dressed in a white Tibetan *toethung shirt*, with its offset chest flap buttoned up with knots, billowing orange-silk pants, a broad leather belt, and woven sandals. It was obvious that Sandy had taken him shopping and encouraged him to go for a princely look, but to me he looked like one of Sinbad's crew. Sandy floated around in raw, sheer silk. The gossamer hint of her body gave all the men—Eastern, and Western—pause.

"I have never been drunk before!" Madhav Sharma, the office manager of Wongchhu's fledgling company, Peak Promotions, gushed. Alex picked him up from behind and dumped him, fully dressed, into the pool! It was obvious that Madhav had never learned to swim. Alex immediately followed him in and thrust him back up onto the tiles, where he flopped around wide-eyed like a landed fish, then burst out laughing. It was pretty damned funny.

Continuing a conversation we'd been having, Catherine turned to me and said, "Okay, I'm going to break up with my fiancé then fly up to the Rockies to live with you," And then she kissed me deeply.

"I'll find us somewhere to live."

MAY 29: David left a message on my machine: "Steve climbed to the summit of Everest, solo, via the North Ridge on May 25. He is back in Base Camp and well. He got a picture of our Vaseline Research flag on the top. It is a good conclusion, and I consider it a summit for our expedition."

JULY 2: Catherine and I stood before Judge Allard in Calgary with my childhood best friend, Jonathan, and my high-school-buddy-cum-lawyer, Richard, as witnesses. Judge Allard said, "I guarantee my marriages." It was what I wanted. I was in love, and marrying Catherine would allow her to stay in Canada. She had hesitated, and then said yes, all things considered.

"The Gift": Ian Tyson

The Letter of Marque by Patrick O'Brian
This House of Sky by Ivan Doig

CHAPTER 14 — LETTING GO

CURTAIN CALLS

Curtain Call is a magnificent 400-foot-high waterfall that forms on the basalt cliffs of Tangle Ridge at the Columbia Icefield in the Canadian Rockies. On a cold late-February morning in 1985, Guy Lacelle, James Blench, and I crunched about on crispy snow that had been scraped onto the shoulder of the Banff/Jasper Highway. Above us, Curtain Call rose as a broad blue column that ended at a halfway ledge. Above the ledge, the second pitch etched a slender pillar. I imagined a Saxon Cross: the upper pillar a line of square-cut sapphires laid into the grip of a sword. The ledge was the cross-guard, and the wider first pitch the blue blade.

"Are you ready, Barry?" Guy's Québécois accent came through on my name, which he pronounced "Bah-ree." "It looks like we have got some ice to climb." His blue eyes were glittering and giddy.

I traversed away from our first anchor with my mind already engaged. I was only twenty-five years old, still building my climbing repertoire, and I needed the ice to help me prepare for difficult alpinism. I looked up and locked into the first placements of my Stubai tools. A groove shot up the middle of the blue blade, a feature medieval knights would have called the "blood gutter." Testosterone plumed up inside of me, and then Guy, ever the clown, said, "James, look at me, I'm belaying Bah-ree Blanchard! THE Bah-ree Blanchard!" I relaxed, smiled, and climbed on.

It was a difficult pitch. It always seemed difficult back then, when Curtain Call would get one or two ascents a year, some years. As I stood

m leading on Oh Le Tabernac, Mt. Wilson,
anff National Park, 1992. Kevin Doyle

at the anchor belaying up Guy and James, I thought about Jeff Lowe and Mike Weis making the first ascent back in 1979. The tools and screws of the day would have added a grade of seriousness to the climb, and so much more so to the mind. Ice equipment continues to evolve. Curtain Call often sees two ascents a day now.

APRIL 1, 1995: *I set out with the best ice climber in the world. I sometimes think that Guy Lacelle came into my life to keep my feet on the ground. He never let me forget that I am no more than what I am, and he did that with his eyes. Guy had beautiful blue eyes.*

Despite our being uncomfortable and unhappy for much of the day, Riptide—on Mt. Patterson on the Icefields Parkway—was as big and blue as ever. It took screws from ground zero, but wave upon wave of wind and snow lashed us. The wall was alive with spindrift, and my hands were clammy, or wet, all day long. It was a fight to scrape them back into clinging gloves every time I took them out, and minute grains of snow found their way into everything.

A lone pillar had formed fifty feet right of where Guy and I stood anchored to the top of Riptide. The tip of the pillar ended in space—looking like the point of a sword, it led to the blue glacier above. Strong winds slapped sheets of snow onto us. The storm had matured into a blizzard, and the avalanche hazard on the slopes below was escalating. I suggested bailing.

"It would be nice to have a better day, but this is the day that we have," he said, winking—a glint of sapphire. It is one of the most precious Zen-liners that he gave me. I treasure it: This is the day that we have. *The day offered 5.8 rock to WI 7 ice, onsight in a blizzard. Guy took us up to the blue glacier; he'd become a master. Yet when I teetered into a trembling balance beside him on top, my forearms felt like they had razor blades in them because I was so spent. I saw his child's eyes again; it was his Christmas morning, and Guy's eyes were glassy with joy, pure joy.*

Back down at the highway, Guy and I parted ways. He was going north to Prince George, and I was heading home to Canmore. Having guided a rock route on Mt. Yamnuska the day before, and then not being able to get to sleep that night, I'd been up for forty hours. I began to hallucinate voluptuous, naked, dark-skinned women lying in the highway. It was time to pull over and sleep.

In 1995, I guided 221 days to pay off a tax debt with bimonthly installments. I hadn't filed my taxes since I'd finished work on Cliffhanger. *Weight gain was not an issue for me. But a year earlier, just after Christmas 1994, Alex Lowe, aka "The Fiend," had come to go climbing with me—"to get after it!"*

DECEMBER 28, 1994: I climbed into the 1990 Isuzu Trooper that The Fiend had driven nonstop from Bozeman, Montana, to Canmore, Alberta, the day before.

"Nine hours," Alex said on arrival.

"What the hell is this contraption?" I held up an artificial climbing hold connected to a bungee cord anchored to the passenger-side door.

"Oh, that's so I can get a pump on while I'm driving. I pull against the fingertip hold and do reps until I can't hang on, then I switch hands."

"Alex, you're a freak."

"I know, I know."

"What's the book for?" I picked up a copy of Patrick O'Brian's *The Letter of Marque*.

"The novels are amazing, all about square-rigged fighting ships in the Napoleonic Wars. I read half of that one on the drive up."

"What the hell do you mean?"

"Well, the roads in northern Montana are really straight and there isn't much traffic, so you're fine if you look up once in a while."

And then I didn't know what to say. But Alex did.

We were heading into the North Ghost River. Half of the 1.5-hour drive was off-road, on progressively more rugged, snow-covered ground that required several river crossings. Alex filled the time telling me about a mountaineering accident on Granite Peak, the highest peak in Montana, in which some climbers on the summit had sport-trundled rocks that hit and killed another climber far below whom they did not know was there. Alex had been called as an advisor to the investigation and legal proceedings, and had had to refine his moral stance to represent the average man as well as friend and fellow climber to the rock pushers. I was impressed with the depth of his analysis, and the conclusions he was drawing, part of which required using me as sounding board. He was a deeply thoughtful man, and I was honored by the trust he placed in our friendship.

Embarrassingly, he placed equal faith in my route-finding ability. Earlier, from the summit ridgeline of the ice climb This House of Sky, I'd spotted an amazing-looking frozen dagger in a drainage that fell northeast from the true north ridge of Mt. Costigan. High above, a slender thread of silver ice led up through steep black rock bands to a broad gully of snow that looked to go to the summit. I knew Alex and I would both love to stand on a summit on one of the shortest days of the year.

We left the Trooper parked below This House of Sky and began walking in, talking about how much we had both enjoyed Ivan Doig's memoir *This House of Sky: Landscapes of a Western Mind* on growing up as the son of itinerant sheep herders in Montana.

"You know, Northern Montana and Southern Alberta are the same country," Alex mused. "Just ask the Milk River."

"I hear you, brother." I panted, trying to keep up with Alex, an impossibility. "Ian Tyson has a line in his song 'The Gift' where God tells Charlie Russell, on Charlie's arrival at the Pearly Gates, 'Kid Russell, I got a job for you. You're in charge of sunsets up in old Montana. 'Cause I can't paint them quite as good as you.'"

"Ha! I love it. I love this land. This place is sacred."

"I'm with you, brother. HOKA HEY!" ("Hoka Hey" means "Let's go!" in the Lakota language. It's reported to be the first part of Crazy Horse's battle cry when riding into Greasy Grass Creek—Little Bighorn—Montana, to confront General Custer. The second part of the cry being, "It is a good day to die!")

At the mouth to our drainage, we turned south-southeast, teetering up snow-crusted river rocks and tiptoeing around pools of water covered with eggshells of dirty brown, wind-ravaged snow. The rest of the morning, and much of that afternoon, Alex and I wandered into side drainages fruitlessly searching for the blue dagger. So much for my route-finding. I was beginning to doubt my memory, and my mind, when late in the day, stumbling up the fourth tributary of our quest, I heard

Alex, who'd strode beyond my sight, bellowing, "Oh ya! We got some ice to climb! We got ice to climb! Yahoo! Hoka Hey!"

I rounded the corner. There was the dagger. It looked magnificent—and scary as all get out. Curtains of blue ice draped over two overhangs, totaling about 150 feet of climbing. The 40-foot-tall blade that touched down was no bigger around than a 50-gallon oil barrel. Alex was running around it like a dog who'd treed a cat.

"I'll take it!" he gushed when I got up to him.

It looked like it very well might fracture with the first ax plant, so I replied, "Okay, it's all yours, brother."

He paused for a moment, thinking of his wife. "I promised Jenni that I wouldn't get on anything like this unless I got rock gear in."

"Was that after you rode that pillar down onto Tackle, Backes, Hanning, and Bancroft?"

"Exactly." In November, Alex had fractured a pillar off a virgin route in Hyalite Canyon, near Bozeman. Dave Hanning had Alex on belay, while Jack Tackle brought up Scott Backes and Bill Bancroft. Alex rode the blue brahma bull down to a ledge, where it exploded and he somehow caught his balance, landing on his feet! But he'd lifted a palm-sized flap of scalp off his forehead. Fifty stitches later, Jenni extracted the promise: rock gear.

"I'm going to see if I can get some pins into that crack up high and in the back," he said.

Alex soon had a couple of pitons buried into a crack thirty feet up and ten feet behind the pillar. I didn't quite get how an arcing swing into the rock was better than riding the pillar to the ground, but Alex was happy with having kept his promise.

"This is so much fun!" The Fiend bellowed, hammering away at the pillar, which was gonging and vibrating under the heaviness of his hand. Alex was not a delicate ice climber; he was happy to hit hard—far harder than I would have. Perhaps it makes no difference whether you stride or tippytoe through a minefield.

Then he was up and off the blade and sinking solid screws; the rope payed out through my hands in a rush. My turn. The climbing was one hell of a lot of fun, given the rope securing me from above. By the time I got to Alex's big, toothy grin, the sun was setting.

DECEMBER 28, 4 P.M.: Time to rappel and get back to Canmore. That evening, Alex stood in my small kitchen in his guide's pants and sweat-stained base layers, delicately slicing up garlic with his scabbed, big-knuckled ranch-hand's hands. Three of his fingers had bruises under the nailbeds.

DECEMBER 29: We climbed into the Trooper in the dark for the second day running and were back at the This House of Sky parking lot at dawn. We had left our ropes threaded through locking carabiners at our anchor so that we could toprope the first pitch. Then we took the ropes off and punched steps up snow and small steps of ice for 1,500 feet. I did my share of trail-breaking and felt good about that. Alex was up front when we came onto the silver strip of ice. He took the first lead, thunking his way up thin, translucent ice with the fairy dust of spindrift occasionally sprinkling down and most of his protection ferreted out of the limestone bordering the five-foot-wide smear.

Alex and I swapped a couple more pitches and then moved together through the upper snow gully. Midafternoon, we stood on top of an 8,900-foot-high sub-peak of Mt. Costigan. We were 3,500 feet above Alex's truck. I could see Mt. Rundle, the massif that runs from Canmore to Banff, to the west, and the broad sweep of Devil's Head to the east. We were mighty happy lads.

"That was so bloody fine, Bubba," Alex said, beaming.

A number of rappels down the way, retracing the first pitch of the upper ice strip, our ropes wouldn't pull, the knot joining them having jammed at the anchors. Alex asked, "Am I going back up?" and started back toward the pitch, while I yarded the ropes sideways, striding across the snow surface. "I guess I'm going back up," he said—a horrid thought, as we were both getting pretty damned tired. But then I got the ropes far enough sideways and at enough of an angle that when I jerked my weight, the knot popped free, leaving me to scramble my feet back under me, and then keep yarding on the freed rope.

"Bubba! You are my hero!"

As we drove away late in the day, Alex said, "You know, on the Montana side of the Waterton-Glacier International Peace Park, there's

Sir Christian John Storey Bonington with me, approaching the northeast ridge of Ha Ling Peak in the Canadian Rockies, 1995. Pat Morrow

the Going-to-the-Sun Road. I think that would be a good name for our route. What do you think?"

A perfect name for a perfect day.

JANUARY 1995: "The series is called *Great Railway Journeys*," the filmmaker Richard Else said over the phone. I'd met Richard Else and his company, Triple Echo Productions, at the Banff Mountain Film Festival wrap party in 1992.

"Chris Bonington is the host for the Canadian episode. We will be riding the train from the East Coast to the West, and I would like to include a climb with you when we reach Canmore."

"*The* Chris Bonington?" I asked in awe (the British mountaineer Chris Bonington was the best-known climber in the Anglophone world).

"Yes, the venerable Christian Bonington himself. Any ideas for a climb?"

"Hell ya, a lot of them. How hard does Chris climb these days?"

"Well, he is sixty, but fit and active. I think he could well manage 5.9 in the North American system, although it would be good to pick a slightly easier climb for the sake of more movement on camera."

"The Northeast Ridge of Chinaman's Peak could fit the bill. It's close to Canmore, and the crux is 5.7." (The derogatory summit name was changed in 1998 to Ha Ling Peak at the behest of the Chinese communities in Canmore and Calgary.)

"Splendid."

"I'll need to ask if I would be getting paid."

"Would $700 per day in Canadian bills work?"

"Why yes, Richard, that would do handsomely."

JULY 12, 1995: "Chris is really worried that he's been getting out of shape riding the train and that he won't be able to keep up with you," Richard said when they arrived in Canmore. "'Blanchard has been guiding and climbing, while I've been eating, sitting on a train, and talking,' is what he said."

"Not to worry—I can lead all the pitches and guide Chris if need be."

"It would be better for the camera to have Chris take some leads. I'll let you decide what might be appropriate."

And then I got to meet the Triple Echo Adventure Film Crew, some of the best climbers, mountain guides, and adventure cameramen in Britain: Brian Hall, Dave (Cubby) Cuthbertson, Keith Partridge, and Duncan McCallum. Along with the Yamnuska guides James Blench and Dave Stark, we got to rig for a couple of days and then shoot for a couple of days.

Chris and I roped up below the Northeast Ridge, and then I led off. The cameras started rolling. When Chris got to my first anchor, I asked, "Would you prefer that I take on the role of the guide?"

"What do you mean, mate?" he asked, puzzled.

"Do you want me to lead all the pitches?"

Chris looked like I'd slapped him, and said, "No way! Fuck you, mate; it's even steven. I love me leading."

"Okay, cool. I have you on belay then, my man." Chris waltzed up the next pitch, and we swapped leads from then on.

Six pitches up, we were off camera when the rain came.

"I'm worried about the weather," Brian Hall, the safety officer, said over the radio. "I think we should all get off of the mountain."

"This will pass over, Brian," I said into my mic, and then asked Bonington, "Do you want to go down, Chris?"

"Hell no! We can sit out a little weather, don't you think?"

"Yes, I think we can—it'll blow over. Chris and I are going to sit here under my guide's tarp and drink some tea," I said into my radio.

"Well, if you are going to stay, we'll stay too."

"A fine idea indeed," Chris said when I set the radio down. The rain came and left; Chris and I were dry and happy.

"The rock will dry out pretty fast," I told Chris.

"Right, then—are there any other tricky bits?"

"You mean cruxes?"

"Yes, please. I'd love to lead them please."

"Okay, the next overhang is all yours."

"Splendid, just splendid."

And Bonners, as Cubby called him, floated the hardest moves of the route. Made me think I could have chosen a more challenging line for the man who was knighted Sir Christian John Storey Bonington the next year, 1996.

OCTOBER 5, 1999: Four years later. Alex Lowe and David Bridges were killed by an avalanche triggered by a large serac that fell 6,000 feet down the south face of Shishapangma, in China, the fourteenth highest mountain in the world at 26,335 feet. They were part of a nine-man team attempting to summit and then film a ski descent of the south face. Conrad Anker had been pummeled by the avalanche too but came to rest on top and survived. Perry Beckham, who had been Alex's brother-in-law for a time, called to tell me what had happened. Catherine and I were in New Zealand working on the Hollywood film *Vertical Limit*. I drove to the production office and told her. She loved Alex like a big brother. She collapsed in tears and said, "I don't care what it costs—we are going to his memorial."

We spent fifty-six hours in the air to spend thirty-six hours on the ground, but it was a very important thirty-six hours.

Four hundred people packed the rustic Springhill Pavilion above Ross Creek tight to the western edge of the Bridger Range. It was classic Montana—no small wonder that Robert Redford shot scenes for *A River Runs Through It* and *The Horse Whisperer* here. More important, it was Alex's country. I could feel him in the soil when I squatted on my haunches and put my right palm to the Earth.

Incense combined with the smell of burning juniper. All attending had a khata scarf draped over their necks upon entering. Farm Boy (Steve House) told me that Conrad had brought the scarves back from Tibet, along with all the prayer flags hanging from every rafter. In my mind, I saw Alex standing beside me at our puja below the Kangshung Face of Mt. Everest five and a half years earlier. I didn't recognize Conrad at first. His head was shaved; cruel triangular scars scabbed his scalp, looking like blows dealt by a battle hammer. When he turned, I saw his haunted pale-blue eyes and I lost it. I hadn't cried until then. Deep, guttural sobs welled up, and I wrapped him in a bear hug. "Conrad, Conrad, it is so good to see you alive, man, so good," I said.

And then I wrapped Jenni Lowe in my arms.

A few months later, Jon Krakauer was to give me a jewel—and he used those words—"a jewel." While in Antarctica with Alex and Conrad on a successful expedition to climb Rakekniven Peak in Queen Maud Land in 1996, Jon had asked Alex for a definition of

Stewart Alexander Lowe joyously smacking his way up the first ascent of the Going to the Sun Highway (Mt. Costigan, Ghost River, Alberta) as the night advances, 1994. A return the next day was called for. Barry Blanchard happiness. Alex had replied, "A day in the mountains with Barry or Conrad."

Catherine and I boarded our return flight to New Zealand early the next morning. The spirit of Alex Lowe caught up with me when I returned to work on *Vertical Limit*. "I see you running off up there every time we break for lunch," Phil Patterson, the first assistant director, said. We were at The Remarkables ski field in Otago, on New Zealand's South Island.

"I'm traversing the ridgeline twenty minutes at a time. Takes me ten to get up there, and ten to get down. Leaves five minutes to cram food into my piehole, but that's enough time," I replied.

"Good on you, mate, good on you. Wish I could be up there too, but first I've got to get this movie made."

I pumped up to the ridgeline and stepped over into the head of the right branch of Doolans Creek. Pristine New Zealand hummocks of dry brown grass stood above the wind-drifted snow, looking like miniature versions of the reed bundles I'd so often seen picketed above clusters of prayer flags in Tibet. A positive force swelled inside my chest. I felt like I could sprint over the ridgeline unbounded by gravity.

I didn't get it at first. Then Alex was there in my mind, beaming his radiant "Let's get after it!" smile. I shouted, "Alex! Alex!" and shredded a swath of the ridgeline. Gravity still did not apply. It was the last time that I felt his spirit in the mountains, but I continue to think about Alex Lowe, to remember him. I concluded that somewhere within himself, Alex knew that he was only going to get forty years. It was the only way I could understand his energy, his insatiable need to move.

DECEMBER 10, 2009: Guy Lacelle was swept from the top of an ice climb in Hyalite Canyon, Montana, by a small, but concentrated, avalanche. Unroped, he died from blunt trauma on impact at the bottom of the climb.

One month later, we held a memorial in Canmore. Afterward, when I walked his wife, Marge, to her car, she handed me a Ziploc bag with a pound of Guy's ashes in it. Over the next couple of months, I spread his ashes over some of his favorite places: Curtain Call, Oh Le Tabernac, The Trophy Wall, and finally, Nemesis.

Guy Joseph Ernest Lacelle on Riptide, 1990. We didn't make it that day and had to come back five years later. Barry Blanchard

JANUARY 2010: I was guiding Nemesis again, feeling beaten down, at age fifty, by too much guiding. Guy, that old joker, had stowed away in the top lid of my pack for one last ascent. I'd meant to sprinkle him around the base as I'd done at the other climbs. Nearing the top, I realized the bag of Guy was still in my pack. I smiled and I laughed. His gray ashes sifted onto the wind-sculpted snow-like volcano dust.

Five days later, I was guiding Nemesis again, and the final thirty feet of steep blue ice was working me. My forearms were on fire, and I had no more ice screws to place to calm my mind. I closed my eyes and breathed and thought about the trace of Guy just above me. I channeled some of his Herculean power into my arms. When I pulled over the top, his gray ashes had melded into the chalk-colored snow and sapphire-blue ice.

I love you, man. Thank you.

Unknown Pleasures: Joy Division
Nebraska: Bruce Springsteen

Kiss or Kill: Confessions of a Serial Climber by Mark Twight
Motel Chronicles by Sam Shepard
Murder of the Impossible by Reinhold Messner

CHAPTER 15 — HOWSE PEAK I

THE PROMISE

I met Scott Backes in spring 1985, on the East Kahiltna Glacier in the Alaska Range. "Some have called it the Diamond Face," he'd said, pointing across to Mt. Hunter. We stood at the edge of the airstrip—a half-mile-long horseshoe stamped onto the glacier. The northern aspect of Mt. Hunter abutted the far side of the glacier, so vast, complex, and abrupt that I paused in awe. We were gazing up at the ramparts of Valhalla.

Planes started buzzing in, and departing climbers scrambled onto them like they were life rafts. It felt like the fall of Saigon. "Funny, they all want to leave, and I want to be up there," Scott said and pointed again to the Diamond.

"I hear you, man. All I want to do is climb."

Eighteen months later, Mark Twight's first article, "Kiss or Kill," was published in Climbing *magazine and I began clicking Joy Division's* Unknown Pleasures *into my Walkman more often than Bruce Springsteen's* Nebraska*. Mark's words were fresh, confrontational, and loud. The article defined the dark side of my obsession with alpinism. Punk rock in the high mountains. Opposition, irreverence, Gothic-style:*

I don't care about the cash.
I don't care about life's "necessary accessories."
I only care when provoked.
I care about climbing, period.

Scott Backes looks on as I sort through pitons and decide which ones to take. If some is good, more must be better. Steve House

I met Mark in December of 1987 and much of the next decade was shaped by parallel relationships that Scott Backes and I formed with him, both of us drawn to the man through his writing. When I asked Mark what his favorite book at the time was, he replied, *Motel Chronicles* by Sam Shepard. "You're fucking kidding me!" I spat. "That's mine, too!" Reading and listening to Shepard led us to the Peruvian poet César Vallejo. Mark, Scott, and I would mentor Steve House in the second half of that decade. When Mark quit climbing in 2000, a part of our foundation fell away.

MARCH 22, 1999: "So, you're sure you'll be back in time for your birthday?" Catherine had a party planned for my fortieth in five days' time.

"I won't miss it. I promise."

MARCH 23, 3 A.M.: Scott Backes, Steve House, and I set out from Canmore. One hundred and seventy-five million years of orogeny and erosion have thrust and carved Howse Peak into a breathtaking pyramid that falls shallowly to the south and west, but sheerly and precipitously to the north and east. The mountain sits at 116°40′53″ west of the prime meridian, and 51°48′49″ north of the equator. The summit is 10,810 feet (3295 meters) above sea level and separates the Pacific drainage (and points south) from the Atlantic (and points east, north, and west). The mountain bears the name of Joseph Howse—a Hudson's Bay Company fur trader and explorer who crossed a pass three miles west-southwest of the mountain in 1810—as do the pass, and the river draining the peak to the northwest.

My history with the mountain began in late August 1981. Tim Friesen and I spent four days climbing and descending from the Northeast Ridge—two more days than we'd planned. When Ward Robinson and I climbed the virgin north face over four days in mid-March 1988, it was the hardest winter route in the range, and I felt that we'd contributed to the evolution of Canadian alpinism.

Steve House poses as Scott Backes skis over the wetness and Howes Peak is bathed in early morning sun. Barry Blanchard

MARCH 23, 6 A.M.: Steve, Scott, and I skied through evergreens, stark and denuded of snow by wind and recent warmth. Heat radiated from my torso into the cool air, sweat glazed my forehead, and I felt the good warmth of working my skis and weighty pack uphill. Up above us, the north and east faces of Howse Peak held far more snow than on an average year—snow mushrooms the size of cars and even houses bulged from the wall. Similar to cornices, they form on flat ledges on steep walls. Large bands of alabaster snow swept from the Northeast Ridge, arcing 3,500 feet east to Mt. Synge. The wall had the shape of a hand sweeping spilled salt.

Like the creases in my palm, three lines of ice suggested passage up the steep black rock. The middle line, so plumb and perfect, was the one we wanted. For two strides, I could see the route framed between tall Engelmann spruce trees. One slash of black rock kept the ice from touching down; fifty feet of dark limestone cut the feet from 300 yards of silver ice.

"It looks good, Bubba. I just hope we can get onto it," Scott said.

"Let's hope there's some cracks there. Someplace to get gear in."

"Ah yes, but that's why we've got The Great White Hope of American Alpinism with us," Scott said and grinned.

"Follow me, you aging assholes," Steve said. "See if you can keep up."

We skied onto the flat white plain of Chephren Lake. Steve stabbed my extra pair of skis into the snow above the shoreline, with their bright-yellow top sheets pointing toward the east slopes of Mt. Chephren. Having firn skis there gave us the option, after our ascent of Howse, of descending via a traverse of the adjacent mountain, The White Pyramid, and then down the eastern side of Mt. Chephren. I would then ski up to retrieve the skis we'd leave standing below the face of Howse while Steve and Scotty chilled, literally.

The lake ends at a lateral moraine that the glacier had bulldozed to its zenith in 1844, thirty-four years after Joseph Howse had passed by the opposite side of the mountain. A few meager dwarf trees clung precariously to avalanche slopes, picketing the entrance to the alpine.

"Good God, man, isn't this place wild!" Scott exclaimed.

We set a zigzag track up the crest of the moraine. Avalanche-prone slopes grew to our left and to our right, though we were on the relatively safer high ground of the crest. Still, images of slab avalanches propagating through ridgelines flickered in my head: deep crown failures held the architecturally defined angles of joined concrete.

I kicked my skis around whenever I felt the snow gain a degree of threat.

The last stunted spruce passed on our left as we entered the true alpine—our crucible of rock, ice, snow, and glacier. For us, this place, rising above most forms of life, was alive with the promise of growth, honor, and adventure.

Why did we do it? Already, in our first hours together, I'd felt the bond of commitment to a dream shared by men I would grow to love; the primal joy of traveling through the forest with the dawn glowing orange against the summit ridgeline, illuminating snow mushrooms like crown jewels; my body heating up in anticipation of three days' trial, when I expected to lose fifteen pounds doing what I believed I was designed for—heavy work in the wilderness and the intricate and intuitive test of meeting risks as they arose. When I did that well, I felt the presence of my totem animal, the gray timber wolf.

As we skied, we snapped pictures in anticipation of sharing—and even selling—our success. The three of us were, to some degree, professional alpinists who needed to keep making significant ascents. The money helped pay the bills, although never more than about 10 percent in my case; I continued to work as a mountain guide. The beauty in our shared bond lay in knowing we would be here doing this regardless of fame or money. We gave no thought to the potential poison of our desire for glory. In the previous five years, reputations had been made through modern mixed-climbing techniques. We felt the competition deeply. The alpinism we practiced had traditionally been the only place to apply mixed climbing. Smugly, I pointed across the valley to a small overhang where several modern mixed routes had been bolted out the roof to gain daggers of ice.

"That's where the kids are drytooling."

"It is the dojo at the bottom of the mountain," Scott replied. "The real test is up there: on the battlefield." He pointed to Howse Peak.

"I wonder what those guys could do up here. Could they deal with the impossible?" Steve added. Reinhold Messner's seminal essay, "Murder of the Impossible," condemned the use of expansion bolts drilled into the rock. He argued that any mountain challenge could be overcome with machinery. Scott called it "guaranteed-outcome climbing."

We carried no bolts. Our outcome was up to us.

The moraine melded into a transitional bulge before laying back into the upper basin. I was in front, about to cut across the convex roll to the right. The snow would be under tension; the thickening of a wind slab was visible in its plump, curving surface. Most slab avalanches are triggered by people disturbing such features.

"You and Scott better hang back here until I get across this," I said, stating the obvious.

I sliced my ski into the slope. Six-inch-deep linear chunks of snow sliced from its edge like knife-cut meringue. Underfoot, I felt the slab thicken. My nerves jacked my heart rate; each stride increased the risk. I sensed the texture of the snow through my feet, gauged its density by the depth of my pole plants. I listened intently for abnormal sounds but heard only the hiss-and-crunch of my advancing skis and the heaving of my breath. At 120 feet on, the slope eased back, and the slab thinned to nothing.

I yodeled for Steve and Scott to follow, one at time, and my voice echoed from the wall of Howse Peak as the sun broke the ridgeline at our backs. All around me, snow that had been flat and gray now glowed bright white. The wall was beautiful: immense ramps of snow, sheer cliffs of black, with patches of gray and tan under overhangs and roofs. Our line was the prize, that thousand-foot strip of water ice dead center, but not touching down.

I stood beside the skis we had thrust into the snow at angles and bound tight into a tipi with a compression strap. We judged them to be out of firing range of the face; to lose our skis to an avalanche would be a costly mistake—the road was a half-day of postholing behind us. Legions of snow mushrooms, some the size of weather balloons, bulged from the upper wall and summit ridgeline—beautiful in the morning sun, but as deadly as a collapsing building in an earthquake if they broke away from the wall.

"I'm more worried about the snow mushrooms than I am about the avalanche hazard on the approach slope," I said. The lower slopes were

riddled with recent slide debris, none of it from slab failures; it was all snow that had slid from the wall because of heat.

"There's way more mushrooms than normal this year, isn't there, Bubba?" Scott replied.

"Ya, we've had a lot of snow and westerly winds. Look at the size of some of them."

"Do I have to?"

The bergschrund lay open in intermittent gaps and above spindrift that had cut chest-deep runnels in the snow. Steve and Scott were ahead, kicking steps in snow soft enough to go without crampons. They looked so bold to me, advancing up snow as white as a wedding train while black rock bulged high above. Linear stains of water wept from the low edges of snow bands, darkening the rock one shade. I caught up with Steve and Scott 500 feet higher. Clumps of moss campion grew from cracks in the shale, and I could see the rich green of life returning with the sun. Then the sun was gone.

"I like warm alpine climbing. There is nothing wrong with warm alpine climbing," I said.

We stamped out platforms in the snow to drop our packs onto.

MARCH 23, 12:30 P.M.: *Thunk!* Steve's pick set into the first exposed ice on the east face of Howse Peak. He pulled up, locked off, and swung again.

"It's good," he called down. "Grade 2. We can solo it."

Three hundred feet higher, I constructed an anchor next to the first technical pitch. Scotty arrived, looked up, and said, "I'll lead this." He left his pack and advanced onto ice that looked like a giant lace curtain. His yellow-and-black one-piece suit popped against the white ice and black rock.

"You look like a bumblebee checking out my grandma's curtains!" I yelled.

"Brother, I wish I was a bumblebee, 'cause then I could hover my ass up this shit! Half of this stuff is useless!" He used a sling to tie off another ice screw that had passed through the lacey ice and bottomed out against the rock. And then his bumblebee butt quivered over the lip and left our field of view.

'm traversing away from the Magic Line to
heck out what would become the first ascent of
116, Howse Peak. Scott Backes

Twenty minutes later, Scott bellowed, "Off belay!" and Steve untied from the green rope. We watched it slither up through the protection, Scotty threw it back down, and I leaned out and hooked it and tied his pack on via an equalizing sling so it would haul upright and be less likely to snag. Some minutes of hauling passed, and then the rope "snapped!" back down from the sky and Steve tied back in.

Steve and I climbed classically, with our packs on our backs, as almost all alpine pitches had been seconded in the first half of the

twentieth century, before jumars and Yosemite big-wall techniques changed all that. We had jumars in our packs but felt that using them would dilute the purity of our ascent. Not that we were beyond them, we just felt better about ourselves when we didn't use the mechanical rope clamps.

"To Bonatti," I said, offering the head of my ax. Steve tapped the head of his to it: "To Bonatti." Walter Bonatti was the greatest alpinist of the twentieth century. He didn't use jumars.

If you were to look at a photograph of Scott leading the pitch, you could conclude that he was on an ice pitch. You wouldn't see the repetitive reaching and swinging and pulling through the lack of structure. Whatever water had been present in October, five months earlier, had frozen to the rock. Since then, the ice had been swept by a thousand waves of spindrift and pounded by avalanches that contained chunks of bonded snow. Snowfall and avalanche had filled many of the holes in the ice at the same time as the ice had delaminated from much of the underlying rock. Within the curtain left selectively bonded to the rock, snow metamorphosed toward ice, and ice toward snow. Much of the resultant material we called "snow ice," or simply "snice."

Snice climbed like vertical glazed meringue and looked like exotic blown glass. Your pick would cut through and you'd have to swing again and again to find enough structure to pull on. Its color hinted at its strength: tin-gray suggested more ice, while stucco-white guaranteed more snow.

The snice reared to vertical, and my arms throbbed and fearful breath charged in and out of my lungs. A total collapse of the curtain was possible. From above, Scotty hauled on the ropes. Mine was cello-string tight and as narrow as a cigarillo, but the pack pulled on me, trying to take me back to the valley floor. My will became the fulcrum between gravity and the rigid rope.

I swung and pulled and soon saw Scotty.

"I think one out of four screws might have held a fall," I said, panting.

"Amen, brother. That was intense. I am so very happy that I didn't try to lead it with my pack on!"

"It felt like grade 6 to me. Though it's hard to compare to water ice. Maybe we should make up a new grading system."

teve is a happy young man after Scott and I—
e forty-year-olds—decide to get after it.
arry Blanchard

"That's already been done," Steve said dryly. The "M" climbing grades—MI through to MI4—had been added to climbing culture to express the difficulty of modern mixed climbing, which is frequently bolted. "What have we got for an anchor?"

"We've got a good half-inch Angle [piton] up here, and I had to stack a long, shallow angle behind this Knifeblade [piton] to feel good about it. We're good; the anchor is good."

The pitons were driven into compact black limestone that offered very few cracks. Scott had excavated several square yards of snow to find the only one. Steve took a picture of the anchor, and I started punching steps up the last of the massive snow bands that transected the face from the Northeast Ridge to Mt. Synge.

Eventually, we anchored and leaned out to look at the Magic Line. The realization of a harsh and somber truth painted serious expressions on my partners' faces: a large roof presented an underbelly of rectangular cobblestones. Above, compact black limestone led to thirty feet of diaphanous and detached icicles—the start of the Magic Line. Blobs of snow clung like sponge between and along the tassels of ice.

"If we touch that thing, it is going to break off thirty feet above. And there aren't any cracks leading to it," I stated. "Not good at all—no cracks. No cracks, no gear...."

"No gear, no go." Steve finished the mantra we'd learned from our friend Alex Lowe.

"What this route is sayin' is, 'Fuck all y'all!'" Scotty sang, pointing his trigger finger to the pistol decal on his helmet.

But the wall held three lines of silver, and my imagination had pieced together a possibility 600 feet to our right on one of those lines.

"We're here now. We should check out the line to the right. I think we can still make it."

"What line?" Steve's focus had been solely on the sword of icicles that hung above.

"It's one I looked at on our way up—I think we can get into the gully that George Lowe and Jock Glidden climbed to finish the Northeast Ridge in '71."

"But in the summer, right?"

"Ya, they climbed it in the summer, but there is ice in it. Big ice, alpine ice."

"Lead on, Bubba," said Scott.

There were two football fields of snow to cross, with 1,500 feet of black cliffs and snowfields below; I found all of the protection that the mountain offered, but it was never enough. Hundred-foot bellies of rope arced across forty-degree snow, an angle that wants to avalanche. Short ice screws bottomed out in the shallow ice that froze from meltwater along the lower borders of the snow. I tied the screws off with slings; when the threads were exposed, I used carabiners because the threads were sharp enough to cut the slings in a fall. Where cracks appeared, I'd dick in rock pro, several pieces if feasible. I did the best I could.

In time, I stood beside a width of gossamer ice. My right hand had gone numb from pounding on a recalcitrant piton, and I had to shake it back into tingling and then sense and functionality. I created a good anchor and belayed the boys over.

"It looks like uncooked pancake batter," Steve said.

"If you like green pancakes." Cups in the snow ice held the faint green of oxidized copper, while the bulges frothed white; the transition between the two looked like the heavy, lower edge of antique windows that had been blown and spun flat, with more glass accumulating at the edges.

"And this serving is yours, Farm Boy," Scotty quipped. "Always bite off more than you can chew—that way you're sure to get your fair share. That's what Twight would say." He grinned at Steve and poured hot coffee from his thermos.

Steve charged from the belay, the rope snaking down below him. I learned later that he was pissed at being expected to perform like a trick pony, but the climbing soon demanded his attention, and his movements slowed as his anger waned. Some pick placements sank true on the first try; others required numerous swings. His breathing ramped up, and I soon heard the rumble and hiss of his powerful exhalations and watched how he choreographed his upward movements to deep draws of breath. And then he was twenty-five feet above his only ice screw and the tension in his core was just noticeable in episodic tremors through an arm or leg.

Scott and I watched wordlessly—a fall would have been horrible. Steve fought to place an ice screw, which he was only able to get twisted in by releasing it to regrip his right tool and swing life back into his left hand, which had been holding the majority of his weight. Then he would return to the screw. One screw wasn't good enough, and I was so proud, and relieved, to see him work through mounting exhaustion to clip a second screw to the red rope. Screws of equal elevation: one on the red rope, one on the green. And then he tacked to the left, and the translucent ice, as seasonal as cottonwood fluff, thinned and reared to just past vertical. At 120 feet out, we could still hear his breathing as we watched him excavate a crack and place a cam with a trembling hand.

Physically he was pushing his threshold; emotionally and intellectually, he didn't flinch. Steve was climbing magnificently, and I thought about how much better he was doing up there than Scott or I could have, even in our prime. Steve was a higher-evolved alpinist, yet Scott and I had both contributed to that evolution, as had the men who'd invented and played the game before us.

Scotty was belaying, and I was taking pictures. He looked over his shoulder and asked, "How is it that House always ends up with the hard pitches?"

"Because God knows," I said. "God knows."

It was Scott's first time climbing with Steve, but I had been climbing with Steve for three years and I knew he had heart. An ardent heart, visible in the calculated determination of his movement. The lead was potentially deadly, but he dealt with that and kept going up. Eventually, he pulled over the top.

MARCH 23, 9 P.M.: The evening dimmed around us. I felt the air get heavier, colder, thicker. Scott and I used the jumars to follow the pitch, and I jugged with Steve's pack hanging low from my harness, below my crampons. The jugs made following faster; we were under the gun to find a place to spend the night. Thus was our ethic eroded. It's true that we climbed steeper and more tenuous ice than Walter Bonatti ever had—our tools had evolved through the ice revolution of the 1960s and '70s—and true that speed is safety in the alpine. But a purely alpine adventure would have required each of us to free climb each foot up the mountain, every inch of the wall.

Steve climbing magnificently up the first WI 7 on the first ascent of M16, on the east face of Howse Peak. Protection was sparse, but ability was abundant. Scott Backes

It was heavy toil going up with two packs, and I was panting deeply when I reached Steve.

"A very-fucking-fine lead Farm Boy," I panted.

"Thanks, Bubba. It definitely felt a grade harder than Scott's pitch."

"Ha! That's why I am so glad it was yours!" Scott cracked.

"My turn," I said. "We need to find someplace to spend the night."

Steve's anchor was constructed with solid ice screws that gave me confidence as I kicked my crampons into another massive, unsupported field of snow. This feature had looked like a giant manta ray to me when I'd pieced the route together in my mind a dozen hours earlier. A hundred feet of rising leftward into the slope, I worked at thrusting my ax shafts head-deep and kicking good, flat, supportive steps. I pressed down the fear of fracturing a slab avalanche and gained some calm from the good feeling of firm snow pressing back against the toecaps of my boots. I focused on moving to the rhythm of my breath while feeling for any variance in the snow's resistance. At 170 feet out, I tried to assure myself that if the slope was going to avalanche, it would have done so by now. At 200 feet, I came to the sole protruding rock, banged in pitons and slotted cams, and yelled, "Secure!"

My hooded buddies looked so small way back down there.

Steve and Scott soon began working up my steps, and I belayed. The weight of the colder and calmer air encompassed me. Oddly, it felt like an embrace, probably because I was still warm from effort. Here was the site of our first bivouac. Far below us lay the flat expanse of the lake, with the oceanic slopes of Mt. Chephren sweeping down to it; farther north, the tumultuous Mistaya River cut deep canyons through the deep-green forest. I felt good, felt that we had climbed well that day, that we'd been effective. I was excited to continue.

My brothers arrived. We coupled several shovel blades to our ice-axes and began the laborious task of hollowing out a snow cave, a job we finished by headlamp.

"Holy shit!" I exclaimed, "There are people below us!" When I yodeled, headlamps swung our way. Faint "yahoos" came in reply.

Two thousand feet lower, two headlamps danced like fireflies as Dave Marra and Dave Edgar, we would later learn, arranged a bivy at the lake. Over the next two days, they would make the first ascent of the third line of silver on the wall, 1,300 feet south of us, a waterfall that they climbed to the top of the ice, before retreating. They called the line "Life by the Drop" and graded it WI 5+.

"I wonder who they are?" Scott said. "Hope they aren't coming up here."

"We're a day ahead of them," Steve observed. "They'll never catch us up."

Beyond the instant niggling of competition, I felt a strange and slender connection to whoever it was: other humans drawn to the mountain. We were not alone. And yet, my territorial, competitive response had come up first, before the compassion.

Our digging bottomed against rock one yard in, so we turned sideways to the left and right of the portal. To the right, we managed a fifteen-foot-long torpedo tube. Scott and Steve got set up in the primary bedroom.

"Holy shit, Backes! How big is your bag?" I asked of the voluminous blue pit as it exploded from its compression sack like biscuit dough from a cardboard tube.

"Six pounds," he replied, laughing and then feigning shock—"Oh no! how did this get in here?"—as he held up an in-flight pillow! "What can I say, I'm aged and saged."

I got the kid's room: six feet long and just round enough for me to slither in after my bivy sack and bag, and then lie down. I felt like a hot dog in a bun.

Steve assembled our stove to start two hours of brewing and eating. The last thing he handed me was a strawberry Pop-Tart, and I thought how considerate it was of him to have catered dessert. I savored every bite.

🎧 "Beat on the Brat": The Ramones
🎧 "Real Wild Child": Iggy Pop
🎧 "The Wait," "Precious," "Tattooed Love Boys": The Pretenders
🎧 "Willin'": Little Feat

📖 *Alpinist 2* by Voytek Kurtyka

CHAPTER 16 — HOWSE PEAK II

THE HIT

In its deepest sense alpinism is the art of freedom. As an exquisite art it offers a creative relationship with the mountain:

> *Every move is a creation,*
> *Maintaining the delicate balance is a creation,*
> *The line is a creation,*
> *Survival is a creation,*
> *Freedom is a creation.*
> *—Voytek Kurtyka, "The Shining Wall,"* Alpinist *No. 2 (2003)*

MARCH 24, 1999, 4 A.M.: The alarm reverberated into my skull. I'd laid my watch on top of my head and inside my toque to keep it warm and to hear it and feel it. My bivy sack crackled with cold. I could feel the bite of frost in the blackness and see the unmoving cloud of my breath when I twisted on my headlight. It was my turn to run the stove. I fired it up and began plopping chunks of snow into the titanium pot. Wrestling onto my elbows, I held the first of the foil-wrapped coffee bags to my nose, then pulled across its scissor line; the waft of fresh coffee smelled like alert eagerness. I repeated that first step twice more, then poked my partners' sleeping bags.

"Wow, Bubba, you've got the stove going already." Steve rose to sitting. I handed him hot coffee and a second mug for Scotty.

"What's for breakfast?"

Cold but happy. I'm thinking that Scott, Steve, and I had just beaten the odds with an injury-free ascent. Steve House

"You don't have your Pop-Tart?"

"What Pop-Tart? I didn't get no Pop-Tart."

"Yeah, you did. We gave it to you last night."

"That was breakfast? I thought it was dessert. I ate it last night."

There was a pregnant pause, then Steve said, "Bummer, dude." Scott started laughing and pointing at me.

"Bubba, you are one no-home-Pop-Tartless-sorry-assed-motherfucker!" Scott laughed some more and so did Steve and so did I.

"My lead, eh, Scotty?" I asked across the cave. "That pitch of snow yesterday didn't count." Each of us cherished leads where we got to test our mettle—plus, we didn't have to climb with a pack! Yet both Scott and I knew that the really hard, serious leads needed to fall to Steve, the best technical climber. A gifted one, in fact.

I backed out of the cave, stood next to Steve, and saw the bewilderment in his eyes as he studied the compact black limestone overhead.

"Where you going to go, Barry?"

"I think up and left—there's a corner system. Leads up to some white stuff that might be climbable. Looks hard up higher, but that'll be your lead."

"So, what's above this wall?"

"A gully takes us up under another big, triangular-shaped wall. That wall is overhanging, so from there we'd most likely traverse right to the couloir that George and Jock climbed in '71."

A patina of iron-gray ice armored the protruding rock of our snow cave. I front-pointed onto it and traversed into the base of a 500-foot-high arc in black rock that wore snow mushrooms and snow bands like rows of pearls. A grisaille of snice was crusted into the arc; that would be our route.

My pitch was magical: grade 4 alpine snow-ice that reverberated like a wooden plank when I smacked it broadside with the head of my ice tool. Reasonable ice screws were hard to get, yet I felt relatively safe because I was climbing well and in control. At the top, in the cold shade of rock, ice, and snow, I anchored to large cams in rock and shouted "Secure!" to Scott and Steve, who were in front of the cave and in the sun...the lucky bastards.

My brothers jumared and manhandled my pack.

"That was one fucking fine pitch, Bubba," Scotty said, grinning, and soon traversed onto more of the snice and into the sun.

"Yo, Scotty! Look back this way, my man." Steve and I snapped photos and Scotty beamed some more. Then the bumblebee charged, tying off ice screws and running it out between placements. The sun swung from the face when he was halfway up. The temperature dropped, but Scott charged on; at the end of the rope, he lashed us into two pitons, a micro-cam, a finger-sized Stopper, and a three-inch cam. Steve and I jugged, and then the Farm Boy launched onto the most inspired piece of climbing that Scott and I had witnessed during our combined forty-plus years of alpinism.

Dark rock arced into a roof over our heads. Elegant lines of snow had been sculpted by spindrift to fill the underlying void with drifts of snow several feet deep. A shale band sat in the crease of the roof, bleeding a bronze tint into the snice below. Steve tapped delicately, yet assertively, up the bronze; three ice screws higher up, he began clearing the overhanging snow from the shale, the snow chunks falling away and disintegrating as they tumbled.

"Your turn, man," I said, as Scott wrestled into his belay jacket, and then added Steve's overtop. "It's getting cold. Can you take the belay?"

"Got it, Bubba." He looked up. "Whoa! That looks like a no-go!"

Fifty feet above, Steve was scoping an overhanging groove of rock choked with snow mushrooms. The very first beachball-sized blob that he touched sheared instantly and yarded at his right tool as it fell free. Scott's brake hand instinctively locked off, and we saw the pull of the snow mass jerk across Steve's shoulders.

"Fuck!" I blurted, thinking that Steve would teeter and fall, but he stabilized himself and got his right tool back onto the rock.

"I don't think so," he shouted down and slowly retreated back to the level of the bronze snice. "I'm going to check out right."

Steve stood at the threshold, his feet bridged wide and front points set on limestone edges; above him, an overhang of rock was draped with a veil of snow. He'd just placed our largest cam, a size 3, and it was good. He could climb back down to us, or lower, and we would retreat. If he pulled over the roof, there would be no coming back. Soon he was advancing, then his crampons danced like a prizefighter's feet as he jousted to find something that would hold them. It reminded me of Muhammad Ali's balletic footwork. Then, he pulled from our view, and Scotty and I inched out the eighty feet of remaining rope.

Three hours later, we heard, "Off belay!"

"Thank Christ," I exhaled, my voice vibrating from the chill that rattled my jaw.

"Amen, brother, amen. Let's hope he has a good anchor."

"He ran out of rope a half hour ago, he must have something."

I thrust my jumar over the roof and had my breath taken away. A strip of chrome-tinged ice two to three feet wide ran up a vertical wall of gray-black rock. It was the perfect actualization of my alpine ideals: high, hard, serious, yet elementally beautiful, like one elegant brush stroke in a Zen painting.

And then I surveyed the mastery of Steve's climbing as I plucked out pitons and micro-cams, some of them marginal and a number very far apart. None of the ice was thicker than one inch, and the flow was interrupted by several four-inch micro-roofs that demanded overhanging moves. At the first roof, I could see the scratch marks of his picks and crampons left and right of the strip, and I knew that he'd tried for rock holds, found some, and failed at others. Over the lip of the roof, I saw a horizontal hold he'd chiseled into a half-inch depth of ice. He'd held his three supporting limbs rigid with core strength as he carefully tapped the ice away to a finger's width by a matchstick long, and then he'd laid the pick of his tool onto it sideways and pulled!

"Holy fuck," I sighed, hardly believing what I was seeing. I'd climbed onto several leads that had similar levels of lethal risk—if Steve had fallen, he would probably have been killed. But none of the leads that I'd been caught out on—and I say "caught" because if I'd known that I would end up risking my life, I would not have done those leads—had involved such tenuous climbing. Yet mine had gone on for similar amounts of time, and I recall how the voice of danger screaming in my head had quieted over the hours. The scream faded; gravity became a song.

The strip of ice was eighty feet long. At its top, our rope ends were tied into five screws drilled into a hubcap of ice that was the only available surface. Three of the screws protruded and had been tied off.

I'm following the first of six rope lengths leading to the top of M16. Scott Backes

Twenty-five feet higher, a cluster of four equally tensioned rock pieces added backup. Steve had reached the rock by tying his two skinny prusiks together and back-roping with them.

I slid my upper jug to the bouquet of ice screws and looked up into Steve's eyes. "Holy fuck, Farm Boy. That is the hardest piece of climbing I've ever seen in the mountains, period."

"It was intense, Bubba—felt like I was in a different place."

"Hang onto that place—we may need more of it yet."

"I don't know if I have any more pitches like that in me."

Scotty jumared close to me on the red rope. "Whatdya think, eh?" I asked.

He bowed his head and rolled it side to side, and then took a big draw of air, looked up, and said, "Maybe I could have followed it. But I bet there are less than a dozen men in the world who could have led it without breaking it. It's the hardest lead I've ever seen."

Ahead lay a broad corridor of easy, angled snow. A shield of tawny summer ice—dyed by the shale overhead—lay visible where avalanches

had scoured away the winter snow. For a moment, I saw the stained summer snow balanced against the dominant white of winter. Then the white snow reared into a standing wave with tendons of pewter hinting at underlying ice. I punched steps to the vertical winter snow and began easing my way up twenty feet of crusted meringue.

Each move was a matter of gently applying pressure to the spongy structure without shearing through it. The icicles could hold my foot but weren't thick enough to take a screw. At the lip, I cast my left pick a dozen times but couldn't find enough strength in the snow to pull over. I quivered, a hair's breadth from falling. My right tool slipped an inch and then caught.

I shouted down, "I think I'm going to fall if I try going up here. I'm coming down and trying the other side."

"You don't get to fall up here," Scott replied.

"I've got you, Bubba," Steve said, taking in slack as I downclimbed.

On the far left, against the rock wall, snow broke away like plaster as I hacked at the wave with my ax. Overhanging black rock lay behind the curtain, but there were cracks, and I placed and pounded gear and stood into my etriers. Aid climbing was slower, but safer. Twenty-five feet higher, I teetered from my etrier into firmer, shallow-angled snow. Overhead, the triangular, overhanging wall defined my vertical horizon: it was overbearing, impenetrable. Snow mushrooms bulged from its upper lip like the hulls of fishing boats seen from underwater. They sat 600 feet above me.

The cobalt sky had paled to aquamarine, and I could feel my clothing stiffen with the cold of the oncoming night. We needed a place to dig in. I tacked rightward across the snow to a sheet of rock that slanted past vertical with a snow ledge underneath. The ledge marked an angle change on the wall topping the 700-foot-high vertical band that we'd climbed that day. Above and left was a narrow snow couloir that led to a steep fan of snow abutting the triangular, overhanging wall. I anchored and shouted down. By the time Scott and Steve arrived, I had already attached a shovel blade to my ice-ax and started digging.

"Maybe we should go higher, Bubba," Steve stated.

"No, man, I think this is the best we're going to get."

"You don't think there'll be something up against the overhanging wall up there?" Scotty asked.

"I think we could waste a bunch of time prospecting for the depth of snow that we already have right here, and get skunked, and have to rap back down."

MARCH 24, 10 P.M.: Night, stars, and cold, yet my hands and back were sodden from hacking hard snow. We took turns squirming into the hole, excavating while we lay on the Ensolite pad that I'd pulled from my pack's back panel. The front man would chunk away, snow would rain down with each strike, and the heat of effort would melt it to merge with our sweat.

"Clang!" The shovel blade hit rock, and my elbow tendons jolted. I spat and turned the arc of the cave sideways and parallel to the rock. It would be another torpedo tube. Steve took over, but fatigue soon smacked us all. We compromised on half a cave.

Steve crawled into the back, and then Scott. I stood outside waiting, anxiously surveying how best to shoehorn the three of us in. Frost was forming inside my bright-orange one-piece suit. Earlier in the day, Scott had said I looked like a road worker, "No! Better yet, a convict!" As the fabric froze, I indeed felt shackled. The cold reached through my layers, metallic against the lower flanks of my back.

"Scott, you're going to have to slant yourself against the outer wall," Steve stated.

"How the fuck am I supposed to do that?"

"Can't you angle your feet and pad?"

Scotty snapped and shouted, "NO! No, I can't! Where is there room for my bag then? Where do I fucking go?" Fatigue, low blood sugar, claustrophobia, stage-one hypothermia, malnutrition—I'd already lost ten pounds on this climb—it all added up to a kind of temporary insanity.

Is alpinism madness? If alpinism is mad, it is a fine kind of madness. That day, Steve had attained a measure of grace, glimpsed some the best within himself, climbed into a special place—an extremely dangerous place—and found a calm acceptance there. It was a place that most of us only get snippets of. Steve, Scott, and I were each granted our moments of grace up there, on the wall, in the alpine.

I made light of Scott's outbreak with a Twight coinage: "Stop torture; handcuff an alpinist." Then added, "It'll work if I sleep with my head and shoulders in the cave and my feet out on the belay ledge. The weather is looking good—it'll be okay."

That night, a storm swept in from the southwest, the opposite side of mountain. The northeast flank of Howse Peak came alive, and awash, in spindrift. We were comatose and unaware.

MARCH 25, 4 A.M.: My alarm shrieked, and I felt the firm, cold clamp of snow bonded across my lower legs, a cone of snow the size of a headstone. My sleeping bag was flat and dead. I had to punch at the snow with gloved fists to break it up. Spindrift hissed through the beam of my headlamp, constant and pulsating, like the spray flanking a waterfall.

We wouldn't be going anywhere. I settled back and tried to lift my bivy sack up with my feet. I wanted the snow to settle into an arch that wouldn't press, and melt, against my pit, but the damage had already been done. Having decided to let my partners sleep, I had no place to go.

"We're not going anywhere in this crap," Scotty stated when he woke up. The dull gray of the new day was a downer.

"We've got enough food and fuel to sit here for a day," I said. "I think we should wait it out. If it clears within the next couple of hours, we could still gun for the top with the plan of returning here. If it doesn't, we can see what the forecast says at 4, when they update it. The worst-case scenario is that we descend tomorrow morning."

"I'll buy that," Scott said.

Steve added, "If we're going to be here for the day, let's dig out the cave."

Two hours later, we'd moved into a fine three-bedroom cave and sealed the portal with snow blocks. Everything went quiet and still. The world of gray, hissing white, and rumbling slides disappeared. We brewed and ate until we were pissing clear again.

"Oh man! Seeing the Ramones live was such a trip." Scotty's gargoyle grin beamed over the steam from his fourth cup of tea. "I was so high, and Johnny played his guitar so low. Nobody holds their guitar lower than Johnny." Scotty chanted the chorus—"Beat on the brat!"—and then broke into cackling, his head jittering down for another long, loud pull of tea.

"I saw The Pretenders in Calgary," I chimed in. "Iggy Pop was backup and did two encores. Then Chrissie Hynde came out and said, 'All right,

Snow cave life: Steve House waiting out the weather and listening to Scott Backes talk about The Ramones, and me enjoying the Pop-Tart I should have saved for breakfast the next day. Photos: Barry Blanchard, Steve House

girls, I am THE lucky girl. I get to kiss the stage that Iggy Pop stood on.' And she kneeled down and kissed the stage, stood up, and blasted into 'The Wait,' 'Precious,' and 'Tattooed Love Boys.'"

As we bantered more about music, with Farm Boy adding that he'd never been a rock convert and ribbing us for being old, he finally confessed, "When I was in high school, I had a picture of Bubba ice climbing taped to the inside of my locker."

"Are you shitting me?" I asked.

"No, God's own truth. I swear," Steve stated, then burst into laughter.

"That, my friend, is priceless," Scotty managed through his cackles.

We talked and slept. Over the day, we solved all of alpinism's problems, globally, then went on to solve all the problems between male alpinists and their romantic partners or spouses (we should have written that down, because it all vanished once we started climbing!). Steve was against the door. Fourteen times, he removed a block of snow to look out; fourteen times, he saw gray and spindrift sweeping down in waves.

MARCH 25, 4 P.M.: Environment Canada updated their forecast, and the three of us lay still, listening to the robotic voice predict a twelve-hour break in the storm tomorrow. We ate again and eventually slept. I thought about the day to come and how much I wanted to succeed, to have Steve's lead legitimize a grand route and not be lost to the catacombs of alpine history, which was where it would end up if we didn't finish. We'd started to refer to his lead as "The Pitch."

MARCH 26, 4 A.M.: Liquid fuel pooled in the burner cup of the stove. I clicked my lighter to it, and orange flames leapt a foot high and danced, illuminating our cave like a campfire. I rubbed my hands over the flame, then the fire collapsed, and I turned the fuel valve on. A ring of bright blue roared to life. My partners slept until I stirred them and handed them coffee. Our day had begun.

An hour later, I asked Steve, "How does it look out there?" He eased a block of snow from the door: "Too dark to tell, but I saw a couple of stars." At dawn, he looked out again: "It looks like a snow version of Niagara Falls." Silence as three hearts sank.

"I guess we're going down," Steve said softly, his eyes falling to the floor.

"Well," Scott said, "let's eat the rest of our food then."

While we ate, I pondered The Pitch. I got pissed off at the storm. Then I started thinking about continuing in spite of the storm.

Scott's head jerked up and his brown eyes flashed as he said, "Hey, guys, why don't we just cinch down the Velcro, strap on our goggles, and go take a look? If it's too mean, we can always run back here. If we make the top, we can descend via the White Pyramid and Mt. Chephren. That's why we left your firn skis down at the lake, Bubba. I'm willing to write off all of my bivy gear if it means making it."

"Man, you've been reading my mail," I said. A wave of shock crossed Steve's face. Later, he told me that he didn't think that Scott and I, the old guys, would want it as badly as he did. His face cracked into a smile. We organized a couple of day packs and stepped out into the storm. We'd split the last of our food—two gel packs and three butterscotch candies each.

"I guess we shouldn't have eaten everything else," I lamented.

"My lead," Scott said and clipped the ice screws and rock rack to his harness as snow fell from the sky and hissed down the face to cover everything. He climbed away; when our ropes came tight, Steve and I followed, removing Scott's protection as we went, so that we all moved together in a fourth-class climbing system.

Snow and rock melded into the gray of cloud. I felt as if we were traversing the waking edge of a dream, my consciousness in one realm, tentatively stepping into another. Everywhere there was the white of the snow and the gray of clouds and in between an ebb and a flow; in the pulsation of the flow, even the black rock hazed to a shade of gray. The only colors available to me were the orange of my suit and the red of the rope. Then there would be an opening in the clouds, and we'd get brief stroboscopic glimpses of the far side of the valley, two miles distant, the peaks washed in gray with horizontal bands of ashen cloud clinging. Snow fell in clusters as Steve and I followed Scott's foot holes. He led 800 feet across phantasmagoric snow arêtes and mushrooms like you'd more typically see in the Peruvian Andes and Khumbu Himal.

Much of the snow was in motion, sweeping the face with spindrift. The snow not already in motion was set into motion with our passing.

I came to feel threatened only when it whited out completely, when even my red rope disappeared into the gray five feet in front of me. And then I would be able to see farther. At moments, the climbing was nothing short of enchanting. I was happy.

Steve and I climbed onto a desktop-sized platform that Scott had stamped into a deep snowdrift with a bulging wall of limestone above. He'd constructed a secure anchor in rock. The exit couloir, the one that Jock Glidden and George Lowe had climbed in the summer of 1971, lay seventy feet down and right.

"Scotty, that was bloody wild. I felt like I was back in the Cordillera Blanca," I said.

"You did a mighty fine job of that, Backes," Steve added.

"Thanks, guys. It was cool, felt old school, like I was back in my day."

It looked like a steep, short rappel would put us onto a traverse line into the gully. "I think we should fix a rope here so we can regain this Peruvian Traverse if we retreat this way," Scott said.

A thirty-five-foot rappel saw us to an anchor. I took the lead, traversing toward an ice bulge at the entrance to the gully proper. Snowflakes the size of postage stamps filled the air. Large, concentrated

spindrift avalanches thundered from the gully every couple of minutes, forcing me to advance timidly against my fear of being swept off. I swung my picks into the frothy surface of the bulge and felt the bite of the emerald ice underlying. The first surge of spindrift smacked me, the charging snow pounding onto my head and shoulders as I clung within the vibration of the onslaught and dropped my chin to my chest to create a channel of air to breathe.

The slide hissed off down the mountain. "You need a SCREW!" screamed inside my skull. I stabbed at the ice with the spike of my right tool to create a starter hole. Scott and Steve screamed, "Avalanche!" A shadow charged, and I saw the churning front of the next spindrift. I slammed my pick into the bulge and held fast for the smack. It came with force and weight, then disappeared with a hiss. The avalanche had erased my starter hole. I frantically swept snow away, then stabbed the ice screw in and got in a couple of turns before I heard "Avalanche!" again, and the next thundering hit.

"Crap, man, he has to come back," Steve said to Scott. Then I disappeared in the slide.

"Holy shit! He's coming back and we're going down. We can't climb up through this." Scott said.

Several times, between slides, I looked to my partners and saw their concerned gazes, felt empathy in the absolute attention they paid to the rope. I knew that if I didn't pull the bulge, we'd be going down. I wanted to do my part for my partners, and I pushed myself.

The screw twisted home, and I clipped it in the calm between slides; then I had to pull the bulge, knowing that if I took one in the chest it would flush me off. I climbed as quickly as I could on nerve-racked limbs, fear sitting like bile in my throat. My heart hammered. What I was doing was mad. If I could just get above the bulge to where the gully widened, I could take cover on the sides and, I prayed, be granted solid ice screws and rock gear. Which I was. At the pitch's end, I anchored securely.

"That was insane, Bubba," Scott said. "Farmy and I thought we were going down. Now we are going up because of you. Good work, my man."

Steve took the lead, and Scott and I tied into the end of our single 8.1-millimeter rope ten feet apart, with Scott clipped to a knot above me. Leaving my stance, I saw the black wave of an exceptionally large

Climbing through some madness as avalanches pour down at one-minute intervals. I fight to twist in a screw. Steve House slide charging down. I screamed, we were smacked, I sensed Scott fall away sideways, and then I felt my harness saw into my waist as his body weight came onto it. The avalanche continued, and then hissed away. Scotty lay entombed in white ten feet below me, the belay rope running up to Steve as rigid as cable. "I'm okay! I'm okay," he shouted and fought back onto his crampons. "Wow, I could feel this skinny rope just stretching and stretching."

"Steve had you snug. You took twenty feet of stretch out of the rope, man. I'm glad it had you when you came tight to me, or I would have gone too."

"Praise be to Farm Boy for that belay."

Four more pitches of dodging avalanches, digging out cracks for rock gear, and drilling screws into ancient, leaden ice. I thought about how certain situations, like climbing up through tons of spindrifting snow, could completely overwhelm us: Ernest Shackleton and five of his crew sailing through the Drake Passage in the *James Caird*—a 22-foot-long open dory; Voytek Kurtyka and Robert Schauer hallucinating in an icy bivouac, having sat through fifty hours of storm at 7,700 meters on the west face of Gasherbrum IV.

Midday, Lowell George's voice rang in my head, and I began singing "Willin'" at the belays.

"This must be what salmon feel like," I said to Steve as we belayed Scott.

"Why salmon?"

"They're nothing but heart, and I'm hoping we can channel some of that spirit. About all we can do to keep them from returning upriver to spawn is build dams they can't get over. Otherwise, they are going back to their birthplace, unstoppable. We need some salmon heart now."

I led the final pitch on the wall. Twenty feet up and right of my anchor, and hidden from view until then, a summit-ridgeline cornice bellied out from one side of the gully to the other. It reached an honest—and horrifying—forty feet out into space, growing in size as I stood there with westerly winds dumping snow over it and into our gully.

Steve arrived and asked, "Do you think we can get around it?"

Then Scott: "Oh, is it my turn?" He started twisting in an ice screw to rappel off of.

We'd silently and unanimously decided to go down. We rappelled 100 feet at a time (the length of our red rope doubled through the rappel anchors, the green one being fixed below at the Peruvian Traverse) and Scotty left a brand-new Black Diamond Express ice screw and HotWire carabiner for each anchor.

"We could drill ice threads," I said. "That way we wouldn't have to leave all your screws."

Scotty turned out from the mountain and bellowed into the storm, "Hell no! Belcourt will give us more swag just for the stories!" Billy Belcourt was our brother in arms at Black Diamond and in charge of Scott's sponsorship there.

The cogged grind of hunger churned in my stomach. "Gentlemen, when we get down, we are heading straight to the Kentucky Fried Chicken in Banff and getting us a family bucket of fried chicken with one of those pint-sized Styrofoam tubs of gravy."

"Oh man, KFC!" Scotty howled. "Yes! Yes! I can taste that secret blend of seven herbs and spices. Colonel Sanders is my man!"

"Do you think one bucket will be enough?" Steve asked.

"If it isn't, we'll walk back in and get a second one," I said. We talked about KFC for the rest of our descent.

MARCH 26, 5 P.M.: We jumared up the rope we'd left fixed to regain Scott's anchor at the end of the Peruvian Traverse. Snow fell in clumps, and our world remained gray. From down in the depths, I heard the reverberating thump of a helicopter. "I wonder if they're rescuing those guys we saw approach the face a couple days ago?" I asked Scott. Then I realized, "Hey, they may be searching for us!" I pulled my radio from my breast pocket.

"Blanchard party on Howse Peak for Parks Canada."

"Yeah, hi Barry, it's Mark here in the helicopter. Where are you?" Mark Ledwidge was a fellow mountain guide and Public Safety Specialist. We'd been friends since the early 1980s.

"We're at about 9,800 feet on the east face."

"Well, we're way below that. How are you guys doing?"

"We're okay. On our way down. It's not real nice here right now. Are you guys looking for us?"

"Your wife called. She's a bit concerned, and we said that we'd check on you. We had a flight to do up this way anyway. What's your plan?"

"We're hoping to reach our snow cave a couple hundred feet below us tonight and to rap the rest of the face tomorrow."

"Need any assistance?"

"No, I think we'll be okay, thanks."

"Well, the storm should break up tomorrow. Happy birthday, Barry. Over and out." The helicopter whumped off to the south. It felt strange to have had contact with the greater world. My body was cooling, and my exposed hand was numb from working the radio. Scott, Steve, and I were still on a big mountain descending through a storm. Scott led back across the Peruvian Traverse.

MARCH 26, 9 P.M.: Snow fell through the beam of my headlamp; the night was moonless and black and cold. I stood side-footed, my crampon points sunk into the step that Scott had hacked into the ice and my anchor leash tight to the shallow Angle he'd hammered until its shaft bent. We'd called it "over-driven." Scott had equalized the pin to an ice screw sunk into the frothy ice. Twelve inches to my left, a limestone wall melded into the night. Ten feet to my right, across the cinereous ice, stood a parallel wall of limestone. I was strapped to rock and ice inside a deep chasm. Far below me, Steve was on rappel, our twin climbing ropes rigid with his weight. I would be the last to rappel and regain the security of our snow cave 185 feet below.

Alone at the anchor, I listened for the soft crunching as six-armed snowflakes—stellars—hit my jacket. I held my breath and clenched my eyes against the steely cold, trying to will blood to my skin as I waited for Steve's "Off rappel!" The seconds stretched; the cold slowed everything. Even the snowflakes. At the beam's periphery, the absolute black grew darker, pulling, disquieting.

"Off rappel!"

I swung my attention to my harness, hauled on the ropes, and folded them into my rappel device, then turned a locking carabiner shut on them. The black folded and flapped like a raven's wing. And then a thunderous *Crack!* exploded through the night. The air was compressed by the roar of a large object in freefall. Now came the booming

Snowfall sets the world and the mountain into motion as I follow Scott across the Peruvian Traverse. Steve House and the barrage. It hammered into me and obliterated my scream with pounding thunder.

The hit was inhuman. I had the illusion of being swept away, scraped from the mountain. Next would come the belly-raising free fall as I shot out of the couloir, and then the muffled crunches of my skeleton shattering. One thought bellowed into my mind: *I will never see her again! Please no, not now, not now.*

But blocks of snow still smashed and pummeled, pounding my body. I realized that I wasn't hurtling down. I was still anchored! Folded in half and rag-dolling in the avalanche flow, as tons of blocky snow surged through the ten-foot-wide hourglass. I was being battered against the rock wall but remained attached by the virtue and grace of a small bulge of limestone that Scott had chosen to anchor under. Six inches to the right—one shoulder-width more exposed—my anchorage would certainly have failed.

The pounding snow backed off in a last surge as the avalanche roared into the night, diminishing to a final dribble of snow that trickled through the hourglass. The flow had stopped.

Only the stellar snowflakes continued to fall faintly on everything.

With shaking hands, I grabbed my anchor leash. Manacles of snow as hard as mortar encircled my exposed wrists. My headlamp's beam slashed left and right as it bobbed around my neck, its strapping ripped from my helmet. Sobs burst out of me; spit and snot and blood from my nose splattered the snow and ashen ice. I quaked with shock and stumbled trying to get onto my left leg. I had felt my right leg break against the rock. Numb and dumb, it would not support any weight; my left leg and hands responded in spastic jerks. The ice screw had failed and now dangled from the anchor cord. Scott's bent, beautiful, over-driven piton alone had held me.

"BARRY, BAARRRY!"

"Ya-a-a..." I moaned.

"Are you alright?"

A knot of fear choked me. I stacked six jittering draws of breath and shouted, "I'm ok-k-kay!" but that was bullshit. My jaw quivered uncontrollably. My fear vibrated into the taut sling connected to the bent pin. I became terrified of the piton pulling out. I broke the snow manacles from my wrists and scraped my damp hands into gloves that did not want to accept them.

My breath still came in staccato draws and sighs, and I continued to sob as I untied the ice screw, twisted it back into the ice, and retied the rap cord to it. Death could still take me. A surge of sorrow swamped my heart as I imagined my mother's face, and Catherine's. I choked and cried and resolved to fight the fucking dark and cold. When I struck the bent piton with my hammer, it rebounded with the sound recoil of firm metal well set. A prayer whispered, *God bless you, Scotty, God bless you.* I untethered from the anchor and began hopping down the rappel.

The darkness swallowed me, and snow fell into the beam of my headlamp. I felt as vulnerable as a young boy lying in bed afraid after domestic violence has shattered the security of home. I was a wreck. At the bottom of the rappel, Steve grabbed me by the armpits and pulled me onto the snow ledge outside our snow cave like a father lifting a child from a swimming pool. His hands were so strong and so assured. It was all that I could do to stand. When he looked into my eyes, I saw the immediate flush of horror in his.

"Oh, Bubba! Fuck man, Bubba!" and he started to cry and bear-hugged me. My chest heaved. "My pack is g-g-gone. I thought I was dead," I sobbed as I leaned into Steve's arms.

"Scott! Scott! Get out here—Bubba's been hurt."

From the sanctum of the snow cave we'd climbed away from fourteen hours earlier, Scott had been insulated from the avalanche. Steve had felt it surge past, but he'd been out of the line of fire and merely awash in heavy waves of spindrift.

My partners took control, and I became the patient. Inside the snow cave, they swaddled me into Scotty's massive blue sleeping bag. My bag lay crumpled and frozen from dampness absorbed on our second night on the wall. Tonight would be our fourth. They sealed the cave portal with snow blocks and boiled a liter of water for me to nestle between my thighs, where it would heat my femoral arteries. Then they used the last of our fuel to make me a cup of tea, while they had nothing.

I undid my helmet and saw that the suspension had fractured. Incredibly, an inch-thick layer of chalk-hard snow was plastered to the inside, so firm you could sink an ice pick in it! With trembling hands, I set it aside and laid back into Scott's bag.

"I didn't even know that Bubba had been hit. What happened?" Scott asked.

"A snow mushroom must have broken off from the top of the triangular face," Steve replied. "I heard one hell of a crack and then a huge whirring sound and then the explosion of the avalanche. It would have fallen free for 500 feet...."

"And funneled down onto Bubba...holy fuck, man...holy fuck!"

Their words faded to white noise in my ears as I settled into their care and tried to get my breathing under control. Overwhelming sorrow and regret ebbed through my heart. I had been so close to dying. I closed my eyes and breathed, in and out, in and out. Then, an epiphany jolted me: At the moment I believed I was dying, when the avalanche smacked me into the wall, love had charged into me. Images of Catherine rose in my mind, and the sorrow slipped away like the last wisps of the avalanche.

A half hour later, I was warm and breathing normally when Steve checked my pulse for the second time. "Eighty—that's way better," he

said. Then, he held his hand over my eyes one at a time to check their reaction to light. "You're not dilated anymore—cool. We should look at your knee." I undid my harness and coaxed my knee from layers of clothing and zippers. It was swollen to the size of a honeydew melon and mottled with patches of yellow and green and dead-blood black.

"Do you think you'll be able to rappel on it?"

"I don't know, but it's more the downclimbing and reversing that big traverse I led on the first day that worries me."

"Ya, I can see that." Eventually Scotty opened the zipper to his sleeping bag and nestled in behind me to spoon. We would both sleep warmer that way, and I needed to keep warm.

"Oh Bubba-man, we are going to be so cozy cuddling, my dear!" Scott declared, eyes wide and playful, and then he erupted into his trademark cackling.

"Be careful," I replied. "Spooning can lead to forking." Scott and Steve erupted in laughter. It was so good to feel that lightness.

"Holy crap, Bubba, you are feeling better!" Scott chortled.

My VHF radio had been blasted by snow crystals, but it still worked. We listened to the first good forecast we'd heard in two days, uttered in the jolting, robotic voice on a set frequency from Environment Canada. I switched the power off, unscrewed the antenna, and stuffed the radio back into my breast pocket to keep it warm.

I surrendered to sleep.

MARCH 27, 2 A.M.: I woke to the pitch-black of the cave pressing into my face. The threat of death came with the darkness. I began to worry about my leg and losing control on our descent and dying. I lay awake in the black and agonized. *Should I call for a rescue?* It felt defeating to call for help.

I'd spent my adult life pursuing the ideal of autonomous alpinism. My partners and I believed in meeting the challenges of the mountain solely with what we carried in our packs. My radio allowed us to listen to weather forecasts once we climbed high enough, and that is how we'd justified bringing it.

It would have been wrong to use it to call for help; not talking to Scott and Steve about it first would have been doubly wrong. But

.aving left the second snow cave, Steve follows
:ott and me on the Peruvian Traverse. March
6, 1999. Barry Blanchard

it would also have been so easy to die up here with my leg broken. I assembled my radio by feel and twisted the power/volume knob, but the small screen did not light up. I repeated the procedure three times. The screen stayed dark. I felt so small and powerless—a child alone in the dark—as somehow the blackness of the cave clamped down even harder. I wanted to see Catherine and my family again, to be with them within the security of our home on the valley floor. It was something to hold onto. I clung to that warmth and hope, and I prayed. An hour passed, and I found calm in committing to myself to talking to Steve and Scott in the morning about rescue.

I had a plan. I slept again. The three of us lay in a snow cave dug into canted snows that had been accumulating on a shattered incline of shale since late September 1999, at 9,500 feet above sea level on the east face of Howse Peak in the Canadian Rockies. Our skis were picketed into the approach slope 2,000 feet below us. It was our fourth night on the wall. In two days' time, I would be turning forty.

MARCH 27: Our third morning in our highest snow cave; our fourth night on the wall. I twisted my headlamp on and gazed at the arched white ceiling. It had glazed over with ice from the heat of our bodies and breath and the warmth and humidity of the stove, back when the stove had fuel. Angular strikes from the shovel blade had sculpted the roof, and I thought about how it looked like the plaster-and-trowel adobe inside a Taco Bell. I smiled, my mouth tacky with viscous saliva and crinkling from the want of hot drinks. I assembled my radio and twisted the power toggle. The screen remained lifeless, and my grin flattened to a grimace. My knee was fat, hard to the touch, and did not want to bend.

"There is no way I'm going to be able to ski," I said twenty minutes later.

"I say we get you to the bottom of the face, Bubba, and then either Farmy or I ski for help. We rally our friends and ski in here and haul you out on a toboggan," Scott said.

"Rescue just doesn't work like that around here," I countered.

"Ya, but we don't need a rescue. We can do this ourselves."

"The rescue guys ARE my friends."

"It's a moot point right now because the radio is dead," Steve said.

"First we have to get off the wall."

It was easy for me to pack up: I had no pack. The avalanche had sheared it from my back.

"Here, Bubba, put this big-ass puppy on," Scotty said, grinning and handing me his enormous red down jacket.

"Thanks, brother. It's been hard to keep from shivering since we quit spooning under your big-ass sleeping bag."

"I miss it too...the bag that is!" And his eyes pinged wide and he started cackling. I replied with my best Clint Eastwood impersonation from *The Eiger Sanction*: "We'll make it." Scotty didn't miss a beat and replied with a heavy Austrian accent, "I don't think so. But we shall continue with style."

"Would you two please shut up?" Steve interjected.

Steve went down first to rig anchors, and I was soon hopping down the first rap on my left foot. As I slid over the standing wave of snow that I'd aid-climbed around three days before, my right crampon snagged, and an electric bundle of pain fired in my brain. I hopped onto my left and swore and clenched my eyes. Next, we rappelled over The Pitch. Coated in snow, it didn't look nearly as stark. Even so, it took my breath away, as did snagging my right foot again.

We rappelled the fall line from there. On our next rap, we got under the cloud ceiling and saw the whole of the valley for the first time in thirty-six hours. I'd jolted my right foot a half dozen more times. I worried about the damage to my knee and even more about reversing our big traverse of the first day and the fact that I wouldn't be able to ski. Midway down the rap, alone, I caught my balance and rested on my left foot. I pulled out my radio. It turned on!

"Climbers on Howse Peak for Parks Canada."

The reply was immediate: "Hi, Barry, this is Gord—how are you guys doing?" Gord Irwin was another mountain guide, Rescue Specialist, and friend. I looked at my radio. Was this my one chance to call for help? Could I make this decision without Steve and Scotty? My trigger finger trembled over the push-to-talk button, and then I pressed it.

"Gord, we could really use some help getting off of Howse Peak."

"Okay, we're on our way." And it was the last time that radio worked, ever.

"I got through to the wardens and called for a rescue," I said, when I reached Steve down at the next anchor. He was aggressively hacking away snow ice with the adze of his ice-ax.

"Okay." He turned back to his work, two hands wrapped around his ax, pulling hard.

"Shit," he said. "I just broke the adze off my tool." The head of his tool looked strange without the adze, like a bird robbed of its plumage. Scotty arrived and we reversed our traverse, with me hopping sideways and stumbling.

The helicopter found us anchored to the top of Scott's grade 6 pitch of the first day. The ship passed slowly by, surveying the situation—our salvation and my form of an angel.

Mark Ledwidge flew into us at the end of a long line hung from the chopper's belly. His bright-orange rescue jacket shone against the gray sky, lighting up the mountain and the timber like a Christmas bulb, but he came in too low and bounced from the wall beneath us.

"Uff-da," Scott blurted. "That's gotta hurt."

The pilot—I later learned it was another friend, Lance Cooper—pulled away and came in again. The down blast of his rotors raked snow over us, and the air thumped with the pounding of the blades. I reached for Mark's cramponed foot and saw him yelling into his microphone as he slowly lowered to level with us. I grabbed his tether and clipped him into our anchor, and then he unhooked from the ship. Lance banked away, and then everything went quiet.

"Hi, Mark. This is Scott Backes and Steve House."

"Welcome to our world," Scott added.

"Hi. How are you guys? Who's hurt?"

"Just me—I'm pretty sure my right knee is broken."

"Okay, well I'll take you off first, then Steve and Scott."

"Scott and I can rappel and downclimb. We don't need to be rescued, just Barry."

"We can take you all. It's no problem."

"No, we're fine to get down from here," Steve reiterated.

"See what you're anchored to?" I added. "That's my spare ice pick. We ran out of pitons."

"Oh, man—you didn't have to tell me that."

Lance Cooper flying Mark Ledwidge in to rescue me, March 27, 1999. Steve House

Lance came back in, and Mark secured himself and me to the 100-foot-long line. Even though I had ridden beneath helicopters as a rescuer in the past, I was still amazed to feel the authority and power of the lift. At the last second, Scott, the eternal opportunist, clipped his pack to the back of my harness to have it fly away so he wouldn't have to carry it down!

We slowly spun to look back on the east face of Howse Peak; it was melancholic to see Steve and Scott shrink from my view and disappear into the face. I felt like I'd abandoned them.

Several minutes later, we put down in a pullout beside the highway. I was soon in the back of a Parks Canada Suburban drinking hot chocolate while Gord exposed my swollen, multicolored knee. Percy Woods, one of the rescue team, drove me to the emergency room in Banff. Catherine was there to meet me.

"You've cracked the head of your tibial plateau," the ER doc said. "Your knee capsule has filled with blood and fluid, but it should get

reabsorbed over the next three weeks. The crack will heal on its own. We'll get you crutches, but you'll want to start weight-bearing on it in a couple of days."

At home I ate a lot, had a hot bath, and then iced and elevated my knee. I imagined Scott and Steve still skiing back to the highway. Soon they called from Lake Louise; they were on their way home.

MARCH 29: Back at our condo after my fortieth birthday party, Steve said, "Bubba, we've got something for you." He went to the fridge and pulled out a breast of the Colonel's finest.

The cold fried chicken was delicious.

MARCH 30, 3 A.M.: I woke beside Catherine. It was the end of my second decade of alpinism. Twice, I had come close to being killed by an avalanche. First, on the Rupal Face of Nanga Parbat in 1988, at the end of my first decade of climbing. And now, on Howse Peak.

Did I want to be an alpinist anymore?

eing rescued by Mark Ledwidge. I felt the mmense power of the helicopter's lift, and I elt safe. Scott's pack is clipped in and Chephren ake and the Icefields Parkway beyond.
cott Backes

A River Runs Through It by Norman Maclean

CHAPTER 17 — HOLDING ON AND LETTING GO I

INFINITE PATIENCE

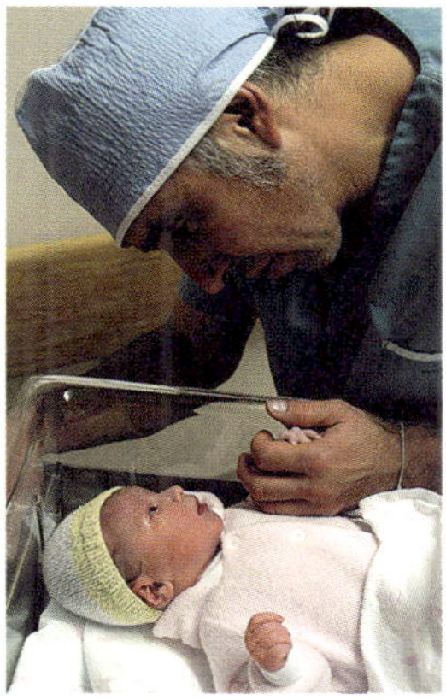

She wrapped her small fingers onto my left index finger...and that was it...a covenant of the heart, for life.

Eric Dumerac and Philippe Pellet called the route Infinite Patience, in deference to attempts I'd made over time: 1989, 1997, 2000, and finally succeeding, with them, in 2002. It was a beautiful line that took more than a quarter of my lifetime to create.

OCTOBER 2002: I had escorted the last of my summer clients out of the mountains; conditions were perfect for alpine climbing. A week of bluebird weather was headed our way, and our prospective line on the Emperor Face of Mt. Robson could go. Farm Boy couldn't get away, so I convinced myself that I had too many other things to do, a career to maintain.

But when Eric Dumerac called, I cleared my calendar. Eric had dragged my sorry ass up some truly sick modern-mixed rigs that were clearly designed to pull my arms out of my torso! But he was also keen to embrace the beauty and battle of traditional alpinism. His passion for *all* of it encouraged me to look beyond my own camp.

Philippe Pellet belaying Eric Dumerac across The Spiral Road on Mt. Robson during the first ascent of Infinite Patience. Barry Blanchard

Above: Unconditionally loving my daughter Rosemary Hawthorne Arwen Blanchard at her birth in Canmore, November 24, 2004. Todd Gynn

Philippe Pellet was on vacation from France to spend two months climbing with Eric. Philippe lived in the alpine village of Briançon (pronounced Brie-*on*-saw; I loved winding him up by saying Bri*an*-con). Philippe was our ace in the hole: The man could climb 5.13, M10, and grade VII in the alpine, and he was a Union Internationale des Associations de Guides de Montagnes member and rescue specialist who spent six months a year slinging into accidents under a helicopter. Philippe was forty-one, a father of three, and spoke little English. Embarrassingly, after a half dozen trips to Chamonix, I still had no ear for French. The bilingual Eric would be our conduit.

We three were headed to climb the King: Mt. Robson.

At 12,972 feet, Robson, the highest peak in the Canadian Rockies, is a full 700 feet higher than Mt. Columbia, the second highest peak in the range. The Secwépemc (Shuswap) First Nation name is Yuh-hai-has-kun, "the mountain of the spiral road," based on the belief that the strata corkscrew a path to the top. Like frozen white flames, immense plumes of rime point skyward from the tops of the mile-long Emperor Ridge—falling to the northwest (first climbed by Tom Spencer and Ron Perla in 1961)—and Wishbone Arête—bifurcating the southwest ridge (Don Claunch, Harvey Firestone, and Mike Sherrick, 1955). These rows of gargantuan ice jewels, "The Gargoyles," rise to a sovereign point on the crown of the King.

The Methodist minister George Rex Boyer Kinney put his all into Robson in the summers of 1907, '08, and then '09, when he erroneously believed he had made the first ascent. The actual first ascent came on July 31, 1913, thanks to Conrad Kain, William Foster, and Albert MacCarthy via what has become known as "The Kain Face." The north face was opened in 1963 by Pat Callis and Dan Davis, and the 7,000-foot Emperor Face was finally climbed, after numerous attempts by a long list of alpinists, by Jaime Logan (then known as Jim) and Terry "Mugs" Stump in 1978. Three years later, Dave Cheesmond and Tony Dick added a second route to the face. In 1989, I started what would become a half dozen attempts, almost always in winter/early spring. Sometimes we'd ski; other times, when we could afford it, we'd helicopter—one of the few places we could do that in the Rockies.

In April 1997, Steve House, Joe Josephson, and I paid for the heli and over a twenty-two-hour day ascended 5,000 feet, opening the

Philippe rappelling over a serac using the two ropes that I'd insisted on, rather than just one with his removable hook—a small aluminum hook rigged with an elastic cord to facilitate single-rope rappels. The rope must be weighted. Once unweighted, it pulls off. Barry Blanchard

key passages of a big emerald-green ice couloir, the "Traverse of the Stubbies," and a triangular ice face. We descended defeated, after somehow dropping the pump to the stove! Three years later, we came back with a film crew who footed the heli costs. We duplicated our 5,000-foot push, but the weather thumped us, and we once again bailed.

OCTOBER 23: Fifteen hundred feet above our exit from the warm helicopter, we encountered our first difficulty, a freshly formed mixed challenge—M5 rock shelled in snow that dead-ended. Philippe took the lead and escaped left across a steep, undercut traverse to reach newborn water ice.

Fifteen feet into seconding Philippe's traverse, I uncovered blocky limestone from the eggshell crust of grainy snow. Philippe had set a hand-sized cam. Two of its lobes were open, but I couldn't get it out. My pack was dragging on me, heating my forearms to a vicious, burning pump. I stepped down, poised hard up against a questionable nut below the cam, realizing I was about to fall in a horrible pendulum if I did not get rid of my pack. I screamed back to Eric, who screamed in French to Philippe; with more screaming, Philippe coiled and hurled a rope to me. I felt my left shoulder failing, elongating. The tasks of tying a knot with one hand and clipping in my pack and shucking it from my back drew out

into anxious and exhausting minutes. I wobbled, then fell into panic and rage when the pack fishhooked on my right tool and dragged on me like a gibbeted corpse. I jerked and jerked; my crampon points rasped and scratched. I screamed a string of vitriol that silenced Philippe and Eric.

They grabbed at the mountain and checked their belays. My pack unsnagged and arced away to *thud!* into the wall below Philippe. Now back in balance, I welded the nut into the mountain with multiple smacks from my hammer and clipped my quivering ass to it, then sorted out the cam and breathed. We ferried the other packs across.

Four hours later, we bivied right of the big couloir. The northern lights burned across the firmament like a wall of jade flame. It was one of the rare nights on a big mountain when there was no wind or spindrift. We sat in our sleeping bags eating and drinking and staring, awestruck, at the radiant aurora borealis.

OCTOBER 24: Eric's early-morning headlamp bobbed from Philippe to rest on me.

"Philippe wants to put in gear and use the rope."

The modern alpinists were opting for less risk! The climbing was superb. A classic gully of ancient green ice led to the "Traverse of the Stubbies," as Jo-Jo, Farm Boy, and I had named it on our first attempt, back in 1997. It was mostly protected on four 10 cm ice screws: stubbies.

Eric led a lovely, snow-covered 5.7 corner to link us to a small, triangular ice face; the sky was blue, the temperatures bearable. Pivoting at one of the anchors, Philippe accidentally elbowed one of his ice tools, which slithered off downslope to ping and bounce, then bound, down the huge couloir. Latinate profanity followed, an impressive amount of it, every bit as loud and colorful as my Anglo-Saxon of the day before. Eric listened intently, and then turned to me and said, "He's pissed, man."

"No, really? I didn't quite catch that, *mon ami*."

Philippe took over at the highpoint that Jo-Jo, Farmy, and I had reached in 1997 and 2000, 5,000 feet up the face with daylight gone but time to bivy on both efforts. We followed a magic strip of ice for four perfect ropelengths. The climbing was near mythical: a three- to six-foot-wide passage of silver ice etched into corners and grooves of solid tawny rock.

The upper reaches of Mt. Robson, picketed with a regiment of "Gargoyles"—rime formations—some seventy feet high. Barry Blanchard

It was—and is still—one of the most sacred lines I have climbed in the mountains.

Eric's block merged us onto the north variation of the Emperor Ridge, an ice gully leading to an ice-coated chimney. Later, by headlamp, we found an established bivy at about 11,000 feet. I pointed out chalk-colored flesh, blanched by the −22°F windchill, on Eric's nose. We put our backs to the bitter west wind as hunks of spiced Italian sausage jiggled and puffed up in a simmering pot of hot-and-sour soup and pad thai noodles. The French really are further evolved culinarily. I'd have brought mac and cheese and tube steak.

"Those pitches had never been climbed," I said. We were talking about how amazing the ice strip had been. Philippe immediately asked for a translation. He wanted to know every word that I said, and Eric had grown weary of these requests.

"Yeah, Bubba said he's badly constipated and has hemorrhoids—he needs your spoon man." It was a classic "Do-mo" crack (what a lot of us called Eric Dumerac). I could read his smirk and see the grim grin on Philippe's face.

OCTOBER 25: I got the gemstone pitch, a foot-wide strand of deep ice recessed in a vertical chimney that I climbed with one tool, adorned with positive edges and ending on the Emperor Ridge proper. Quite frankly, it just doesn't get any better. Above, we tacked up the Emperor Ridge for many an hour. Philippe's block ended by turning a steep step on the frost-locked 5.9 terrain of the Emperor Face. As he belayed, he accidentally elbowed off his remaining ice tool. As it disappeared, he opened his mouth and set a route record for volume, length, and scale of profanity.

"He's pissed," Eric said.

"No shit."

"Oh wait—this is good. He says that in twenty-five years of climbing, he's never dropped a tool, and if he drops one more, I'm supposed to take him to the nearest mental hospital and check him in."

Above us the King rose still. Any other route in the range would have been over.

Philippe on top of Gargoyle number 8. Soon we would leave the Gargoyles and follow the Spiral Road. Barry Blanchard

OCTOBER 25, LATE AFTERNOON: I surmounted Gargoyle number 10. We were at 12,000 feet, and more than a half mile of Gargoyles stretched before me in toppling legions along the ridge. We would never get through them that day. The words of the Shuswap Nation came to me, Yuh-hai-has-kun, The mountain of the spiral road. I sprinted out right onto the "Spiral Road," and for ten ropelengths we traversed a 40-degree ice band held in place by Robson's strata.

The immersion into cold night started, calf muscles so exhausted that we sprinted to belays, to anywhere we could get a foot sideways.

OCTOBER 25, 9 P.M.: Eric's block gained us the couloir that tops the Wishbone Arête. Philippe ground on in the lead, and Eric and I followed on brittle, glassy ice, with one tool each and one gloved palm gliding over the skin of the mountain. When it got steep, we'd hook a finger into Philippe's pick holes. Our other three limbs penetrated the ice by force and the bite of forged metal.

OCTOBER 26, MIDNIGHT: Eric and I crunched onto the summit shelf and wobbled over to clamp Philippe in our arms. We were all teary-eyed. Language was superfluous; the moment spoke spirit to spirit to spirit. We pointed our headlamps to the firmament and HOWLED!

NOVEMBER 2004: We knew we'd be having a girl. Catherine pushed for twenty-four hours, using up pretty much all the hot water in the Canmore Hospital while standing, supported by me or one of her girlfriends, in the shower. There was a duel between the doula and the doctor, at least until I told the doctor we were going to bring in Tibetan monks and incense and start chanting. His double take became a smile. In the next hours, he said, when it could start to get dangerous for the baby, he would initiate a cesarean with the backing of legislation. "Danger to the baby" was all we needed to hear; into the operating room we went.

I got to hold our daughter first, carrying her with her misshapen head—it looked like there was a hockey puck under the crown of her scalp—to the warming table. Her hazel eyes were wide with the most genuine and pure amazement I have ever seen. After the nurses cleaned her up and clothed her, I saw her next in her baby trolley. I bowed my face to hers and looked into her gorgeous eyes. Life would never be the same for me.

Catherine named our daughter Rosemary Hawthorne Arwen Blanchard. "I carried her for nine months. I get to name her," she declared. I should have put up some resistance, should at least have spelled Hawthorn like the tree on her Registration of a Live Birth.

Rosemary came with us to back-to-back ice festivals in Munising, Michigan, and North Conway, New Hampshire. She was not yet three months old.

FEBRUARY 2005: My mother's voice broke when she called to tell me that my brother Steven had died of a drug overdose. I crumpled to the floor, weeping. My little brother, whose deep-brown eyes had welcomed the world with as much amazement as Rosemary's. He'd been such a beautiful boy. What had happened? I had him come and live with me in Canmore when he'd first started getting trouble with the law in 1984. I took him climbing in Canada, then again in Peru in 1987. When I'd gone alone to the north face of Kusum Kanguru fourteen years earlier—after realizing that my marriage was failing, mostly due to my own actions, and not feeling good enough—climbing helped. I guess it wasn't the fix for him.

Some losses are never accounted for. I often return to Norman Maclean's words from *A River Runs Through It*, "It is those we live with and love and should know who elude us."

CHAPTER 18 — HOLDING ON AND LETTING GO II

AGING ALPINIST

David Cheesmond, Tim Friesen, and I made the first ascent of the Andromeda Strain, along the Icefields Parkway, in 1983. I was an unmarried twenty-four-year-old. In 1989, Greg Golovach and Joe McKay linked a direct pitch, one climbed previously by Jim Elzinga, to the crux pitch of the Andromeda Strain—the A Strain Direct. I had always wanted to climb it.

APRIL 2006: Jonathan Carpenter (aka "Blitz") and Billy Belcourt showed up to go alpine climbing. Nancy Feagin was home in Salt Lake City with Connor, Blitz's and her year-old son. I was forty-seven, a husband for the second time, a father for the first. Rosemary was sleeping in her crib. Perhaps the Andromeda Strain would provide a fitting bookend to my hard years of alpinism.

APRIL 4: Billy, Blitz, and I stepped our skis gingerly across spits of jagged talus to link up expanses of snow on the approach to Mt. Andromeda. At the base of the peak, Billy and Blitz punched a track up the steep, avalanche-prone slopes leading to the bergschrund. Despite our best intentions, we were late in pitching the tent below the route. Still, I was happy to be sitting in the vestibule with my feet hanging in the slot I'd dug for them. The stove purred away, melting snow.

Billy Belcourt scrapping his way up the Andromeda Strain Direct in the Canadian Rockies, April 5, 2006. Barry Blanchard

Billy was the head of climbing-hardware design at Black Diamond (BD). For fifteen years, he'd been enticing me to leave Grivel and come to BD, except for his year as president of Grivel North America (GNA), when he was happy to have me as an ambassador. Billy and Mark Twight had both run GNA (Mark from 2002 to 2008) and sponsored four ambassadors: Vince Anderson, Steve House, Marko Prezelj, and me. While Billy slurped down his minestrone soup, he said, "I'll sponsor anyone who can cause Blitz to be in pain." Then he grinned wickedly and giggled.

"Gonna take more than your skinny ass to put me in pain, buddy," Blitz shot back.

I told Billy about how I'd farted so rankly at the top of the Moonflower Buttress (Mt. Hunter, Alaska) that Blitz had gagged and choked and ripped the zipper to the tent door open in fear that he was going to vomit. Billy laughed so hard he passed minestrone through his nose, and then said, "Bubba, you are golden for life."

"Ya, you just enjoy that, buddy," Blitz commented. I grinned seeing how much like brothers they were.

APRIL 5: Blitz and Billy's track led us through the dark morning. Dawn saw us on the face, with Billy and me fourth-classing behind Blitz for several hundred feet until we stood beneath the Golovach/McKay direct start.

My lead. I launched onto polished ice, getting good screws until the ice ended against a steep, flaky corner. Remarkably, a two-inch-wide vein of ice sealed the spine of the corner and took my picks as deeply as I needed. Ten feet up, I found dependable gear and advanced by bridging and tapping in my picks.

Thirty feet higher, I had squirmed into a chimney between vertical rock and a snow mushroom. A solid-looking crack rode the left edge of my peripheral vision, and I scraped my elbow around to slot my pick into it, torquing lightly on that tool's shaft. Then, the outer edge of the crack drifted away as a square yard of rock—the size of a large stingray—sheared.

"Rock! Rock! Rock!" I bellowed.

It roared through space like a concrete panel failing from a skyscraper and crashed into the polished ice below, exploding into shrapnel and smoke. I heard a scream, then Blitz moaning and cursing, then growling as he hid his left shoulder.

"Are you guys okay?" I shouted.

"Ya...just wait a minute!" Billy yelled, "Blitz took a hit!"

Anxious seconds. *Please let Blitz be okay.*

"Yes, he says he's okay!... He's whining like a little kid."

Blitz interrupted, "Bloody fine! Couldn't be better!"

"You better check the ropes," I called, a request that they weren't expecting. They were shocked to find a core shot toward the middle of our red rope.

The rockfall had scared me. I had to breathe the adrenaline away before stepping onto the hard part of the pitch. Centered again, I made an airy step onto a fist-sized blob of ice, and then several strenuous lockoffs and long reaches to where the ice was thicker. My front points teetered on small rock edges, and I knew that I could fall and break bones, or worse. Rosemary's beautiful, inquisitive face came to me. I paused on the razor's edge of engagement for three beats of my heart and decided that I would not fall. I would fight for her. I blew out my fear and reached and pulled through the threat.

I'd sewn the pitch up with numerous pieces. When Billy clipped into my anchor, he said, "You are a master, Bubba." I'd uncovered a solid, shallow Angle placement in a frozen, mud-filled crack and whaled on the piton until the mud displaced and the spine and edges of the pin bit into solid stone.

Billy rallied for the crux pitch, one that I'd led over four hours split between an afternoon and a morning twenty-three years earlier. As it had then, it took time to clear several armchair-sized snow mushrooms and numerous smaller ones.

"How's your shoulder?" I asked Blitz during a lull in the blocks of snow Billy was hacking away and dropping.

"Bruised but not broken. Billy pushed on it everywhere, and it's just fine."

Three hours passed before Blitz and I started climbing. I'd forgotten how hard breaking onto the right traverse was.... Then again, I hadn't climbed with a pack on the first ascent.

Blitz led an awkward step of black rock and got us established in the upper couloir. I grabbed the gear and started swinging my tools into antediluvian ice, frothy and sea green. I climbed slower than when I was twenty-four, when I'd felt like a sled dog lunging against its harness, with David and Tim not able to follow fast enough. At forty-seven, I reflected on the quality of the A Strain: solid ice, firm snow, and relatively sound rock. Then I passed under an old anchor hanging tattered and out of reach ten feet up the rock wall. The couloir had lost five feet of ice depth over the years. This realization made me close my eyes and sigh for the route, and the mountain.

"What do you think—can you handle this?" Blitz asked Billy. To our right lay the exit; it bulged from the wall like a massive pale emerald.

"Ya, I think I can." Billy was wide-eyed and chuckling like a kid. He eased over to the ice, got in a solid screw, and tapped his way into the dusk. We seconded Blitz's next pitch by headlamp. Cornices rimmed the summit amphitheater; a scary, house-sized one sat perched to our left.

Climbing with Billy was like hanging out with Q in a James Bond movie. Because of his work at BD, he had many cool toys.

"Use this headlamp, Bubba. We call it the 'Eye of Sauron.'"

The Eye lit up the amphitheater like a floodlight and illuminated a passage through the overhanging snow. It also burned through four AA batteries in an hour! Just after midnight, I rose to my feet on the shallow backslopes on top of the route. I walked downslope to the southwest, excavated a hollow in the snow, and knelt to brace myself. I belayed in the ropes that connected me to Blitz and Billy, just as David had done for Tim and me all those years ago. I could see David then, as I thought about how he'd died on the Hummingbird Ridge of Mt. Logan in 1987 when his daughter, Tserin, was four. An overwhelming pulse of melancholy choked out a sob in me, and I trembled, thinking about how much I loved seeing Tserin because I could see his face in hers.

Blitz and Billy pulled over the edge. I stood and walked to them and gave them powerful, life-affirming hugs. We started down into the night and back to our tent.

DECEMBER 17: My guests and I climbed toward the high camp on the Vinson Massif, its summit 16,050 feet above sea level, although

Billy evaluating the route ahead and wanting to get after it on the Andromeda Strain Direct. Jonathan Carpenter the thinning atmosphere over the poles made the altitude feel 4,000 feet higher. Vinson is the highest peak in Antarctica. I gazed south to a low-lying white cloud layer and held that illusion for thirty seconds until reality slapped me. "Holy shit!" I blurted. "That's the continental icecap!"

As I stood and stared, I suddenly knew there were too many airplanes in my life. At home in Canada, Catherine was pregnant with our second child. I needed to cut back on my time away if I wanted to be a good father. From then on, I guided only one trip a year abroad and would be away for no longer than three weeks. My expedition climbing would be shelved until my children were older.

JULY 2007: Eowyn Jasmine Thetis Blanchard was born. Also named by her mother. When Eowyn's eyes opened, I cradled her in my arms and took her to the windows in the Canmore Hospital and whispered, as I'd done with Rosemary, "These are your mountains; this is your valley."

Becoming a father changed alpinism for me, as did my age. Early in my climbing career, my fear was reflexive. The mountain would move with rockfall, avalanche, or serac collapse, and fear would charge inside me. Over time, fear became very specific: If I was out of range

of the event, I could view it with relative nonchalance—although a size 3 or 4 avalanche or the collapse of a football-field-sized serac always command attention. Events of that weight made me feel cornered, even though I might not have been.

Storms create a veil of fear in me, like being immersed in thick fog while fighting with broadswords. A deadly blow could come from any quarter. Storms can spit spindrift or create the constant motion of snow falling with gravity that draws you into a world of motion, almost like being in the ocean. Large surges of spindrift can hit with a pressure like waves.

Whiteouts are different. When my eyes lose the horizon and there is nothing to focus on—inside the ping-pong ball—I am usually on shallower ground with snow or glacier underfoot. There, I fear falling into a crevasse; even on a rope, some crevasse falls are fatal, and I know that a collapsing snow bridge has enough mass to break my neck or press the breath from my chest. Or, if I can't see a cliff edge or cornice—I could plummet into the void.

The fear of falling can suffocate me when falling could mean dying, when the protection is poor and will not hold. Reflexes—speed of thought and hand—have a lot to do with not falling. By age forty-seven, my reflexes had slowed by milliseconds. Less testosterone left me less willing and able to take risks. My lungs couldn't pull as much oxygen, or as quickly; nor could my heart maintain the workload of two decades earlier. My heart now held the responsibility of Rosemary and Eowyn's hearts and lives. Love made me more wary of the ways I could get hurt or killed up there.

Down in the valley floor, spousal love slipped away for the second time, and Catherine and I separated in 2011.

2013: Troy Kirwan and his wife, Sophie, played matchmaker between me and Nicole Toner, who was Sophie's best friend. Nicole had been working as a public-health nurse in Canmore and had vaccinated Rosemary when she was an infant. Catherine and I would often run into her walking her dog when we were walking ours. Nicole and I found love and created a family. We are growing older together. I love her with my whole heart.

MARCH 29, 2019: My sixtieth birthday party was held at the Royal Canadian Legion, where my mother had been a barmaid for thirty years. I was surrounded by family, friends, climbing partners past and present, exes, and the whole climbing tribe. Folks came up from the States and over from Europe. My buddy's daughter who was in kindergarten came, as did an esteemed elder of the Calgary Mountain Club who was 102.

Cassidy, Troy's darling daughter, was eight, and got on with Rosemary and Eowyn like a house on fire. Eowyn and Rosemary, then eleven and fourteen, were shocked to see a projected photo of their father and Troy Kirwan smoking cigarettes on the way out of K2 in 1993. They were both closer to the age I was in that picture than I was at sixty. They will learn more about their father but, I suspect, not as much as I will continue to learn from them. They grow my heart.

Four years earlier, Troy had been dealt a hard hand: amyotrophic lateral sclerosis (ALS). It's a ruthless motherfucker of a disease that shut him down from his fingers and toes inward. Troy and I would sit in his back yard in Revelstoke, BC, and watch our daughters play and play and play. He was in an electric wheelchair then and had a feeding tube. He typed with his eyes. His tablet put what he wrote into words, and he and I talked about the climbs of our younger years while we watched our girls.

"I am so happy that you and I get to do this, buddy," he said to me. "I didn't think this was going to be in the cards for you and me." ALS couldn't take that away; death couldn't either. I loved the guy, and told him so on June 3, 2020, when he passed away at home. He's with me still. I talk to him.

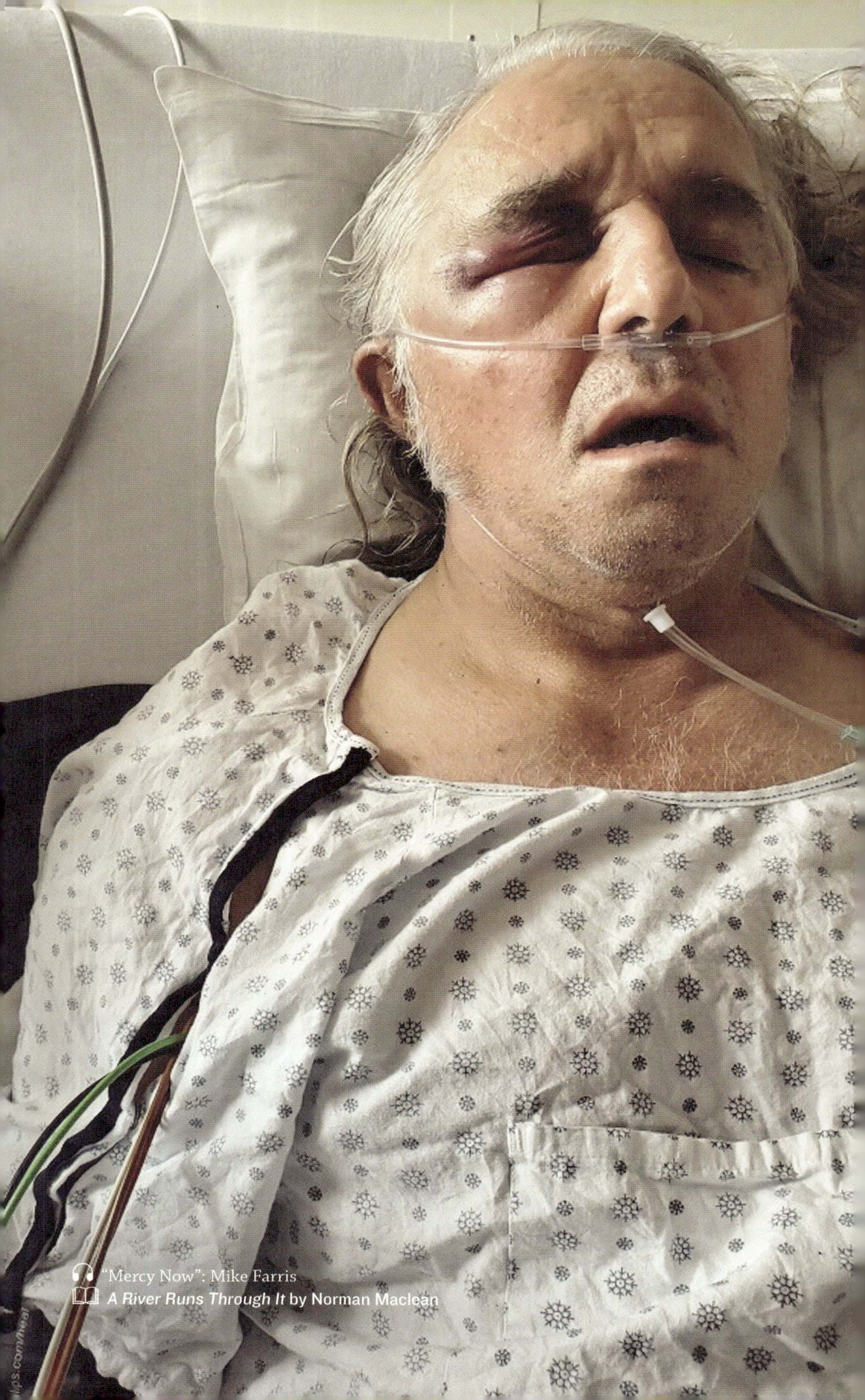

"Mercy Now": Mike Farris
A River Runs Through It by Norman Maclean

CHAPTER 19 — HOLDING ON AND LETTING GO III

THE FALL

Eventually, all things merge into one, and a river runs through it. The river was cut by the world's great flood and runs over rocks from the basement of time. On some of the rocks are timeless raindrops. Under the rocks are the words, and some of the words are theirs.

I am haunted by waters.

—Norman Maclean, A River Runs Through It

AUGUST 7, 2021: Flat-as-a-plate Saskatchewan. My buddy Scott Davies' farmhouse is a two-story log home that he built, and it bears the wrath and rage of the unfettered prairie winds. The only thing standing between Scott's house and the wind is the occasional head of cattle.

The last thing I remember was sharing Mike Ferris's cover of "Mercy Now" with Scott and his wife, Lorilee. It was something we always did on the first night of my family's annual trip to their farm. Our four girls had gone up to bed. The three of us adults—Nicole had to stay back home for work—were sitting at the laptop on the kitchen counter and sharing the best songs we'd discovered over the last twelve months.

The evening stretched on for another couple of hours, but I don't remember that. Scott tells me that just before midnight he was walking me down the thick wooden steps, canted at 45 degrees, leading to the basement, where I'd be sleeping. I must have tripped.

Unconscious and suffering with eleven skull fractures and a traumatic brain injury in Regina General Hospital, Regina, Saskatchewan. When my head hit the stair, Scott knew I was in trouble. Scott Davies

I tumbled right past Scott down the long flight. "When I heard how hard your head hit the bottom stair, I knew that we were in trouble," Scott told me later. It had taken four months before he was ready to talk to me about it.

Scott had been with the Regina Fire Department for over twenty years and he had seen his share of injuries. "Yours was the second worst crack to the coconut that I've ever seen," he continued. "The other guy didn't make it."

While Lorilee called 911, Scotty raced down to me. "You were on the concrete floor muttering and just losing consciousness," he recalled. "Blood was coming out of your mouth, and blood and fluid were draining out of your left ear. Your arms stiffened up and your wrists were so curled in I couldn't straighten them, even with all my might. Your back was arched, and you were choking on your own blood. I sucked it out of your mouth and gave you some mouth-to-mouth for a half hour until the ambulance showed up."

The EMT did not want to intubate me because of my head injury. The way I'd stiffened up—decerebrate posturing—concerned him, and he called for the air ambulance. It was out on another call, so he made the decision to transport me by road. Scott got into the ambulance and bag-valve masked me for the thirty minutes it took to get to the Regina General Hospital. I was intubated in the ICU and given IVs and eventually a nasal canula. My head was CAT scanned four times over the week that I spent in the ICU.

Nicole arrived from Canmore with my ex-wife, Catherine, who would bring the girls home and take care of Rosemary, who had fallen and broken her wrist swinging from a tree in Scott's yard that morning. For the second time in twelve hours, Scotty had been en route to the hospital in Regina.

Fourteen-year-old Eowyn, Nicole, my sister Kim, and Scotty all visited that day, one at a time due to Covid rules. I looked pretty beat up. A basal skull fracture had swollen my eyes shut, and I had the most impressive black eyes of my life, streaked with magenta. The right side of my face was swollen, and my mouth lay open and slack. I was unconscious. When Eowyn first saw me, she ran to the washroom, locked herself in, and cried—she thought that her dad was dead at sixty-two. She wasn't far from wrong. My skull was fractured in eleven places, and the doctors had found three potentially dangerous hematomas caused by bleeding within the skull. It was possible that they would have to operate to relieve the pressure on my brain.

Kim and Nicole, who had earned her PhD in nursing, took turns by my hospital bed for days.

I have no memory of my first week in the hospital. For the first few days I was sedated whenever my consciousness started to return, to keep me from going into a fight-or-flight reaction and tearing out everything that had been attached to me.

AUGUST 9: Nicole's father, John, drove four hours from Prince Albert and stayed for a number of days. His was a reassuring voice for her, "He is getting better, Nic. I can see improvements each day."

The nursing staff had been trying to stimulate a verbal response, but they had fixated on calling me by my middle name, Kenneth. "Kenneth! Can you wake up Kenneth?"

The first word I said, and would repeat, was "bacon."

The first sentence I voiced was "Who is feeding the cat?"

AUGUST 14: I was moved to the surgical recovery ward, even though I hadn't had surgery. I had started to find some words but couldn't find people's names. And sometimes I didn't even recognize the people closest to me. One day, a very attractive young nurse with brunette hair was paying me extra attention and care. When she went to hug me, I said, "Whoa! Wait. We can't do this! I have a girlfriend in Canmore. She is older than you and she's blonde." It was Nicole, of course, but I didn't realize it. I asked her to call "the other woman," referring to Kim. Nicole couldn't get ahold of her, so she called my mother, handed me the phone, and said, "Someone wants to talk to you, Barry."

"Oh, Bear," my mother said. Nicole saw my face and chest settle. My body relaxed, and all the guarding fell away. "Mom" was the first name that I'd found, and it is so poignant to me that I recognized my mother's voice without the sight of her face. My mother is the human whom I have known the longest, and that will be the case until one of us passes on. I think of my mother as a tigress, viciously protective and supportive of her young. It brought tears to Nicole's eyes, and then anxiety to her heart when she asked herself, "What if he doesn't remember my name?" Karin, her childhood friend from Prince Albert, drove to the farmhouse that night and talked to Nicole for several hours.

During my long hours of sleep that night, my brain reestablished a connection that had been lost. When Nicole walked in the next day, I blurted, "Oh, you are Nicole. You can hug me." Tears again, happy tears. She told me that I'd been acting like a nervous animal who wouldn't make eye contact. It was so good to be back.

I have several other gossamer memories of my second week. Images of people seen through the window staying in the adjacent section of the hospital, medical staff moving about, some computer time, some television. Vehicles stopping at houses across the street or driving away along the road. One night alone in my bed, I stood and balanced my hand against the wall and teetered a half dozen steps to the washroom to urinate. That was a major victory.

Another victory was when I was able to stand and take a shower on my own a few days later.

I remember I overheard a guy on the ward asking a nurse if he could get just one glass of liquor and the nurse rebuking him, "Now, you know I can't do that." I was also wheeled into the elevator and taken for my fifth CAT scan, the only one I actually remember. Both pieces of information that my brain was able to shelve into memory.

AUGUST 19: The good news was that my hematomas had resolved and I wouldn't need surgery. On my last full day in Regina General, Kim, and our cousin Cindy got the okay to put me in a wheelchair and push me around the main floor, where we visited with an administrator at the First Nations and Métis Health Services. Then they took me outside, a place I hadn't been in two weeks. It was so miraculous to feel the sun. Later, Nicole was with me when my attending physician released me for ambulance transport to the hospital in Canmore.

The ride back to Alberta the next day took ten-odd hours. My EMTs organized a much appreciated stop at a Wendy's in Medicine Hat. Of course, I had a burger—and it was delicious.

When we finally got to Canmore, my dear friend Kat came to my gurney and hugged me. If there is a word to express the importance in

Lorilee and Scott Davies on a Zoom call with Nicole and me during my recuperation.
Barry Blanchard

that connection, it is *love*. I felt so *loved*. It felt so good to be back in my hometown, with my people.

I spent four days in the Canmore hospital before I was set free. Eowyn, Rosemary, and Nicole were with me as much as they could be, and I started training with my physiotherapist, Mitch, and my occupational therapist, Michelle. Initially Mitch had me working on balance, just standing on one leg with my hand against the wall. Michelle got me to hold objects like a pencil and try to write. I would work with them for months, and they helped me immensely. By mid-October, they told me that they'd done everything they could, right after Michelle gave me a pass on my home-cooking exam. I think that I made bacon, eggs, and toast. Old habits are hard to change for old dogs.

My buddy Glen wasn't using his bottom-floor condo in Canmore and was happy to have us stay there until Christmas. That was a godsend. My daughters and Nicole did not want me trying to negotiate the dozen cement stairs to our condo on the high and steep side of the valley.

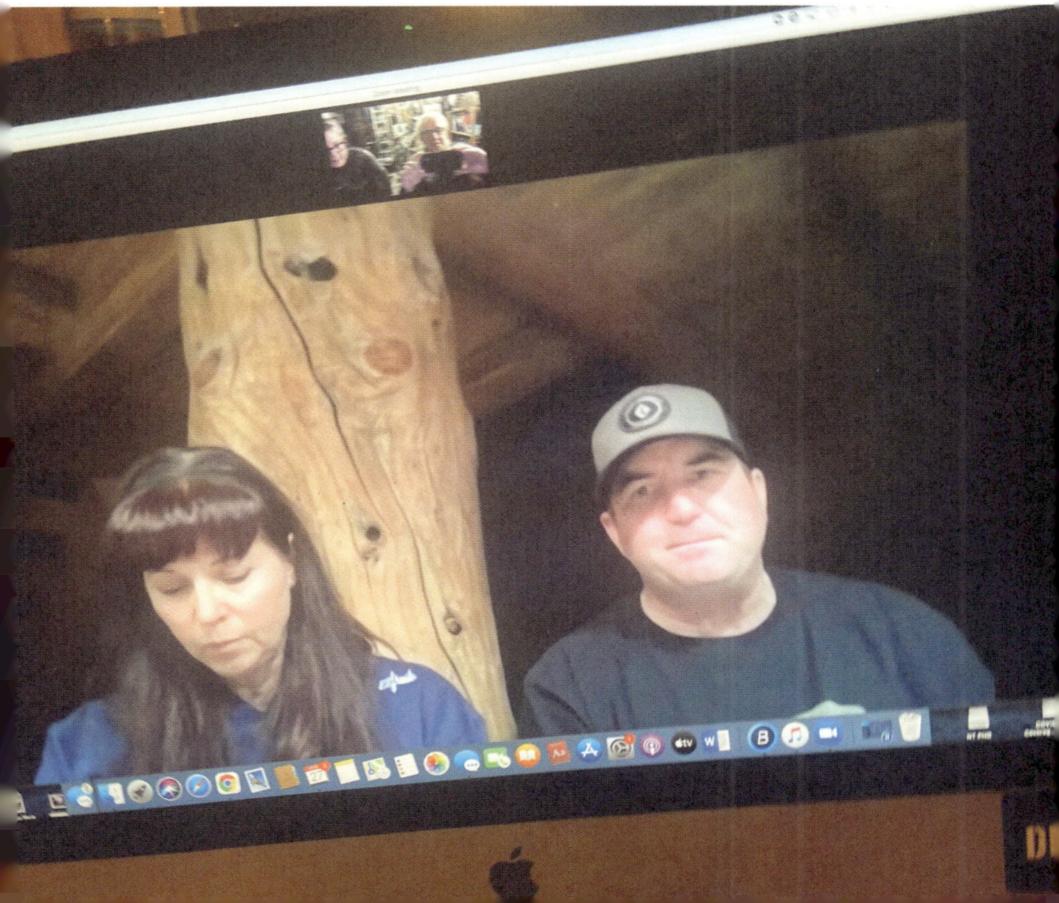

I needed to continue to build up my strength and confidence. Nicole and I started working with the law of expanding circles. Every morning, we would walk as far as my compromised balance could tolerate. At first it was one lap around the condo, then up one block and then down the other, eventually expanding to a circuit of the neighborhood, a rectangle of a half dozen streets. It took me a couple of months to achieve as my balance slowly recovered. I feared not being able to climb again.

But I'd lost more than balance and conditioning. The first time I chose to watch TV, Nicole handed me the remote and I stared at it blankly. She became my remote controller until the neuroplasticity in my brain found the connections and allowed me to choose the streaming channels on my own.

When I was in my forties, I'd watched Ingmar Bergman's 1968 film, *Hour of the Wolf*. The theme of being haunted at 3 a.m., when the wolf comes, had been in me before and has stayed with me since. At Glen's condo, the wolf would come between 2 and 3 a.m., and I would wake to a dark silhouette of fear. What if I couldn't climb again—then what would I be? I'd lie there terrified until I got up and slowly stood, remembering the times I'd come close to toppling over when I'd come onto my feet too quickly. I'd reach out and balance against the wall. The night world. I'd look into the darkness to find whatever lights stayed on outside the window, to confirm reality with my eyes. While I stood, another thought would come. *What if I couldn't ski again?* Humorously I'd answer myself: *Oh well, I had some fun skiing*. The wolf threatened my climbing, but the coyote joked about the skiing, which had never been my raison d'être anyway.

"Do you think that I could go to the climbing wall?" I had asked my doctor two months after my fall. He said yes, it could help with my recovery, but he wanted me to wear a helmet—and that proved to be something I just couldn't do. In my defense, I never did any leading at the climbing gym and wasn't exposed to any falls of consequence—if I was on a toprope all the time, could I ever hit my head at the gym?

The condo was a two bedroom. There wasn't room, nor did I have the mental capacity at that time, for Eowyn and Rosemary to spend every second week with Nicole and me, as they had been doing for ten years, ever since their mother and I had separated. The girls would have dinner with us every week, and it was always so good to see them, to smell the top of their heads, their hair. To kiss them there and hug them deeply and feel the ardent heat of my heart.

In early December, Nicole and I moved into a big, four-bedroom house with a ground-level walkout, and Eowyn and Rosemary resumed their weeks with us. They were excited about their spacious new rooms, as was I to live in a house that was quite a bit larger than any I had ever lived in.

Another benefit to the new house was that we could assume the previous owners' bed-and-breakfast. Nicole set us up as Blanchard Mountain Bed and Breakfast, with the idea that it was something I'd be able to manage as I recovered. She had taken a leave of absence from her work, and the days and months that she put into organizing the new paradigm of our lives carried extra mass every time she said, "I love you."

DECEMBER 18: Blanchard Mountain Bed and Breakfast received its first guest, and from then on, much of my time was spent running it.

JANUARY 6, 2022: Every medical expert that I'd seen over the previous four months, and the ones whom I would see in the next six months, all reiterated that I could not take another hit to the head. And I wasn't allowed to drive. So, I was driven a dozen times to either the Peter Lougheed Center or the Foothills Medical Center in Calgary for appointments with my occupational therapist, physical therapist, speech therapist, social worker, neuropsychologist, or physiatrist. Driven by my brother Dave, or my longtime climbing partner Jim Elzinga, or Nicole. There was always a side trip to Atlas Pizza for Dave, and one to Dairy Queen for Jim.

JANUARY 24: An encouraging day for me. My occupational therapist and doctor had sent reports to Alberta Transportation and a letter arrived informing me that I could drive and that I wouldn't need to retest my motorcycle or car licenses—not that I'd driven a motorcycle in rather a long time. I would have to retest the taxi license I'd gotten for driving passenger vans, but not having to drive passenger vans anymore was a good deal in my books. The next couple of trips I made to the hospitals in Calgary didn't cost me a stop at Atlas Pizza or Dairy Queen. I drove myself.

FEBRUARY 22: I was recovered enough to undergo double knee surgery, a procedure I had been waiting to have for a couple of years. Nicole drove me to the South Health Campus in Calgary, where I had a final chat with my surgeon and was then wheeled off in a gurney. My old friend Josh Briggs, who'd been a wellsite geologist and mountain guide, and was now an anesthetist, was scheduled to work on me. When he saw "Barry Blanchard" on the docket, he said to himself, "There can't be two of them," and recused himself. Nonetheless, it was great to see Josh and get caught up recalling our times in Canmore. A different anesthetist injected adductor canal blocks of bupivacaine into the insides of my thighs, put a spinal into my back, and made me dozy.

When I started to get my wits back, I was still in the operating theater but my surgeon was gone. I learned that he had finished in only an hour and a half. Later he told me that I'd worn the outside of both knees down to stage-four osteoarthritis (bone on bone), but that the rest of my knees were fine. That meant that instead of the full replacements he'd been prepared for, he'd done only partial replacements. I was surprised by the time he'd taken as I'd assumed it would have taken longer.

Josh and his wife, Laurie, brought homemade chicken soup and cycling magazines. When I asked Josh if the brief hour and a half that it took my surgeon made sense, he assured me that he'd observed him operate. "He is a master carpenter who knows what he needs to do, and doesn't waste any time or make any mistakes," Josh reassured me. Wow, I'd known that my surgeon was good, and now I knew he was the best.

FEBRUARY 23: The anesthesia wore off in the night. It became a rough one. So hard to not move or to find a way to escape the hurting. When morning came, with the help of a physiotherapist, I was able to stand and walk with crutches. When my surgeon asked me if I'd like to go home, I replied, "Yes, please." I called Nicole and went home, where I lay in bed for the next three days.

MARCH 2: I leaned heavily on the banister as I descended one level of stairs to the B&B, wearing a climbing pack stuffed with bedding and supplies so I could carry stuff down. Nicole and I walked back into the law of expanding circles: up and down the street, then around the block, and within three weeks I was able to go through the neighborhood using a couple of trekking poles. Soon, I didn't need the poles.

My strength was returning and my balance was much improved, but things were different. My sense of time had changed since my head injury. Before the fall, I had held time within my mind like blocks in an orderly stack. Now, seconds, minutes, and hours felt spherical and adrift within the space of my mind, like varisized cotton balls floating in air.

Could I go back to guiding? Did I even want to?

"The Dead" by James Joyce

CHAPTER 20 — HOLDING ON AND LETTING GO IV

SPINDRIFT

A few light taps upon the pane made him turn to the window. It had begun to snow again. He watched sleepily the flakes, silver and dark, falling obliquely against the lamplight. The time had come for him to set out on his journey westward. Yes, the newspapers were right: snow was general all over Ireland. It was falling on every part of the dark central plain, on the treeless hills, falling softly upon the Bog of Allen, and farther westward, softly falling into the dark mutinous Shannon waves. It was falling, too, upon every part of the lonely churchyard on the hill where Michael Furey lay buried. It lay thickly drifted on the crooked crosses and headstones, on the spears of the little gate, on the barren thorns. His soul swooned slowly as he heard the snow falling faintly through the universe and faintly falling, like the descent of their last end, upon all the living and the dead.
—James Joyce, "The Dead"

APRIL 19, 2022: "We are going to change the storyline of your film," Andy said. "We want to include your accident." My dear friends Kat Wiebe, Andy Arts, and Nikki Tate had been working on a film about my life for six years. When they joined forces with director Ivan Hughes and my old buddy Hank Van Weelden as producer, mass accumulated, as did momentum. "Ivan thinks that we have to include your fall and what that has done to Eowyn, Rosemary, Nicole, and the rest of your family," Andy continued.

Hugging Mark Twight hard after he introduced *Spindrift, The Barry Blanchard Story* at the Bozeman Ice Festival. Hearts in parallel.
Andy Arts

"You guys are filmmakers. I'm a writer, and homie don't do filming. Whatever the moviemaking crew wants to do is fine by me. Let me know if you need more writing."

"Okay, we will, but we are going to need you to do some acting."

"Cool, if I just need to play myself, I can't really make any mistakes. That, I like."

MAY 14: And so I found myself—just shy of three months after having both my knees partially replaced—climbing up, crossing, and descending the edge of a lateral moraine with Mt. Athabasca framed by passing clouds 5,000 above. Trekking poles aided in my balance, and confidence, as I kicked steps into the remnants of the winter's snowpack. It was the closest I'd been to an alpine mountain since the fall. As I looked up to Athabasca, I wondered if I would ever climb it again. If I would ever again climb any alpine route.

Several days later, Andy and Ivan filmed Eowyn, Rosemary, and me above the Bow River with Mts. Allen, Lougheed, Charity, Rundle, and Norquay as backdrops. I was walking well and felt loved and appreciated by my daughters as we talked and I wrapped my arms over their shoulders, smelled them, and kissed the tops of their heads.

The dark turquoise of the Bow flowed on below us, as it has for the last fifty thousand years. Like drops of rain, Rosemary, Eowyn, and I have been added to the river; we are part of it, part of its journey from Alberta into Saskatchewan.

MAY 23: I walked to the top of the Yam Bluffs with sixteen British Army soldiers and three fellow guides. These sandstone cliffs—up to fifty feet high—are part of the Belly River Group (fifty million years old), over which Mt. Yamnuska (five hundred and forty million years old) itself had been thrust. The bluffs are where I had started the rock-climbing part of my guiding career forty years earlier. In a sense, I was restarting my guiding career. Or, if things didn't go well, possibly ending it.

It was a good day. I guided, albeit tentatively and cautiously. My guiding world had contracted, and that awakened a deeper empathy for my clients. I had drifted back to when I was a beginner climber. For the next two days, my fellow guides and I returned to the bluffs with different groups of soldiers. I was back to guiding.

In early September of 2022, my daughters, now teenagers, had a private screening of *Spindrift, The Barry Blanchard Story*. Eowyn sent a text to Andy, "I watched the film, and I thought it was probably the most honest thing I've seen produced about him."

OCTOBER 30: *Spindrift* premiered at the Banff Mountain Film Festival. Eowyn, Rosemary, Nicole, and my brother Dave were there; Andy, Ivan, Hank, and I introduced the film. So many people had prayed for me after the fall. Many were in the audience. When everyone rose to their feet with the communal reverberation of two hands clapping, hundreds of hands clapping, I felt supported, loved, like I was climbing back. By December, I was guiding one to six days a month. I was on rock, ice, and my skis and it all felt good. I hadn't been in the alpine and my balance sometimes took me up to a minute to attain before I moved. My confidence was growing.

Hank, Andy, and I drove to Bozeman, Montana, to present the film at the Bozeman Ice Festival. Mark Twight introduced me.

"They say that when you save another man's life, he becomes your responsibility." Mark shared that he had saved my life thirty-four years earlier on Mt. Everest, and since that time I had saved his, and that most of our lives were now behind us. Our ponytails held more gray now than black—much more gray. As Mark came off stage, we embraced. I felt the bond of unconditional love transmitted between his heart and mine, aligned to the heart side of our bodies. Hearts in parallel.

FEBRUARY 11, 2023: One last standing ovation for *Spindrift* at the Michigan Ice Fest in Munising. I had walked to the theater through moist snow, some of it six inches thick over sidewalks that had yet to be shoveled clean. My boots pressed halos of translucent slush, slush that would freeze to ice overnight. The assailing hand of Lake Superior pushed its winter wind onto my left flank. There is almost always wind coming from north of Superior, the largest freshwater lake by surface area on the planet. The trees on its southern side are different from the trees in the mountains of western Canada. They are eastern trees.

The people watching *Spindrift* that night were mostly Easterners, but they were also climbers. Kitty Calhoun and Conrad Anker were there. I had climbed with them both and had instructed many of those present and at previous Ice Fests. The audience rose to its feet in response to the film for the first time in the festival's thirty-plus years, I was told later.

MARCH: The number of days I spent guiding had increased to as much as sixteen per month, but that was too much. I've settled into guiding no more than ten days a month since then. My age had increased, and my abilities decreased.

JUNE: As I write this, 694 days have passed since I tumbled down the stairs in Scott's house; thirty-six days from now, I will reach the two-year mark. Others who've suffered traumatic brain injuries and concussions have told me it took two years to get back to normal—or to their new normal. By anyone's measure, I have had a good recovery.

One of the longest lingering effects has been my impaired balance. For most, if not all, of the days out rock climbing, I've experienced thirty seconds to a minute of vertigo when I first touch the rock, just as

I had when I returned to the climbing gym. Out at the ice, I came close to toppling over several times. So I stopped leading on the ice and had expert partners safeguarding my rope from above. When my heart rate increased with exertion, I would have to stop and hold myself fast to my ice tools and crampon points until the vertigo passed.

When I shared that with the people at the head-injury clinic, they pointed out that the brain is 2 percent of the body's weight but needs 20 percent of its oxygen. I was instructed to stop moving and exerting myself when my balance faltered and to use deep breathing to get my heart rate down and more oxygen to my noggin. It helped significantly and became one of my workarounds.

Nordic skiing challenged my balance, too, but in a good way. I chose the easiest trails at the Canmore Nordic Center; if I concentrated on the downhills, I could stay on my skis. After a half dozen one-hour trips up and down the green (easiest) Banff Trail on separate days, my balance resolved itself. Not so on my one day of downhill skiing before knee surgery, when I went with Joe, a guest at the B&B, to Lake Louise. The increased speed over Nordic challenged my proprioception and balance all day, and on the one blue run that I tried I lost my edge, smacked down onto my hip, and slid downslope thirty feet.

Knee surgery put an end to both forms of skiing for the rest of the winter, and I spent time out hiking in the snow and eventually getting on my mountain bike. Summer saw me back on the road bike, and often going with Jim Elzinga on thirty-five-mile rides. I was improving.

This past winter, I have guided some days out on the ice, with even more days spent on my skis. Now I am back to guiding and climbing on rock, and in the last month the vertigo has finally left me for good. My brain continues to repair itself, a wonderful and engaging process and a complex one because it is all happening within my brain—which is observing itself.

My left ear, where blood and fluid drained out when I fell, has felt like there is some sort of stuffing in it for the last twenty-three months. But as Nicole says, "That ear saved your life. It doesn't owe you anything." She is right, I have nothing to complain about...nothing. Two days ago, I saw Rosemary graduate high school. I have so much to be grateful for.

My daughter Rosemary and Kat Wiebe on Minihapa, July 1, 2023. Rosemary had graduated high school two days earlier, and now she was learning about her ancestors. Barry Blanchard

JULY 1: A couple of days after she graduated, Rosemary came rock climbing with my friend Kat and me for the first time since my fall. Kat safeguarded me with her belay, a skill Rosemary will need to brush up on. We went to Cascade Mountain, near Banff. I had once heard Stoney Nakoda Chief John Snow call it "Welcoming Mountain," because, as you travel up the Bow Valley, the mountain welcomes you.

Our connections to this land run deep. My family history is all around. One of Rosemary's close friends is Chief Snow's granddaughter.

The climb we did is called Minihapa, which means "mountain where the water falls" in Stoney.

"The Stoney believe that it is the voices of the ancestors, the grandmothers and grandfathers, we hear speaking from the waterfall," I said.

"Oh, I can hear it," Rosemary said and smiled.

"Literally the voices of the ancestors?" Kat asked.

"Yes, both women and men," I replied, and then added, "Above Minihapa is a route called Battle of Seven Oaks. I guided it three days ago before coming to your graduation banquet that evening, Rosemary. The route was put up by Joe McKay, who is Métis and a distant relative of ours. His family is from the Qu'Appelle in Saskatchewan just like ours."

"Oh, ya," Rosemary chimed in. "His daughter is in Eowyn's class!"

"Yes, and your ancestor Cuthbert Grant led the Métis at the Battle of Seven Oaks in 1816. A trace of your ancestors is here, too." Rosemary smiled, and I explained our family's lineage to Cuthbert to Kat, who had grown up in Manitoba and knew of the battle and had seen the monument that stands where the battle occurred in what is now modern-day Winnipeg.

Minihapa starts with two ropelengths just north of the falling water. On the third pitch, you step over the water as it diagonals across a rock shelf, to finish the route south of, and not thirty feet from, the waterfall. The ancestors' voices are all around.

Rosemary and Kat loved the route, and while we sat on our packs up top and ate and drank, Rosemary said, "That was fun, Dad. I want to do more rock climbing. I'd go back to the climbing gym with you."

My turn to beam. "We can definitely do more, sweetie, and it would be great to get out ski touring again this coming winter." The string connecting my heart to hers strummed.

We stood and shouldered our packs. I gathered my ancestral voices and heard, from my heart, that this chapter in my life was about supporting, loving, and helping Rosemary and Eowyn as they matured. It was all that I could ask for, and it is more than enough. I thanked the land and all the humanity that had touched it and left a trace and their words upon it.

JULY 16, 5:30 A.M.: The rain fell with weight. It was the second time that my guests Erin and Phuong and I were getting pelted and pulling on our rain pants. The dawn had risen just as this curtain of rain had fallen, and I tucked my ice-ax under my left arm, bit on my right glove, pulled it from my hand, and reached up to click off my headlamp. In my left hand I held some coils from the rope that connected me to Erin and Phuong. We were walking, with crampons on, across the glacier below the north side of Mt. Athabasca at the Columbia Icefield of Jasper National Park. We had started at 2 a.m. The summit would require another five hours of ascent. I was guiding in the alpine again, and feeling good.

I had logged over 100 ascents of Mt. Athabasca since my first time up it in 1979, forty-four years before this climb. The mountain was an ancestor to me, but an alpine one, more complex and dynamic and less knowable than the rock peaks I'd learned from. Athabasca has been a mentor, and very occasionally a menace and a threat. Crunching up the glacier that day with Erin and Phuong, I felt some benevolence from Athabasca. After the rain had passed, the sun came out, and the snow we eventually walked onto felt firm and bonded, with no threat of avalanche until the sun perhaps heated it to oatmeal slop.

That avalanche hadn't happened yet. I forced my ax spike into the snow and kicked steps and advanced up Athabasca. The wolf hour and the terror and the nightmare that had risen in me at 3 a.m. so many nights since the fall...well, the wolf had taken one last look at me over its left shoulder as it loped away. Erin, Phuong, and I climbed through the darkness and into the dawn.

EPILOGUE

JANUARY 2026: I have spent many thousands of days on the sides of beautiful, beautiful mountains in the company of good men and women. A handful of those days were black and cruel; death took lives on some of those mountains, indifferent to humankind despite their beauty. I think of David Cheesmond, Alex Lowe, and Guy Lacelle often. I feel them in the mountains, no longer through their presence, but rather in remembrance. They live on in my heart.

The mountains I climb now, I climb predominantly as a guide.

I am blessed. First, in hearing the mountains call. And last, in realizing that love was calling me all along.

I'm descending from Mt. Athabasca, July 16, 2023. The hour of the wolf was over, and the wolf loped away. Erin Lind

Sunset on the mountains of my life.
Barry Blanchard

GLOSSARY

A0
A difficulty rating system used in aid climbing. The aid scale runs from A0 through A5, with each increment denoting more technical and dangerous aid climbing in which the placements may no longer hold a fall but just body weight, and the potential falls get longer.

AID CLIMBING
Aid climbing, or "artificial climbing," involves directly weighting the protection to make upward progress, versus free climbing, in which you place the protection solely to safeguard a fall. The aid climber stands in stirrup-like etriers to place the next piece.

ARÊTE
A thin, almost knifeblade-like ridge or rock created by two glaciers eroding parallel U-bottomed valleys. The word is applied to all like structures in the mountains, whether they are composed of ice, snow, or rock, or various combinations of the three.

ASCENDING HITCH
One of a number of hitches that can be used to climb up a rope, including autoblock, prusik, French prusik, climb heist, and more.

BACK-ROPING
Used by a solo climber. A length of rope is secured and placements are clipped to it as a safeguard against falling. The rope is secured at the top and the climber descends it to back-clean the protection pieces and retrieve the rope.

BELAY
To hold, manage, and secure your climbing partner with a rope, catching them in a fall or enabling them to rest.

BERGSCHRUND
German for "mountain cleft," the standing crevasse that separates flowing glacial ice from the stationary rock, ice, or snow of the mountain above. Often difficult and delicate to climb over. Climbers shorten the name to just 'schrund.

BIVOUAC/BIVY
Sleeping in the open without a tent, though you may have a sleeping bag, bivy sack, or pad. An open bivy at altitude, exposed to the cold and the elements, can be uncomfortable or even deadly.

CAM/CAMMING DEVICE

An umbrella-shaped, removable type of active protection (vs. passive protection like wires). Springloaded, cams contract with the pull of a trigger and then expand inside the crack. Unlike passive protection, they also work in parallel crack systems.

CARABINER

A metal snap-link used to clip the rope into protection. These building blocks of the roped climbing system come in all shapes and sizes, including the locking carabiners used in belay anchors.

CHIMNEY

A crack so wide that a climber can fit entirely inside; climbers scale chimneys by pressing their back and butt against one wall and their legs against the other.

CLIMBING GRADES

Globally there are many scales to grade the technical difficulty (how hard it is to advance your body upward on rock, ice, and snow) as well as grades that express the seriousness of the climb. Some scales combine both the technical grade and the seriousness grade.

In the pages of this book, reference is made to the Yosemite Decimal System (YDS) to grade the technical difficulty of rock climbs from the very novice—5.1—to the intermediate—5.5–5.8—and the expert—5.9. Originally 5.9 was the ceiling of difficulty, but rock climbers just kept getting better and better, and 5.10 was added along with subgrades of a–d (note that the difference between 5.10b and 5.10c is a full grade and equivalent to the difference between 5.6 and 5.7). When I started rock climbing in the mid-1970s, 5.12 was the hardest people could climb, and there were precious few who could. With climbers ever improving their skills, the precious few are now knocking on the door of 5.16a.

The extended YDS included six classes of climbing, from walking on even ground—class 1—to scrambling up exposed ridges without a rope—class 3—to tying-in to the rope and using it to safeguard a fall while both climbers move together, either with the mountain's features or running pieces of protection—class 4. Class 5 climbing is technical climbing where only one of the climbers moves at a time and is safeguarded via a belay from the other climber. Class 5 is where the technical grades of 5.1 to near 5.16a exist. Class 6 is direct aid climbing where climbers use the support of climbing equipment to advance, as opposed to just their hands and feet, as in class 5.

Direct aid climbing grades are abbreviated to A0 through to A5, with A0 being where pitons are used as hand- or footholds, A1 being simple and secure aid, and A5 representing a number of placements that will just support body weight; if you jump on them they will rip out, and your subsequent "zipper" fall (because of the unzipping of a number of placements) will be at least seventy feet.

The YDS grade for seriousness and length of a route is expressed by the Roman numerals I–VII, with grade I being a climb that takes an intermediately skilled team one to two hours to complete. A grade IV would take the same team a day, and a grade VII would take an expert team a week or more.

The Union Internationale des Associations d'Alpinisme (UIAA) grade system for seriousness has its origins in the rock difficulty grades of VII (easiest) to I (hardest) developed by the Austrian mountaineer Fritz Benesch in 1894. The great German alpinist Willo Welzenbach inverted the scale and applied it to alpine routes with grade V being the hardest. The UIAA added grade VI when it adopted the scale in 1947. Reinhold Messner's manifesto, *The Seventh Grade,* argued the scale into open-endedness on its publication in 1974.

The Canadian water-ice grading system applies to waterfall ice climbs and is represented with a commitment grade, a Roman numeral from I to VII that mirrors the seriousness grades of the YDS system but takes into account the winter threats of cold and avalanche. A grade VII will take days and have a fifty-fifty chance of getting the chop (killed). The technical grade on waterfalls is open-ended, starting at WI 1, which is frozen lakes or creek beds. WI 4 has up to eighty feet of vertical ice. WI 7 is a full ropelength of vertical ice that is very thin or a long overhanging technical column of dubious adhesion (a very physically and emotionally demanding pitch).

Mixed climbing grades are expressed by the M grade and have come into use with the popularity of modern mixed climbing, which can largely be viewed as the winter equivalent of sport climbing. Instead of chalked-up hands and rock shoes, a winter climber uses ice tools and crampons to cling to combinations of rock, ice, and occasionally snow. M grades are a technical grade and have been compared to similar physical experiences on the YDS. M4 feels like 5.8, M9 feels like 5.12, M12 feels like 5.13+.

CRAMPONS

Metal plates with downward and sometimes forward-pointing spikes that affix to mountain boots for traction on snow and ice.

CRUX/CRUX PITCHES

The most difficult section on a one-pitch climb or the hardest pitches on a multipitch climb; the toughest climbing on a given route.

DOWNCLIMBING

Climbing down the rock—reversing a sequence or pitch to get out of a sticky situation, usually.

DÜLFERSITZ RAPPEL TECHNIQUE

Developed by the German climber Hans Dülfer, this technique requires straddling the rappel rope, or ropes, and then wrapping the rope over the dominant hip, up and across the chest to the non-dominant shoulder, and then taking it into the dominant hand. The rappel is then controlled by friction with the body. Dülfer was killed at Arras during WWI; he was twenty-three years old.

ETRIER
A short rope or sling ladder to stand on and advance while aid climbing. In North America they have been commonly constructed, or tied, out of webbing. In Europe it is more the custom to incorporate metal or plastic rungs and tie them in sequence with small-diameter rope.

EXPANSION BOLT
An expanding fastener (also used in construction—in concrete) used as permanent climbing protection. The route equipper drills a hole, pounds the bolt in, and tightens it until a sleeve expands inside the hole, giving the bolt its holding power.

FACE
A smooth, open panel of rock.

FIRN SKI
A ski marketed by Kastle for skiing on glaciers in the summer. Climbers call them approach skis.

GRIGRI
An assisted-braking belay device that cams onto and pinches the rope when the cord moves quickly, such as in a fall.

HARNESS
A nylon contraption with a waist belt, leg loops, and usually a belay loop that a climber wears to tie into the rope.

HEXENTRIC/HEX
An eccentric hexagon constructed from extruded aluminum. Hexes were invented and patented by Yvon Chouinard and Tom Frost in 1976 and they were an innovation on the six-sided engineering nuts that climbers had been inserting into cracks to gain protection. The Hexentric had the ability to fit into three different sizes of cracks with the smaller two dimensions also exerting a camming force on the crack.

Hexentric is a registered trademark of Black Diamond Equipment, Ltd.

ICE-AX
The mountaineer's principal tool. Present-day models range from 15 to 35 inches in length and always have a pick and an adze comprising their head (as opposed to an ice hammer, which has a hammer head and pick).

JUMARS/JUGS

The first marketed versions of a handled eccentric cam ascender, or "ascender." Jumars debuted in 1958 and were soon incorporated into the developing big-wall techniques in Yosemite Valley. Spring-loaded cams clamp onto climbing rope and allow the climber to ascend ropes, including free-hanging ones, via the device's handgrips.

KLEMHEIST KNOT

A ratchet knot that slides up the rope if you push on it, but it grabs the rope if you pull down on its loop—or fall.

KNIFEBLADE PITON/ KNIFEBLADE

A flat-bladed spike driven into rock cracks. They vary from one to three inches in length by about three-quarters of an inch wide.

OFFWIDTH

A crack that is too wide to jam with the sides of your fist, but too narrow to squeeze your body into. Offwidths are notoriously difficult to climb and often involve wrestling to insert your knee, shoulder, and elbow, all on one side of the body.

ONSIGHT

To climb a route on your first try without any prior knowledge.

PENITENTE

A pyramid of ice that forms on high-altitude glaciers, from the Spanish for "penitent-shaped" snows.

PITCH

A single ropelength of rock climbing.

PITON

Blade, angle, and Z profile of metal hammered into cracks in rock to gain anchorage and protection via a carabiner clipped into the piton's eye. Piton lengths normally range from one to four inches with widths being one half to one inch. Also referred to as pins or pegs.

PRO

Short for "protection." Any piece of equipment inserted, hammered, screwed, or threaded into the mountain to anchor the climber. Friends, nuts, wedges, cams, ice screws, pitons, threads, chickenheads, spikes, and trees are all examples of protection.

PRUSIK

A friction hitch that is tied onto a climbing rope. Two prusiks can be used to ascend the rope with inchworm-like movement; the climber is said to be prusiking or to have prusiked the rope. Named for the Austrian mountaineer Karl Prusik, the alleged inventor, in 1931.

RAPPEL

To descend a rope or ropes from an anchor, using a rappel device to generate friction and control your rate of descent.

RAPPEL DEVICE

A device used to generate friction on the rope or ropes while rappelling; most belay devices also double as rappel devices.

ROCK HAMMER

A hammer specifically designed to hammer pitons into cracks. Rock hammers often have a blunt pick opposite the hammer to help extract pitons and nuts.

SALOPETTES

Bibbed trousers with shoulder straps similar to overalls but usually made of shell material, sometimes insulated, meant to be worn as an outer layer. Salopettes can also be made out of insulation fabrics alone or integrated with shell fabrics. The term originally referred to French skiwear from the seventies.

SERAC

Ice cliff that collapses catastrophically where a glacier cannot maintain its integrity while flowing over a steep drop on the underlying mountainside. Seracs also form as isolated columns from the crosshatching of crevasses where a glacier is under tension in several directions.

SIRDAR

The leader of a Sherpa climbing/ trekking team.

SIMUL-CLIMB

To climb together as a rope team without stopping at belay anchors. Instead, the climbers, tied into either end of the rope, keep a string of protection clipped between them, such that if one climber falls, the other climber—and the protection system—will keep them both from being pulled off the wall. This risky technique is most often used in the mountains and when vying for speed records on big-wall climbs.

SNOW MUSHROOM

A large, dense formation of snow that grows on very steep mountain sides and can weigh a number of tons. Very destructive when they avalanche.

STOPPER

A wedge-shaped nut placed into a constriction in a rock crack for protection. Also called "wedge."

Stopper is a registered trademark of Black Diamond Equipment, Ltd.

TOPO

A hand-drawn schematic map of a typically multi-pitch climb that shows relevant landmark features like cracks, corners, ledges, overhangs, and so on.

VERGLAS

Water that flows over rock then freezes to ice.

Tenzing at our camp below the southwest face of Kusum Kanguru, unclimbed in 1991. Barry Blanchard

ACKNOWLEDGMENTS

My people are the Métis, and I am so proud to carry that bloodline and to have now passed it onto my daughters, Rosemary and Eowyn. I feel my ancestors in the mountains, and I pray to them and to all my relations.

I hold and return to some of the important climbing writers who have influenced me: Heinrich Harrer, Walter Bonatti, Lionel Terray, Gaston Rébuffat, Giusto Gervasutti, Reinhold Messner, Fosco Maraini, Tom Patey, Warren Harding, Yvon Chouinard, James Salter, Mark Twight, Al Alvarez, Joe Tasker, Peter Boardman, Geoff Powter, and Jon Krakauer.

My literary pantheon has diminished over time. Ernest Hemingway, Paul Bowles, Norman Maclean, Sam Shepard, Cormac McCarthy, Thom Jones, Charles Bukowski, César Vallejo, and Jalād ad-Dīn Rūmī are all gone, several before I was born. John Irving and Bruce Springsteen are still here.

I am again grateful to Patagonia Books. Thankful to my editors Sharon AvRutick, Matt Samet, and especially Virginia Durksen, who taught me comparative literature at the University of Alberta in 1987 and agreed to come on board and help me with *The Echo*. Virginia suggested the title to this book and improved it with her gentle editorial hand. Kyle Sparks has been a pleasure to work with, selecting pictures for the book. This is my second book guided by my publisher, Karla Olson. Thank you so much Karla. My gratitude to Christina Speed and Jeremy Dean for the layout and design.

Hard to believe that I've been with Patagonia for thirty-three years, and I am eternally grateful to Malinda and Yvon Chouinard for what they created and astounded at how they and their children, Claire and Fletcher, have made the Earth Patagonia's sole shareholder.

I've been blessed to share a rope with Carl Tobin, Mark Twight, Peter Arbic, Troy Kirwan, Steve Swenson, Alex Lowe, Guy Lacelle, Christian Bonington, Scott Backes, Steve House, Eric Dumerac, Philippe Pellet, Jonathan Carpenter, and Bill Belcourt. What a blast to be out in the mountains with you gentlemen.

My admiration to Nikki Tate, Kat Wiebe, Andy Arts, Hank Van Weelden, and Ivan Hughes, the team that created *Spindrift, The Barry Blanchard Story*.

All my love to Nicole, Rosemary, and Eowyn.

INDEX

Previous spread: Guy Lacelle on Riptide in very thin conditions, 1990. Barry Blanchard

H

I

J

K

Q

R

S

ABOUT THE AUTHOR

Photo: Tim Davis

Canadian mountain guide and alpinist Barry Blanchard was born in Calgary on March 29, 1959. A six-month trip to the French Alps in 1980 set the course of his life: to climb the steepest and most complicated faces of the world's great glaciated peaks. He has enjoyed some success, including many first ascents, but more importantly, Barry has enjoyed all of his outings. His previous book, *The Calling* (2014), is now available in paperback. Barry lives in Canmore, Alberta, with his fiancée, Nicole; his daughters, Rosemary and Eowyn; two cats, Orion and Lemmy; and a dog, Strummer.

Scan here for more about Barry and his adventures, including a link to *Spindrift: The Barry Blanchard Story*, other climb videos, a reader's guide, Barry's playlists and reading list, and links to the e-book and audiobook.